Workshop on Resources and Technologies for Indigenous, Endangered and Lesser-resourced Languages in Eurasia (EURALI 2022)

Held at LREC 2022

Marseille, France
20 - 25 June 2022

Editors:

Atul Kr. Ojha
Sina Ahmadi
Chao-Hong Liu
John P. McCrae

ISBN: 978-1-7138-6119-5

Printed from e-media with permission by:

Curran Associates, Inc.
57 Morehouse Lane
Red Hook, NY 12571

Some format issues inherent in the e-media version may also appear in this print version.

Association for Computational Linguistics
209 N. Eighth Street
Stroudsburg, Pennsylvania 18360

Phone: 1-570-476-8006
Fax: 1-570-476-0860

acl@aclweb.org

Additional copies of this publication are available from:

Curran Associates, Inc.
57 Morehouse Lane
Red Hook, NY 12571 USA
Phone: 845-758-0400
Fax: 845-758-2633
Email: curran@proceedings.com
Web: www.proceedings.com

LREC 2022 Workshop
Language Resources and Evaluation Conference
20-25 June 2022

Workshop on Resources and Technologies for Indigenous, Endangered and Lesser-resourced Languages in Eurasia (EURALI)

PROCEEDINGS

Editors:
Atul Kr. Ojha, Sina Ahmadi, Chao-Hong Liu, John P. McCrae

Proceedings of the Workshop on Resources and Technologies for Indigenous, Endangered and Lesser-resourced Languages in Eurasia (EURALI 2022)

Edited by:
Atul Kr. Ojha, Sina Ahmadi, Chao-Hong Liu, John P. McCrae

EAN: 9782493814074

For more information:
European Language Resources Association (ELRA)
9 rue des Cordelières
75013, Paris
France
http://www.elra.info
Email: lrec@elda.org

Preface

Eurasia is the largest continental area comprising all of Europe and Asia. It is also home to seven families of more than 2,500 languages spoken. Despite the rich linguistic diversity in this area, the respective language communities are under-represented while their languages are low-resource, endangered and/or systematically politically oppressed in history. Others, such as Kurdish, Gilaki, Santali, Kashmiri, Laz, and Abkhaz, are not only endangered but also understudied. One interesting characteristic of these languages is the influence of communal languages on their lexicon through borrowed words and a partially shared vocabulary of phylogenetically related words (cognates). Furthermore, contact-induced similarities can be observed to some extent even in the syntax of the languages, despite typological differences across different language families. In addition, relying on a lingua franca, many of these linguistic communities are facing standardization issues, particularly in the written form of their respective languages. This commonly results in the use of other scripts by speakers of these under-resourced languages.

In line with the necessity of language technology for under-resourced and understudied languages, this workshop aims to spur the development of resources and tools for indigenous, endangered and lesser-resourced languages in Eurasia. The goal is to increase visibility and promote research for these languages in a global arena. Through collaboration between NLP researchers, language experts and linguists working for endangered languages in these communities, we aim to create language technology that will help to preserve these languages and give them a chance to receive more attention in the language processing realm.

Seeing that this is the first edition of the EURALI workshop, we are very happy to have received many submissions, on various aspects regarding Eurasian languages. In the EURALI 2022 Proceedings, 18 research papers are included, dealing with no fewer than 18 Eurasian languages. We would like to thank all the colleagues who submitted their work to the workshop, the LREC 2022 organisers, as well as reviewers for making the first EURALI workshop a success.

Workshop Chairs

Atul Kr. Ojha, Sina Ahmadi, Chao-Hong Liu and John P. McCrae

Chairs

Atul Kr. Ojha, National University of Ireland Galway, Ireland
Sina Ahmadi, National University of Ireland Galway, Ireland
Chao-Hong Liu, Potamu Research Ltd, Ireland
John P. McCrae, National University of Ireland Galway, Ireland

Program Committee:

Agata Savary, University of Paris-Saclay, France
Alina Karakanta, Fondazione Bruno Kessler (FBK) / University of Trento
Akanksha Bansal, Panlingua Language Processing LLP
Atul Kr. Ojha, National University of Ireland Galway, Ireland & Panlingua Language Processing LLP
Bharathi Raja Chakravarthi, National University of Ireland Galway, Ireland
Bogdan Babych, Heidelberg University, Germany
Chao-Hong Liu, Potamu Research Ltd
Daan van Esch, Google
Daniel Zeman, Charles University, Prague
Deepak Alok, Panlingua Language Processing LLP
Dorothee Beermann, Norwegian University of Science and Technology (NTNU)
Esha Banerjee, Google
Ekaterina Vylomova, University of Melbourne, Australia
George Rehm, DFKI GmbH, Germany
Jamal Abdul Nasir, National University of Ireland Galway, Ireland
John Ortega, New York University, USA
Jonathan Washington, Swarthmore College, USA
John P. McCrae, National University of Ireland Galway, Ireland
Joseph Mariani, LIMSI-CNRS, France
Katharina Kann, University of Colorado at Boulder, USA
Kevin Patrick Scannell, Saint Louis University
Khalid Choukri, ELDA/ELRA, France
Massimo Monaglia, University of Florence, Italy
Nicoletta Calzolari, CNR-ILC, Italy
Richard Sproat, Google, Japan
Rico Sennrich, University of Zurich, Switzerland
Ritesh Kumar, Agra University, India
Saliha Muradoglu, Australian National University, Australia
Sina Ahmadi, National University of Ireland Galway, Ireland
Sourabrata Mukherjee, Charles University, Prague
Sunipa Dev, Google
Theodorus Fransen, National University of Ireland Galway, Ireland
Valentin Malykh, Huwaei Norah's Ark lab

Table of Contents

Conference Program

Monday, June 20, 2022

09:00–10:00 Inagural Session

09:00–09:10 *Welcome*
Workshop Chairs

09:10–10:00 *Keynote talk*
Dr. Jonathan Washington

10:00–10:30 Oral Session-I

10:00–10:30 *NLP Pipeline for Annotating (Endangered) Tibetan and Newar Varieties*
Christian Faggionato, Nathan Hill and Marieke Meelen

10:30–11:00 Coffee break/Poster and Demo session

10:30–11:00 *Towards an Ontology for Toponyms in Nepalese Historical Documents*
Sabine Tittel

10:30–11:00 *Semiautomatic Speech Alignment for Under-Resourced Languages*
Juho Leinonen, Niko Partanen, Sami Virpioja and Mikko Kurimo

10:30–11:00 *How to Digitize Completely: Interactive Geovizualization of a Sketch Map from the Kuzmina Archive*
Elena Lazarenko and Aleksandr Riaposov

10:30–11:00 *Word Class Based Language Modeling: A Case of Upper Sorbian*
Isidor Maier, Johannes Kuhn, Frank Duckhorn, Ivan Kraljevski, Daniel Sobe, Matthias Wolff and Constanze Tschöpe

10:30–11:00 *Bringing Together Version Control and Quality Assurance of Language Data with LAMA*
Aleksandr Riaposov, Elena Lazarenko and Timm Lehmberg

10:30–11:00 *Automatic Verb Classifier for Abui (AVC-abz)*
Frantisek Kratochvil, George Saad, Jiří Vomlel and Václav Kratochvíl

Monday, June 20, 2022 (continued)

10:30–11:00 *Dialogue Act and Slot Recognition in Italian Complex Dialogues*
Irene Sucameli, Michele De Quattro, Arash Eshghi, Alessandro Suglia and Maria Simi

10:30–11:00 *Digital Resources for the Shughni Language*
Yury Makarov, Maksim Melenchenko and Dmitry Novokshanov

10:30–11:00 *German Dialect Identification and Mapping for Preservation and Recovery*
Aynalem Tesfaye Misganaw and Sabine Roller

10:30–11:00 *Exploring Transfer Learning for Urdu Speech Synthesis*
Sahar Jamal, Sadaf Abdul Rauf and Quratulain Majid

10:30–11:00 *Towards Bengali WordNet Enrichment using Knowledge Graph Completion Techniques*
Sree Bhattacharyya and Abhik Jana

10:30–11:00 *Enriching Hindi WordNet Using Knowledge Graph Completion Approach*
Sushil Awale and Abhik Jana

10:30–11:00 *A Digital Swedish-Yiddish/Yiddish-Swedish Dictionary: A Web-Based Dictionary that is also Available Offline*
Magnus Ahltorp, Jean Hessel, Gunnar Eriksson, Maria Skeppstedt and Rickard Domeij

10:30–11:00 *An Online Dictionary for Dialects of North Frisian*
Michael Wehar and Tanno Hüttenrauch

10:30–11:00 *Towards a Unified Tool for the Management of Data and Technologies in Field Linguistics and Computational Linguistics - LiFE*
Siddharth Singh, Ritesh Kumar, Shyam Ratan and Sonal Sinha

Monday, June 20, 2022 (continued)

11:10–11:50 Panel Discussion

11:50–12:50 Oral Session-II

11:50–12:20 *Universal Dependencies Treebank for Tatar: Incorporating Intra-Word Code-Switching Information*
Chihiro Taguchi, Sei Iwata and Taro Watanabe

12:20–12:50 *Preparing an endangered language for the digital age: The Case of Judeo-Spanish*
Alp Öktem, Rodolfo Zevallos, Yasmin Moslem, Özgür Güneş Öztürk and Karen Gerson Şarhon

12:50–13:00 ***Valedictory Session***

Proceedings of the EURALI Workshop @LREC2020, pages 1–6
Marseille, 20 June 2022

NLP Pipeline for Annotating (Endangered) Tibetan and Newar Varieties

[1]Christian Faggionato, [2]Nathan Hill, [1]Marieke Meelen
[1]University of Cambridge & [2]SOAS University of London and Trinity College Dublin
{cf566,mm986}@cam.ac.uk, nathan.hill@tcd.ie

Abstract

In this paper we present our work-in-progress on a fully-implemented pipeline to create deeply-annotated corpora of a number of historical and contemporary Tibetan and Newar varieties. Our off-the-shelf tools allow researchers to create corpora with five different layers of annotation, ranging from morphosyntactic to information-structural annotation. We build on and optimise existing tools (in line with FAIR principles), as well as develop new ones, and show how they can be adapted to other Tibetan and Newar languages, most notably modern endangered languages that are both extremely low-resourced and under-researched.

Keywords: Tibetan, Newar, Corpora, Segmentation, POS tagging, parsing, Information Structure

1. Introduction

There are numerous varieties of Tibetan and Newar languages of the Bodish and Himalayish branches of the Sino-Tibetan language family respectively. These varieties share common innovations, but are often not mutually intelligible. In this paper we present a comprehensive NLP pipeline to create annotated corpora of historical Tibetan texts from the earliest Old Tibetan period (8-11th c.) onwards. We aim to present off-the-shelf tools that researchers can use to create exactly the type of linguistic corpus they need, i.e. standardised & normalised text (re)converted to Tibetan Unicode script (1), text with (word and sentence) segmentation (2), with morphosyntactic annotation (3), with parsed phrase structure (4), or deeply annotated corpora including all of the preceding, but further enriched with information-structural annotation, such as animacy for noun phrases, as well as topic and focus phrases (5).[1] In Section 2, we present our tools and the three phases of our annotation pipeline, with concrete examples from the most challenging part of our historical Tibetan corpora: the Old Tibetan *Rāmāyana*. In Section 3, we first show how this pipeline can be adapted to work for related historical Tibetan varieties like South Mustang Tibetan, but also more distantly-related languages, like Classical Newar. Finally, we demonstrate how these tools can be adapted to endangered modern varieties like Sherpa and Lhomi Tibetan and Kathmandu, Dolakha and Lalitpur Newar. Our pipeline and tools are important, because they can deal with extremely low-resource and under-researched languages that are highly endangered. Off-the-shelf tools like these with instructions on how to adapt them will give researchers the opportunity to use this as a blueprint for any (Asian) language for which no resources are available.

2. Annotation Pipeline

We develop our entire three-phased pipeline (Fig. 1) in accordance with CLARIN standards and FAIR Data Principles, making our resources and tools **F**indable and **A**ccessible, whilst ensuring **I**nteroperability, and **R**eusability (Wilkinson et al., 2016). This means that wherever possible, existing tools are adapted and optimised, rather than reinvented. In addition, our pipeline is deliberately semi-supervised, with two optional stages of manual correction if perfect gold standards are required.

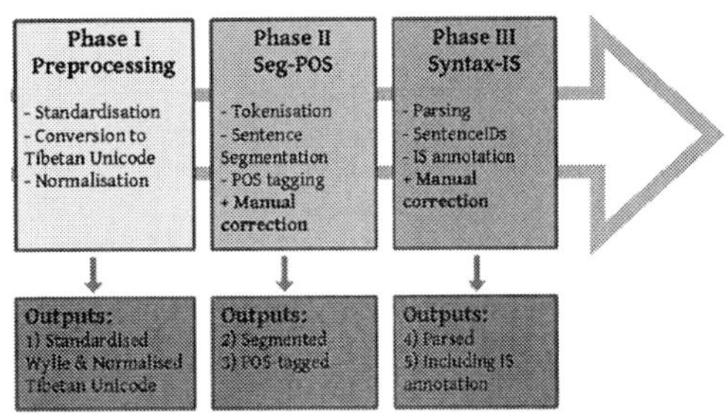

Figure 1: Historical Tibetan Pipeline and Outputs

In this section, we use example input from the Old Tibetan *Rāmāyana* (Fig. 2) to illustrate each stage of the annotation process for historical Tibetan and all output formats underneath.

2.1. Preprocessing

In the preprocessing phase of our annotation pipeline we use as input an adapted version of the Wylie transliteration system from the Old Tibetan Documents Online (OTDO) website (Fig. 2a). We standardise the OTDO Wylie to normal Wylie using a set of replacement rules, and we clean the text from the OTDO editorial conventions using a set of regular expressions (Fig. 2b). In the end we convert the standardised Old Tibetan Wylie into Old Tibetan Unicode script (Fig. 2c) through the THL's Online Tibetan Transliteration Converter, which can also be integrated into our overall pipeline using the more optimised Python implementation developed by Esukhia. The second step of the Preprocessing Phase consists of the normalisation of the Old Tibetan Unicode script. Old Tibetan presents differences in orthography compared to Classical Tibetan. Through a

[1]Code and links to corpora can be found at http://github.com/lothelanor/actib.

a)	**OTDO input**	nga	nI	tsangs pha	'I	long spyod	la	ma	chagste	
b)	**Standardised**	nga	n-i	tsangs pha	'-i	long spyod	la	ma	chagste	
c)	**Converted**	ང་ནཱི་ཙངས་པ་འཱི་ལོང་སྤྱོད་ལ་མ་ཆགསྟེ								
d)	Normalised	ང་ནི་ཚངས་པ་འི་ལོང་སྤྱོད་ལ་མ་ཆགས་ཏེ								
e)	**Segmented**	ང་	ནི་	ཚངས་པ་	འི་	ལོང་སྤྱོད་	ལ་	མ་	ཆགས་	ཏེ
f)	POS tags	p.pers	cl.top	n.prop	case.gen	n.count	case.all	neg	v.invar	cv.sem
g)	**UD tags**	PRON	PART	PROPN	ADP	NOUN	ADP	PART	VERB	PART
h)	Animacy	+human		+human		+inanimate				
i)	Parsed	(CP-MAT-SPE (NP-TOP (NP-PRO (FS+human)(p.pers ང་))(cl.top ནི་)) (PP (NP (NP-NPR (FS+human)(n.prop ཚངས་པ་)(case.gen འི་)) (NP (FS+inanimate)(n.count ལོང་སྤྱོད་)))(case.all ལ་)) (NEGP (neg མ་)) (VP (v.invar ཆགས་)) (cv.sem ཏེ་))								
j)	**Translation**	'As for me, I'm not attached to the enjoyments of Brahma.'								

Figure 2: Example from the Old Tibetan *Rāmāyana*

set of rules written in the Constraint Grammar formalism (Cg3) and python, we deal with these differences (with $> 99\%$ accuracy in 'normalisation' into Classical Tibetan) (Faggionato and Garrett, 2019) so that we can employ existing NLP tools for Classical Tibetan for further annotation. Classical Tibetan texts that are often available as eTexts in Tibetan Unicode can skip this Prepocessing Phase and go directly to Phase II (described in Section 2.2).

2.2. Segmentation & POS tagging

Since the Tibetan script does not indicate meaningful word or sentence boundaries (only syllables are marked in Fig. 2d), we first need to segment our standardised text. For word segmentation (tokenisation), we optimise a syllable-based tokeniser (Meelen and Hill, 2017), inserting missing *a chung* (transcribed as ') in cases where they were cut due to regular sandhi-like mergers in the Tibetan script. Reinsertion of these characters is effectively a form of lemmatisation of all nominal categories ending in *a chung*, e.g. *mkha'i* > *mkha' 'i* 'of the sky'. Similarly, we optimise a sentence segmentation script (Faggionato and Meelen, 2019), extending it with more detailed rules, e.g. rules which automatically capture direct speech based on common Tibetan direct speech markers like *na re, zhes*, etc. Sentence boundaries at this stage are marked by `<utt>`. To make automatic parsing and manual correction more feasible (i.e. avoiding extraordinarily long sentences that are impossible to correct on a screen), we also split consistently after semifinal particles (`cv.sem` in Fig. 2f), even though syntactically they can often function as subordinate clauses. For POS tagging, we extended an existing Tibetan tagger (Meelen et al., 2021) to facilitate downstream tasks related to the identification of information-structural (IS) features, e.g. by adding a specific tag for the topic marker *ni* (`cl.top` in Fig. 2f). In addition, we provide the option of converting the detailed tag set developed for historical Tibetan (Garrett et al., 2015) to the Universal Dependencies (UD) tag set (Fig. 2g). Since the Global Accuracy of the overall segmentation and POS tagging is $>95\%$ (especially with these improvements), the output can be fed directly to the next Phase. However, if Gold Standards or simply better downstream results are required, we recommend a round of manual correction with Pyrrha (Clérice et al., 2022). This online user-friendly annotation tool facilitates efficient manual correction by providing fixed tag lists as well as useful lists of occurrences throughout the corpus with bulk-correction options (Fig. 3).

Figure 3: Pyrrha - Manual Correction of POS tags, Word and Sentence Segmentation

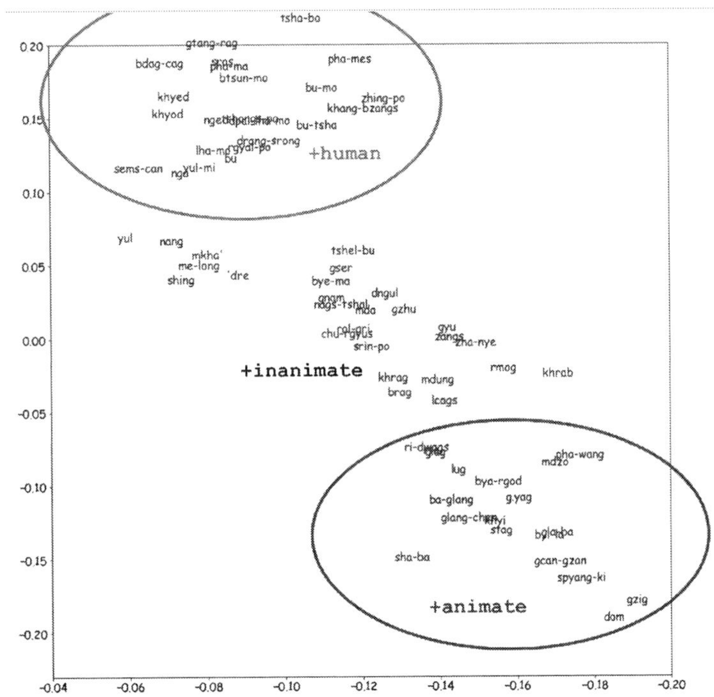

Figure 4: SVD of 100D vector representations of nouns showing Animacy clusters.

2.3. Syntax & Information Structure

We focus on constituency-based phrase structure as it is a better fit for our research questions regarding egophoricity, but dependency-based parsing is also possible (Faggionato and Garrett, 2019), (Faggionato, 2021). Conversion to/from either format is still an option at any time. Although constituency-based parsers are available for historical Tibetan (Meelen and Roux, 2020), these only provide rudimentary phrase structure. We extend these existing parsers to be able to capture complex Noun Phrases (`NP`) embedded within Postpositional Phrases (`PP`) as well as focus and topic phrases (`NP-FOC` and `NP-TOP` in Fig. 2i). The detailed tag set extensions thus help to identify important aspects of Information Structure already, i.e. **topics** and **foci**. The topic marker *ni* is classified with the POS label `cl.top`, for example (cf. Fig.2f). This is an Aboutness Topic (Frascarelli and Hinterhölzl, 2007), which can be translated into English as 'as for NP'. Similarly, Old and Classical Tibetan have focus markers, for example those marking narrow focus through particles like *kyang* 'even', which are labelled as `cl.foc`. Again, these detailed POS tags can help us derive syntactic phrase labels like `NP-FOC` automatically.

Finally, we annotate the **Animacy** of all Noun Phrases, providing them with a `+human`, `+animate` or `+inanimate` label that is integrated into the parsed bracketing format (Fig.2h and i). Animacy labels are assigned through a combination of feature-based rules and a dedicated Semantic Textual Similarity (STS) cluster-based classifier, which assigns Animacy labels based on KDTree distance measures to an average vector of tokens that are manually labelled as `+human`, `+animate` or `+inanimate`.[2] In addition, labels for certain tokens can be derived from POS tags. Tibetan personal pronouns, for example, can only refer to humans (demonstratives are used to refer to animals). Since our detailed POS tag set makes a distinction, we can automatically derive `+human` Animacy labels for NPs containing personal pronouns. Similarly, a combination of detailed POS tags and syntactic annotation allows us to automatically distinguish `+human` proper nouns, i.e. personal names, from place names (`+inanimate`), because humans typically have agentive case markers, whereas place names often occur with locatives. These rules are refined with dedicated verb classes and known argument structure information (Solmsdorf et al., 2021), (Lugli et al., 2021) and the Interactive Tibetan Valency Dictionary). Finally, we manually compiled a list of frequently-occurring animals, which allowed us to compare the semantic vector representations[3] of all new noun phrases with the labeled clusters of pronouns and personal names, animals and place names. Unseen NPs are categorised according to their highest cosine similarity to any of the clusters shown in a preliminary SVD plot in Fig. 4.

[2]For a full discussion and detailed evaluation, see (Meelen, 2022) and (Hill, 2022).

[3]These are based on FastText embeddings trained on the $185m$-token ACTib corpus (Meelen and Roux, 2020).

After automatic parsing and IS annotation, both can be manually corrected with the dedicate user-friendly tool Cesax (Komen, 2013). In addition to facilitating quick and easy correction of syntax and information structure, Cesax provides the option of semi-automatic coreference resolution based on predefined features, enhancing our IS annotation further with **topic chains**. Fig. 5 shows a screenshot of the 'tree view' option of the Cesax interface where both syntax and information structure can be corrected manually. Cesax allows for automatic conversion of parsed (`.psd`) files to TEI-compatible XML files (`.psdx`), but other outputs, e.g. FOLIA XML (compatible with ANNIS), plain text files with bracket structure shown in Fig. 2i, or UD-style CoNNL-U formats. In addition, it can export query results to R or other statistics tools. Altogether, this means the annotated corpora can be queried and analysed in many different ways (e.g. using customised XQuery or CorpusSearch (Randall et al., 2005)) catering to any kind of linguistic research.

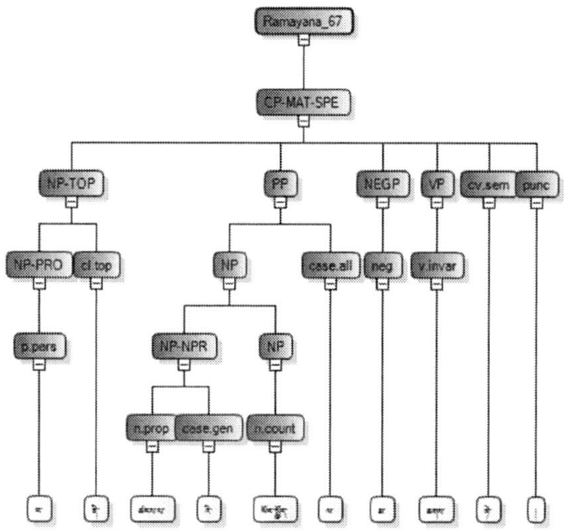

Figure 5: Syntax and IS correction in Cesax

3. Extension to Other Languages

Our pipeline with its accompanying tools can be easily adapted to other historical as well as modern, endangered Tibetan and Newar languages.

3.1. Other Historical Varieties

For **historical South Mustang Tibetan**, we can use transcriptions on the Tibetan social history project website. These transcriptions are done in Wylie, so we enter them into our pipeline at the Preprocessing Phase converting the Wylie transliterations back to Tibetan Unicode script for which we have optimised downstream NLP tools. Since historical South Mustang Tibetan is very similar to other historical Tibetan varieties, we can use the exact same tools and pipeline afterwards. For **Classical Newar**, we deal with two different sources. The first source consists of manuscript images that need to be transcribed into roman script with additional diacritics commonly used in the field. This is done using the Handwritten Text Recognition (HTR) tool Transkribus (Colutto et al., 2019), trained using Ground Truth data available for Sanskrit manuscripts written in a similar Pracalit script (Otter, nd), (Shakya and Bajracharya, 2001). The second source consists of PDF scans of romanised Newari texts. In order to properly OCR these PDFs and render all the diacritics in the texts we use Tesseract (Patel et al., 2012) with a model trained on the International Alphabet of Sanskrit Transliteration (IAST), a transliteration scheme for Indic scripts. These transcriptions are already segmented, but before running the POS tagger and applying the rest of the pipeline, we need to cut off the case suffixes from (pro)nouns to produce an accurate tokenisation similar to that of our historical Tibetan corpus.

3.2. Modern Endangered Varieties

When working with endangered or vulnerable languages there are many challenges for standard NLP pipelines. First of all, the lack of writing systems poses an intricate challenge in terms of language documentation, which creates a bottleneck at the transcription phase due to the lack of standardised conventions. Second, the limited amount of data means off-the-shelf NLP tools usually cannot be applied (Anastasopoulos et al., 2020). For Modern Tibetan and Newar varieties, all source material comes from fieldwork on language documentation projects. For this paper, we test our historical NLP pipeline for both *vulnerable* modern languages (i.e. Hile Sherpa - on the road to extinction - and Kathmandu Newar) and *endangered* ones (i.e. South Mustang Tibetan, Dolakha Newar, Lalitpur Newar and Lhomi). There are at least three different varieties of Modern Newar. Dolakha Newar spoken in a more remote region east of Kathmandu is not mutually intelligible with the varieties spoken in the Kathmandu Valley (Genetti, 2009). For **Kathmandu Newar**, we start with the fieldwork stories kindly provided by Austin Hale (Hale, nd) since the texts are in FLEx format, i.e. transcribed into IPA, segmented and glossed. This means that in our Preprocessing Phase we only need to extract the line with segmented morphemes and glosses. This gives us $10k$ tokens we can use to start training a Part-of-Speech (POS) tagger. $10k$ tokens is not nearly enough for any off-the-shelf neural-network-based taggers, but it is enough to start incrementally training a Memory-Based Tagger like the TiMBL MBT (Daelemans et al., 2003). Even though this is not a recently-developed tool, it is one of the most effective methods for developing a POS tagger from scratch since it can learn from specific features like initial and final characters as well as the context, yielding high accuracies even for extremely small data sets (Meelen et al., 2021). Once more fieldwork data (also for closely-related **Lalitpur**

Newar) has been collected, we can use this preliminary POS tagger to annotate more texts, which we will then correct with Pyrrha to create larger Gold Standards that will improve the Global Accuracy. The result can then be fed into the remaining Syntax and IS Phase of our pipeline. For **Dolakha Newar**, we can follow the same route, but only after digitising the stories published in Genetti (2009). **South Mustang Tibetan** with 1800 speakers is a severely endangered language spoken in a number of villages in Mustang, Nepal, with fieldwork data from the 1990s (Kretschmar, 1995). As these are also not available in digital format, we will collect new data in Mustang and archive it alongside romanised and IPA transcriptions after which it can enter the POS-tagging stage of our pipeline, following the same incremental annotation procedure sketched for modern Newar above. For Modern Newar varieties (as well as Sherpa and Lhomi below) the sentence segmentation is straightforward, since they are indicated with a *daṇḍa* in the case of Classical Newar and Sherpa, and a full stop in the case of Lhomi, Modern Newar and South Mustang Tibetan. **Sherpa** is a vulnerable language mainly spoken in Solukhumbu, northeast Nepal (Graves, 2007). The only Sherpa text at our disposal was a New Testament translation in Devanagari script, which is used since most Sherpa speakers read Nepali in Devanagari, but is very unsuitable for Sherpa phonotactics, which is why we convert it to romanised script (like our historical Newar). The preprocessing is then straightforward and in line with what we did for our Tibetan texts. After the script conversion, we clean it from unwanted non-textual materials (headers, footnotes, page numbers and cross-references) with a set of regular expressions. Again, similar to Classical Newar, we improve existing tokenisation by cutting off case markers from (pro)nouns, which means we can use similar downstream tagging tools. The last low-resourced Tibetan variety that we tested is **Lhomi**. Lhomi is another extremely endangered language mainly spoken in the Sankhuwa Sabha district in East Nepal. The estimated total number of speakers is in between 4000 and 7000, but this number has declined rapidly in the last 8 years (Vesalainen, 2016). The only available text is again a translation of the New Testament (NT) this time written in IPA (like the Modern Newar stories). Just like for Sherpa, Lhomi Preprocessing involves only cleaning the text with regular expressions, with the added stage of cutting off case markers. Having the same NT text available for Sherpa and Lhomi helps us in retrieving sections and verses, which are missing from the Sherpa data.

4. Conclusion

In this paper, we provided a fully-fledged annotation pipeline for historical Tibetan. The strength of our method not only lies in the fact that we build on and optimise existing tools (in line with FAIR principles), as well as develop new ones (for IS annotation in particular), but also that we can adapt these tools to other Tibetan and Newar languages in any input format (from manuscript to fieldwork data), most notably modern endangered languages that are both extremely low-resourced and under-researched. This easily adaptable pipeline will greatly help researchers working on any language for which no resources are available yet.

5. Acknowledgements

This research is AHRC-funded (AH/V011235/1).

6. Bibliographical References

Anastasopoulos, A., Cox, C., Neubig, G., and Cruz, H. (2020). Endangered languages meet Modern NLP. In *Proceedings of the 28th International Conference on Computational Linguistics: Tutorial Abstracts*, pages 39–45, Barcelona, Spain (Online), December. International Committee for Computational Linguistics.

Clérice, T., Jolivet, V., and Pilla, J. (2022). Building infrastructure for annotating medieval, classical and pre-orthographic languages: the pyrrha ecosystem. In *Digital Humanities 2022 (DH2022)*.

Colutto, S., Kahle, P., Guenter, H., and Muehlberger, G. (2019). Transkribus. a platform for automated text recognition and searching of historical documents. In *2019 15th International Conference on eScience (eScience)*, pages 463–466. IEEE.

Daelemans, W., Zavrel, J., van den Bosch, A., and Van der Sloot, K. (2003). Mbt: Memory-based tagger. *Reference Guide: ILK Technical Report-ILK*, pages 03–13.

Faggionato, C. and Garrett, E. (2019). Constraint grammars for tibetan language processing. *Proceedings of the 22nd Nordic Conference on Computational Linguistics: 12-16.*

Faggionato, C. and Meelen, M. (2019). Developing the Old Tibetan treebank. In Nikolova Temnikova Angelova, Mitkov, editor, *Proceedings of Recent Advances in Natural Language Processing*, pages 304–312. Varna: Incoma.

Frascarelli, M. and Hinterhölzl, R. (2007). Types of topics in German and Italian. *On information structure, meaning and form*, pages 87–116.

Garrett, E., Hill, N. W., Kilgarriff, A., Vadlapudi, R., and Zadoks, A. (2015). The contribution of corpus linguistics to lexicography and the future of tibetan dictionaries. *Revue d'Etudes Tibétaines*, 32:51–86.

Genetti, C. (2009). *A grammar of Dolakha Newar*, volume 40. Walter de Gruyter.

Graves, T. E. (2007). *A Grammar of Hile Sherpa*. PhD thesis submitted to the Faculty of the Graduate School of State University of New York at Buffalo.

Hill, N. (2022). Does Tibetan have a passive voice? *International Association of Tibetan Studies - Tech Panel presentation: Prague, Czech Republic.*

Komen, E. R. (2013). Corpus databases with feature pre-calculation. In *Proceedings of the twel h workshop on treebanks and linguistic theories (TLT12). Sandra Kübler, Petya Osenova & Martin Volk (eds)*, pages 85–96.

Kretschmar, M. (1995). *Erzählungen und Dialekt aus Südmustang*, volume 1. VGH-Wissenschaftsverlag.

Meelen, M. and Hill, N. (2017). Segmenting and POS tagging Classical Tibetan using a memory-based tagger. *Himalayan Linguistics*, 16(2).

Meelen, M. and Roux, É. (2020). Meta-dating the PArsed Corpus of Tibetan (PACTib). In *Proceedings of the 19th International Workshop on Treebanks and Linguistic Theories*, pages 31–42.

Meelen, M., Roux, E., and Hill, N. (2021). Optimisation of the largest annotated Tibetan corpus combining rule-based, memory-based & deep-learning methods. *Transactions on Asian and Low-Resource Language Information Processing*.

Meelen, M. (2022). Tibetan word embeddings: from distributional semantics to facilitating Tibetan NLP. *International Association of Tibetan Studies - Tech Panel presentation: Prague, Czech Republic*.

Patel, C., Patel, A., and Patel, D. (2012). Optical character recognition by open source OCR tool tesseract: a case study. *International Journal of Computer Applications*, 55(10):50–56.

Randall, B., Taylor, A., and Kroch, A. (2005). Corpussearch 2. *Philadelphia: University of Pennsylvania*.

Solmsdorf, N., Trautmann, D., and Schütze, H. (2021). Active learning for argument mining: A practical approach. *arXiv preprint arXiv:2109.13611*.

Vesalainen, O. (2016). *A Grammar Sketch of Lhomi*. SIL International.

Wilkinson, M. D., Dumontier, M., Aalbersberg, I. J., Appleton, G., Axton, M., Baak, A., Blomberg, N., Boiten, J.-W., da Silva Santos, L. B., Bourne, P. E., et al. (2016). The FAIR Guiding Principles for scientific data management and stewardship. *Scientific data*, 3(1):1–9.

7. Language Resource References

Faggionato, C. (2021). Constraint grammars for Tibetan dependency parsing - DOI 10.5281/zenodo.4727200, April. Funded by the UK's Arts and Humanities Research Council (grant code: AH/P004644/1).

Hale, A. (n.d.). Collection of stories in Kathmandu Newar. *unpublished*.

Lugli, L., Garrett, E., Faggionato, C., Rode, S., Solmsdorf, N., and Pagel, U. (2021). Visual Dictionary of Tibetan Verb Valency: Data - DOI 10.5281/zenodo.5596064, October.

Meelen, M. and Roux, E. (2020). The Annotated Corpus of Classical Tibetan (ACTib) - Version 2.0 (Segmented & POS-tagged) - DOI 10.5281/zenodo.3951503. May.

Otter, F. (n.d.). Transcription of RAS Hodgson MS 23: Madhyamasvayaṃbhūpurāṇa. *unpublished manuscript*.

Shakya, M. B. and Bajracharya, S. H. (2001). Svayambhū Purāṇa. *Lalitpur: Nagarjuna Institute of Exact Methods*.

Proceedings of the EURALI Workshop @LREC2020, pages 7–16
Marseille, 20 June 2022

Towards an Ontology for Toponyms in Nepalese Historical Documents

Sabine Tittel
Heidelberg Academy of Sciences and Humanities
Heidelberg
sabine.tittel@hadw-bw.de

Abstract

Nepalese historical legal documents contain a plethora of valuable information on the history of what is today Nepal. An empirical study based on such documents enables a deep understanding of religion and ritual, legal practice, rulership, and many other aspects of the society through time. The aim of the research project 'Documents on the History of Religion and Law of Pre-modern Nepal' is to make accessible a text corpus with 18th to 20th century documents both through cataloging and digital text editions, building a database called Documenta Nepalica. However, the lack of interoperability with other resources hampers its seamless integration into broader research contexts. To address this problem, we target the modeling of the Documenta Nepalica as Linked Data. This paper presents one module of this larger endeavour: It describes a proof of concept for an ontology for Nepalese toponyms that provides the means to classify toponyms attested in the documents and to model their entanglement with other toponyms, persons, events, and time. The ontology integrates and extends standard ontologies and increases interoperability through aligning the ontology individuals to the respective entries of geographic authority files such as GeoNames. Also, we establish a mapping of the individuals to DBpedia entities.

Keywords: Ontology, Nepal, Place Names, Toponymy, Linked Data, Text Edition

1. Introduction

Recent years have witnessed a growing estimation of modeling language data as resources of the Semantic Web. Linguistic resources in increasing numbers are converted into Linked Data (LD), a set of standard practices for representing and interlinking structured data on the web using Resource Description Framework (RDF). Ontologies of numerous domains provide the necessary structures to formalize the information in the resources and to embed the resources in a cross-discipline, cross-domain and cross-linguistic context. We here describe a proof of concept for the creation of an ontology suitable for the modeling of Nepalese place names and their entanglement with other place names, events, persons, and dates. The ontology, called NEPALPLACES, will be part of a bigger vision (LINKEDOPENNEPAL): to build a set of LD data resources with a text corpus as its focal point. The text corpus is part of the Documenta Nepalica[1] and comprises texts and documents on the history of religion and law of pre-modern Nepal. LINKEDOPENNEPAL will further comprise an ontological model also for person names, and a lexicographic module. NEPALPLACES is the outcome of a collaboration of domain experts of South Asian studies[2] and of ontology engineering.

The Nepalese language is the official language of Nepal. In a country with 92 (to 124) different languages (and language varieties, resp.) [in 2001] (Diwasa et al., 2007, 10), it is the mother tongue of approx. 45% of the population of >29MM people [in 2021][3], serving also as a lingua franca (Hutt (1988, 23); van Driem (2001, 1125–1128; 1130f.; 1142)). It is also spoken in north-eastern India, Myanmar, and Bhutan (Riccardi, 2003, 539–541). Through different historical periods, Nepali has developed a large body of literary works (Hutt (1988, 71–76); van Driem (2001, 1136f.)), catalyzed also by the legal code from 1854 (the *Mulukī Ain*, see Khatiwoda et al. (2021)) written entirely in Nepali (Riccardi, 2003, 544). Nepali literature is clearly under-represented in the digital context, in particular with respect to historical language stages. The aim of NEPALPLACES ($\subset$ LINKEDOPENNEPAL) is, thus, to not only increase the visibility and re-usability of the valuable historical Nepali documents but also to establish interoperability with other language resources. This is particularly relevant in the context of South Asian countries and societies that are historically connected to and share geographic, cultural, economic, philological and linguistic aspects with Nepalese society. The challenges of this task lie in extending existing ontological models, in ambiguities within the data to be modeled, linguistic hurdles, complex relations between toponyms and connected information as witnessed by the documents.

The paper is structured as follows: We describe the linguistic resource that provides the data in section 2 and introduce the paradigm of Linked Data, together with related work, in section 3. Section 4 shows the steps

[1]Cf. `https://nepalica.hadw-bw.de/nepal/`. All web pages have been accessed 03-17-2022.

[2]We particularly thank S. Cubelic, M. Grujovska, and A. Zotter for many fruitful and intense discussions during the cooperation, and we also thank M. Bajracharya, R. Khatiwoda, A. Michaels, and Ch. Zotter for their valuable input.—Moreover, we would like to give our thanks to the reviewers for their thorough proofreading and commenting.

[3]Cf. `https://www.worlddata.info/languages/nepali.php`, `https://knoema.de/atlas/Nepal/Bev%C3%B6lkerung`.

from the linguistic resource towards a Semantic Web resource, with a motivation in section 4.1, the digital status quo in section 4.2, the development of the ontology in section 4.3, and discussions guiding the ontology engineering process as well as ongoing work in section 4.4. We close with a conclusion in section 5.

2. The Linguistic Resource 'Documenta Nepalica'

The research project 'Documents on the History of Religion and Law of Pre-modern Nepal' (Heidelberg Academy of Sciences and Humanities, with research units in Heidelberg, Germany, and Patan, Nepal) makes accessible for the first time a corpus of historical texts from the early Śāha (1769-1846) and Rāṇā (1846-1951) periods. This rich textual material is held by the National Archives of Nepal[4] and other archives and collections. It consists of temple documents and administrative and legal documents, and it essentially lays the ground of our knowledge about topics still to a large extent unexplored: the history of religious institutions in Nepal, of legal practice in South Asia, the developments entailed by the formation of the Himalayan state, such as the restructuring of social institutions, elite cultures, the legitimization and affirmation of rulership, and the expansion of Hindu rule.[5]

The project's research results accessible through the Documenta Nepalica consist of a comprehensive catalogue of descriptive metadata of the documents (>65,000 entries) and of scholarly digital text editions (>450) including English translations, comments, notes, and facsimiles (published in open access and partly already with DOIs, in cooperation with Heidelberg University Library)[6]; for an example, see Fig. 1.

The creation of an accompanying, comprehensive bibliography and a glossary growing into a future dictionary is also underway. A newly added task is the identification of named entities within the corpus (person and place names with significant spelling variation) and their organization within a register. The digital research results are groundbreaking in their contribution to text-based empirical studies on the history of Nepal. However, they constitute a typical data silo (Berners-Lee, 2009), i.e., a valuable resource in the World Wide Web (WWW) but with limited access to the catalogue and text editions, not allowing queries beyond the implemented possibilities; the glossary and named entity register are currently not open to the public, the bibliography only partly. Thus, interoperability with related resources is not given. To address this problem, we adopt the paradigm of Linked Data.

[4]Cf. http://narchives.gov.np/.

[5]Cf. the project's website https://www.hadw-bw.de/Nepal.

[6]Effective 03-18-2022, cf. https://nepalica.hadw-bw.de/nepal/.

3. Linked Data

Over the last years, the paradigm of LD (LOD respectively, with the 'O' symbolising open access) has developed into a widespread, powerful means to turn the heterogeneous, unstructured information of the WWW into machine-readable, semantically accessible data (Berners-Lee, 2009; Bizer et al., 2009). As the most solid grounding of the Semantic Web it provides a set of best practices for the interlinking of datasets, with *Resource Description Framework* (RDF, Cyganiak et al. (2014)) as a standard data model (Wood et al., 2014, 4–12). RDF represents data in the form of graphs, i.e., triples with a source node (a subject), and a target node (an object), connected trough a directed edge (predicate) pointing from the former to the latter; subject, object and predicate are each identified through URIs that must be accessible via HTTP (the object can also be a literal described as a string).

There are many advantages to representing linguistic resources as LD, such as structural interoperability (through same format and same query language), conceptual interoperability (through shared vocabularies and ontologies), uniform access (through the use of standard Web protocols), and resource integration (linking resources) and federation (cross-resource access); cf. Chiarcos et al. (2013).

3.1. Related Work

Given the potential of LOD to create interoperability crossing borders of disciplines, content, languages, original formats and places of publication of resources, the last decade has witnessed a significant growth in contributions to the LOD ecosystem. This is also reflected by the strong increase of the LOD cloud (Gandon et al., 2017, 2) with resources from geography, life sciences, (political) administration, social media, etc., showing semantically interconnected information across all fields.[7] Also in linguistics, many proposals have been made to integrate language resources and their lexical, semantic, and morpho-syntactic aspects into the Semantic Web (Declerck et al., 2015; Aguado de Cea et al., 2016; Jarrar et al., 2019; Bellandi et al., 2018); for the recent state of the art see Bosque-Gil et al. (2018) and Cimiano et al. (2020).

Also for the modeling of text editions as LD, we can build on previous work. Approaches to transform text editions from XML/TEI (TEI Consortium, 2017) into RDF have been proposed, e.g., a mapping of TEI markup to CIDOC CRM (Crofts et al., 2003) in Eide (2014 2015, 23-38), a formalization of the TEI data model into an ontology (Ciotti and Tomasi, 2016 2017), and the integration of RDFa (Herman et al., 2015) into XML/TEI (Tittel et al., 2018), adapted by Cimiano et al. (2020, 253-262). All approaches depend on an interpretation of each individual TEI markup; however, efforts to define a binding mapping of TEI and OntoLex

[7]Cf. http://lod-cloud.net.

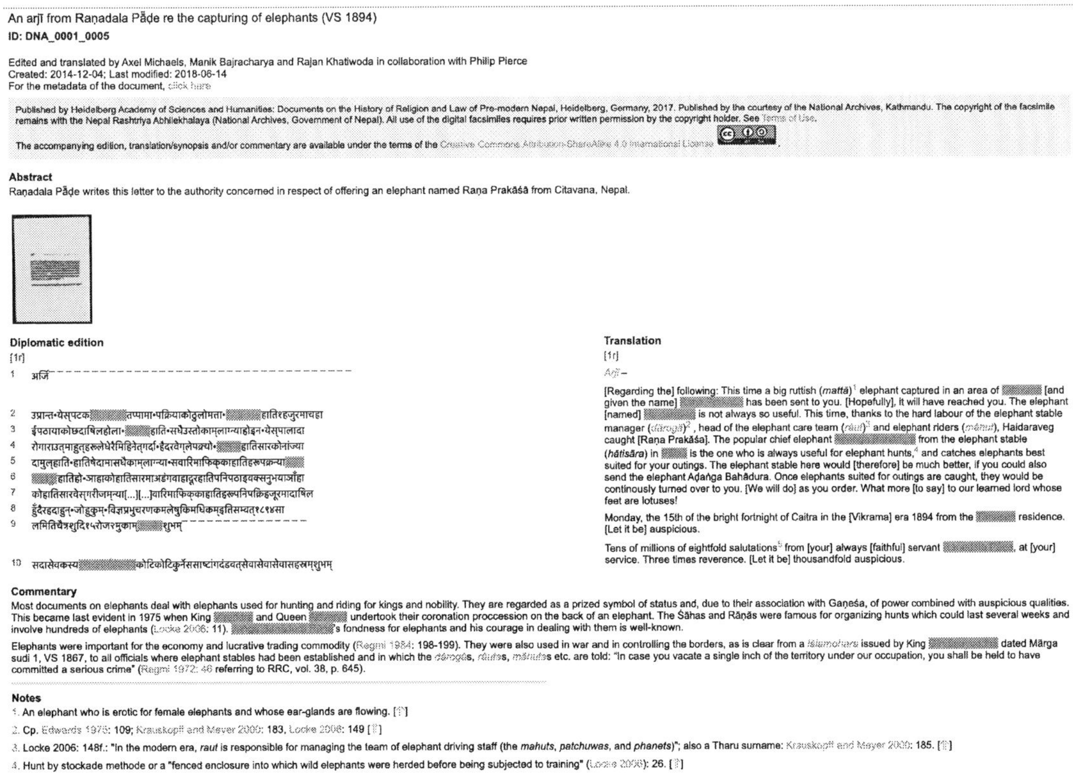
An arjī from Raṇadala Pā̃ḍe re the capturing of elephants (VS 1894)
ID: DNA_0001_0005

Edited and translated by Axel Michaels, Manik Bajracharya and Rajan Khatiwoda in collaboration with Philip Pierce
Created: 2014-12-04; Last modified: 2018-06-14
For the metadata of the document, click here

Published by Heidelberg Academy of Sciences and Humanities: Documents on the History of Religion and Law of Pre-modern Nepal, Heidelberg, Germany, 2017. Published by the courtesy of the National Archives, Kathmandu. The copyright of the facsimile remains with the Nepal Rashtriya Abhilekhalaya (National Archives, Government of Nepal). All use of the digital facsimiles requires prior written permission by the copyright holder. See Terms of Use.

The accompanying edition, translation/synopsis and/or commentary are available under the terms of the Creative Commons Attribution-ShareAlike 4.0 International License.

Abstract
Raṇadala Pā̃ḍe writes this letter to the authority concerned in respect of offering an elephant named Raṇa Prakāśā from Citavana, Nepal.

Diplomatic edition
[1r]
अर्जि

उप्रान्त•येस्पटक तप्पामा•पक्रियाकोठुलोमत्ता• हातिश्हजुरमाचहा
ईपठायाकोछदाषिलहोला• हाति•सधैउस्तोकाम्लाग्न्याहोइन•येस्पालादा
रोगाराउत्माहुत्हरूलेधेरैमिहिनेत्गर्दा•हैदरवेग्लेपक्र्यो• हातिसारकोनांज्या
दामुल्हाति•हातिषेदामासधैकाम्लाग्न्या•सवारिमाफिक्काहातिहरूपक्रन्या
हातिहो•ञाहाकोहातिसारमाअडंगवाहादूरहातिपनिपठाइवक्सनुभयाञाँहा
कोहातिसारवेस्गरीजम्न्या[...][...]वारिमाफिक्काहातिहरूपनिपक्रिहजूरमादाषिल
हुँदैरहदाहुन्•जोहुकुम्•विज्ञप्रभुचरणकमलेषुकिमधिकम्इतिसम्वत्१८९४सा
लमितिचैत्रशुदि१५रोजरमुकाम शुभम्

सदासेवकस्य कोटिकोटिकुर्नससाष्टांगदंडवत्सेवासेवासेवासहस्रम्शुभम्

Translation
[1r]
Arjī –

[Regarding the] following: This time a big ruttish (*mattā*)[1] elephant captured in an area of [and given the name] has been sent to you. [Hopefully], it will have reached you. The elephant [named] is not always so useful. This time, thanks to the hard labour of the elephant stable manager (*dārogā*)[2], head of the elephant care team (*rāut*)[3] and elephant riders (*māhut*), Haidaraveg caught [Raṇa Prakāśa]. The popular chief elephant from the elephant stable (*hātisāra*) in is the one who is always useful for elephant hunts,[4] and catches elephants best suited for your outings. The elephant stable here would [therefore] be much better, if you could also send the elephant Aḍaṅga Bahādura. Once elephants suited for outings are caught, they would be continously turned over to you. [We will do] as you order. What more [to say] to our learned lord whose feet are lotuses!

Monday, the 15th of the bright fortnight of Caitra in the [Vikrama] era 1894 from the residence. [Let it be] auspicious.

Tens of millions of eightfold salutations[5] from [your] always [faithful] servant , at [your] service. Three times reverence. [Let it be] thousandfold auspicious.

Commentary
Most documents on elephants deal with elephants used for hunting and riding for kings and nobility. They are regarded as a prized symbol of status and, due to their association with Gaṇeśa, of power combined with auspicious qualities. This became last evident in 1975 when King and Queen undertook their coronation proccession on the back of an elephant. The Śāhas and Rāṇās were famous for organizing hunts which could last several weeks and involve hundreds of elephants (Locke 2006: 11). 's fondness for elephants and his courage in dealing with them is well-known.

Elephants were important for the economy and lucrative trading commodity (Regmi 1984: 198-199). They were also used in war and in controlling the borders, as is clear from a lālmohara issued by King dated Mārga sudi 1, VS 1867, to all officials where elephant stables had been established and in which the dārogās, rāutas, māhutas etc. are told: "In case you vacate a single inch of the territory under our occupation, you shall be held to have committed a serious crime" (Regmi 1972: 46 referring to RRC, vol. 38, p. 645).

Notes
1. An elephant who is erotic for female elephants and whose ear-glands are flowing. [↑]
2. Cp. Edwards 1975: 109; Krauskopf and Meyer 2000: 183, Locke 2006: 149 [↑]
3. Locke 2006: 148f.: "In the modern era, *raut* is responsible for managing the team of elephant driving staff (the *mahuts*, *patchuwas*, and *phanets*)"; also a Tharu surname: Krauskopf and Meyer 2000: 185. [↑]
4. Hunt by stockade methode or a "fenced enclosure into which wild elephants were herded before being subjected to training" (Locke 2006): 26. [↑]

Figure 1: A text edition as part of the Documenta Nepalica (annotated named entities are highlighted in green).

(Cimiano et al., 2016) are underway.[8] Textual corpora have received less attention (Cimiano et al. (2020, 43), overview ib. 61-87; 89-122).

Some work has been conducted in the field of Nepalese studies with respect to LD and ontologies. Pokharel et al. (2014) discuss the use of ontologies for improving the effectiveness of farming in Nepal facilitating resources with statistic and administrative data, and weather, soil and crop growing days information. The research project "Opportunity Recognition Model of Nepalese Entrepreneurs" seems to be grounded on an ontology, as well.[9] CRAI[10] provides a geographical thesaurus with information downloadable as RDF, with a microthesaurus also for Nepal; however, only four Nepalese place names are recorded. Open Knowledge Nepal[11] is a non-profit organization making Nepal data openly accessible, providing data-driven services and education of citizens, government, etc.; even though RDF is said to be one of the data formats available (see the FAQs), RDF datasets are hard to find; the included geographical dataset (i) is not available as RDF, and (ii) focuses on modern administrative boundaries.

4. From the Documenta Nepalica to a Semantic Web Resource

The overall goal is to model the Documenta Nepalica as LinkedOpenNepal, a set of stand-alone features 'text editions', 'person names', 'places names', and 'glossary', yet aligned to a multifaceted Semantic Web resource.

Adapting the approach described in Tittel et al. (2018), we give a minimal data sample with RDF data from the edition of document ID K_0440_0007[12] that includes a toponym (we use the English translation for the code example, the Devanagari transcription of the Nepalese original is shown in Fig. 2): *The guṭhi for the cakrapūjā [...] 4 ropanīs near Deupāṭhaṃ.*[13]

[3]

[8]Cf. `https://github.com/elexis-eu/tei2ontolex`.

[9]Cf. `https://tinyurl.com/24u2vp9d`.

[10]University of Barcelona, *Centre de Recursos per a l'Aprenentatge i la Investigació*, cf. `https://vocabularis.crai.ub.edu/en/thub/concept/thub:981058505354306706`.

[11]Cf. `https://oknp.org/`.

[12]A royal donation, cf. `https://nepalica.hadw-bw.de/nepal/editions/show/8637`.

[13]For sake of brevity, namespaces are assumed defined the usual way. For the yet unpublished resource we use the common `<http://example.org>`, see also in the following code examples. We also use the prefixes 'occ' (occurrence) for `<http://example.org/K_0440_0007.xml/#>`, 'gloss' (glossary entry) for `<https://nepalica.hadw-bw.de/nepal/words/viewitem/>`, 'place'

52 वालाचतुर्दसिकादीन‾‾‾‾ कावंमा
53 हाचक्रपुजाकोगुठी‾‾‾‾‾‾
...
56 रोपनी४देउपाटंछेउको

Figure 2: Text edition of K_0440_0007.

```
1  The
2  <seg about="occ:210"
4   property="rdfs:seeAlso" resource="gloss:931">
5   <w property="rdfs:label" lemma="guṭha"
6   type="n.">guṭhī</w>
7   <gloss property="skos:definition">endowed lands or
8   other sources of revenue for financing religious
9   and charitable functions</gloss>
10 </seg>
11 for the
12 <seg about="occ:213"
13  property="rdfs:seeAlso" resource="gloss:2002">
14  <w property="rdfs:label" lemma="cakrapūjā"
15  type="n.">cakrapūjā</w>
16  <gloss property="skos:definition">worship in a
17  circle</gloss>
18 </seg> [...] 4
19 <seg about="occ:235"
20  property="rdfs:seeAlso" resource="gloss:2051">
21  <w property="rdfs:label" lemma="ropanī"
22  type="n.">ropanīs</w>
23  <gloss property="skos:definition">unit of land
24  measurement in the hill region, including the
25  Kathmandu Valley, comprising four murīs</gloss>
26 </seg>
27 near
28 <seg about="occ:176" property="rdfs:seeAlso"
29  resource="place:28">
30  <w property="rdfs:label" lemma="Deopatan">
31  Deupāṭhaṃ</w>
32 </seg>
```

Listing 1: Data sample from a text edition of the Documenta Nepalica with XML+RDFa.

For RDF to be Linked Data it must adhere to principles defined by Berners-Lee (2009), one of which reads: "When someone looks up a URI, provide useful information, using the standards" (called a dereferenceable URI). The reference to the Deopatan entry (normalized spelling) of the named entities register in l. 28–31 does not meet this condition.[14] To enhance the information provided and to reach compliance with other resources, a link to the respective entry in a gazetteer or an authority file in the domain of geographic references can be added. These are, e.g., the *Getty Thesaurus of Geographical Names* (TGN), GeoNames, the *Virtual International Authority File* (VIAF), and the *Gemeinsame Normdatei* (GND).[15] The city of Kathmandu, for example, can be connected to GeoNames ID 1283240, GND 4030036-5, TGN 1083294, and VIAF 158284130.

Also, a mapping to each corresponding DBpedia entity is established, e.g., for the Trishuli River, http://dbpedia.org/resource/Trishuli_River, see List. 3, l. 19.

However, many of the geographic names found in the Documenta Nepalica (cities, mountains, rivers, etc.) are not registered by these authority files. The marginalization of less 'developed' countries in global gazetteers such as GeoNames and TGN with respect to coverage, balance, and completeness is a known issue (Acheson et al., 2017). Furthermore, field names for, e.g., a grove, a pasture, a lot, a place related to a religious site—all playing a potentially important role for events such as rituals and lawsuits—are, to the best of our knowledge, not represented. One example is the Pashupati Aryaghat, a socially important ghat on the banks of the Bagmati River serving as a cremation ground for the Nepalese nobility (Michaels, 2008, 5f.).[16] Also, these authority files focus on present day toponymy and, hence, their suitability is limited for the mapping of diachronic changes and historic place names, such as aforementioned Deopatan, a historic town in the Kathmandu Valley and now a city quarter of Kathmandu.

And the problem is more complex: Even with an existing reference, the information returned when navigating to the entry of an authority file is not in an LD standard, thus, it is not 'useful' in the sense of LD. We tackle this problem with an ontology for Nepalese toponyms.

4.1. Why an Ontology for Toponyms

The texts of the Documenta Nepalica attest complex connections of norms, ideas, and rules to places, practices, persons, castes, and the material world. This makes them "such exciting material" (Cubelic et al., 2018, 1) and a key component for understanding the history of Nepal. However, they have not yet been sufficiently studied, neither as a self-sustained textual category, nor as source material for a historiography of South Asia, nor in relation to other texts, such as inscriptions, shastric texts, chronicles, belles lettres, etc. Their content is varied: festivals and rituals of religious communities, emerging scribal and administrative elites, court proceedings and litigation, the development of bureaucratic policies, offices, social roles, military positions, and state duties, cp. ib. 11–13. They also give insight into the social and cultural circumstances and forms of slavery in Nepal (and South Asia) differing significantly from better-studied African and North American forms, being more familiar and strongly related to land and landownership

for <.../nepal/ontologies/viewitem/> (Nota bene: Both resources will be made open access in the course of 2022).

[14]Note that this is also true for the references of *guṭhi*, *cakrapūjā*, and *ropanī* in l. 2; 12; 19 to the entries in the glossary of the Documenta Nepalica.

[15]Cf. https://www.getty.edu/research/tools/vocabularies/tgn/, https://www.geonames.org/, http://viaf.org/, http://www.dnb.de/gnd.

[16]Attested in numerous documents, e.g., in doc. RRC_0062_0180, https://nepalica.hadw-bw.de/nepal/editions/show/47509).

(Bajracharya and Michaels, 2022, 1f.). All aspects are entangled with places, and all require a careful regional contextualisation to enable a deeper understanding of Nepalese socio-historical development, especially considering trans-regional migration patterns (e.g., of scribal groups) and fluctuating borders with emerging or perishing kingdoms, cp. Khatiwoda et al. (2021, 47–56).
Therefore, as a major step towards a LOD transformation of data from the Documenta Nepalica, we develop an ontology that will provide the necessary classes and properties for a modeling of this entanglement. We will populate the ontology with individuals taken from the Documenta Nepalica, turning it into a means to create a bird's eye view on the interlacing of Nepalese places with events and personalia through time.

4.2. Digital Status Quo

While the format of the text editions is in XML conform with the standard TEI P5 (published online as HTML) and can thus be utilized for a future automated transformation into RDF statements, the entries of the named entities register are formatted using HTML:

```
<p>
capital of Nepal, declared capital by
<a href="/nepal/ontologies/viewitem/178">
Pṛthvīnārāyaṇa Śāha</a> on 21 March 1770;</p>
<p>
a district in Central Nepal, part of
<a href="/nepal/ontologies/viewitem/651">
Bagmati Province</a>
</p>
```

Listing 2: HTML entry for Kathmandu.

The code example shows three aspects that are perfectly suited for the current data use but that are shortcomings with respect to automated data processing: (i) all entries of the register are annotated as undifferentiated hyperlinks: in the example, the person name Pṛthvīnārāyaṇa Śāha, a king, and the toponym Bagmati Province; (ii) the information relevant for the classification of the entry is an unstructured string, in this case, the fact that Kathmandu is both the capital of Nepal and a district; (iii) the founding date of Nepal's capital is not annotated. For the time being, we resolve this by extracting the information manually.

4.3. Ontology Development

We construct a conceptual model through the Protégé v5.2.0 desktop version[17] which we formalize in OWL (Bechhofer et al., 2004), integrating existing standards for cross-resource compatibility. As for metadata, this is straightforward: We use DublinCore properties (`creator`, `title`, `issued`, `description`, `rights`)[18] and VANN (`vann:preferredNamespacePrefix`, `vann:preferredNamespaceUri`).[19]; the license is defined as Creative Commons Zero. We also use RDF, RDFS (Brickley and Guha, 2014), and the datatype `xsd:dateTime` (Fallside and Walmsley, 2004). However, to represent the information in focus, this does not suffice. Two aspects are crucial: the establishment of the classes and properties that will enable (i) a classification of the individuals of the ontology (e.g.: city of Kathmandu) and (ii) a modeling of their entanglement with other individuals, i.e., toponyms, events, dates, agents, etc. (e.g.: Deopatan is a historic town in the Kathmandu valley, now part of the city of Kathmandu). For the first point we are fortunate to be able to adopt the ontology established by DBpedia, starting with `Place` as the hierarchically highest class and including only classes relevant for our data.[20]
The second aspect is more time-consuming. It is work in progress: The incremental population with entries from Documenta Nepalica as ontology individuals leads to repeated revisions of the created properties (and, to a lesser extent, of classes). At this point, the properties are as generic as possible, with specifications focusing on rivers (with object properties `hasTributary`, `isTributaryOf`, `flowsIntoRiverAt`). The property `connectsTo` with `Place` as its domain and `Person` as its range facilitates the connection to the person name ontology NEPALPEOPLE, see infra. For alternative designations of a toponym we use the GeoNames property `alternateName`.[21]
We give an example for the river related properties with the modeling of the Triśūlī river, serialized with Turtle Syntax (Prud'hommeaux and Carothers, 2014):

```
###  https://example.org/nepalplaces#
    Trishuli_River
:Trishuli_River rdf:type owl:NamedIndividual ,
                         :River ;
    :flowsIntoRiverAt    :Devghat ;
    :hasTributary        :Marsyangdi_River ;
    :isLocatedIn         :Nepal ;
    :isTributaryOf       :Narayani_River ;
    rdfs:label           "Triśūlī"@ne ;
    gn:alternateName     "Trisūlagaṅgā"@ne ,
    "Trisūlī nadī"@ne , "Triśūla Gaṅgā"@ne ;
    rdfs:comment "One of the major tributaries
    of the Narayani River basin in central
    Nepal; originates in Tibet as a stream
    and enters Nepal at Gyirong Town; joins
    the Narayani River at Devghat."@en ;
    rdfs:seeAlso <https://nepalica.hadw-bw.de/
    nepal/ontologies/viewitem/213> ;
    owl:sameAs dbr:Trishuli_River .
```

Listing 3: Individual Trísūlī river.

Currently, 57 individuals, 76 classes (used 39 times), seven object properties (used 47 times), and 15 annotation properties are registered in NEPALPLACES.

4.4. Ongoing Work

The ontology development is a joint activity with domain experts from the research project's team resulting

[17]Cf. http://protege.stanford.edu.
[18]Cf. http://purl.org/dc/terms.
[19]Cf. https://vocab.org/vann/.
[20]Cf. http://mappings.dbpedia.org/server/ontology/classes/#Place.
[21]https://www.geonames.org/ontology/documentation.html#alternateName.

in and profiting from numerous fruitful discussions, exemplified in the following.

4.4.1. Identification of Shortcomings of the Class Structure

NEPALPLACES must provide the means to map Nepalese toponyms to a class. As mentioned above, we can draw on the DBpedia ontology. However, the DBpedia ontology proved to be (i) not fine-grained enough and (ii) not accurate for the modeling of Nepalese reality and—for that matter—of the reality of the Indian subcontinent. Thus, we extend it, integrating new subclasses into the hierarchy. This is a process driven by several aspects:

Population with Individuals. The population of NEPALPLACES with data from the named entities register from Documenta Nepalica uncovers shortcomings of the class structure in a straightforward way. E.g., the aforementioned Pashupati Aryaghat is a ghat and needs to be classified as such in the ontology. Since this is not possible with the DBpedia ontology we introduce `Ghat` as a sub-class of `ArchitecturalStructure` (on the level of `Building`), annotated with the comment "A set of steps leading down to a body of water with a platform for bathing typically situated at their base", cf. Fig. 3. We said already that Pashupati Aryaghat is also used as a cremation ground with high social significance and also needs to be mapped to this concept. Thus, we also introduce `CremationGround` to the ontology, where the pre-existing `Cemetery` "burial ground" is not accurate. So far, with currently 57 individuals, twelve classes have been added [effective 03-12-2022].

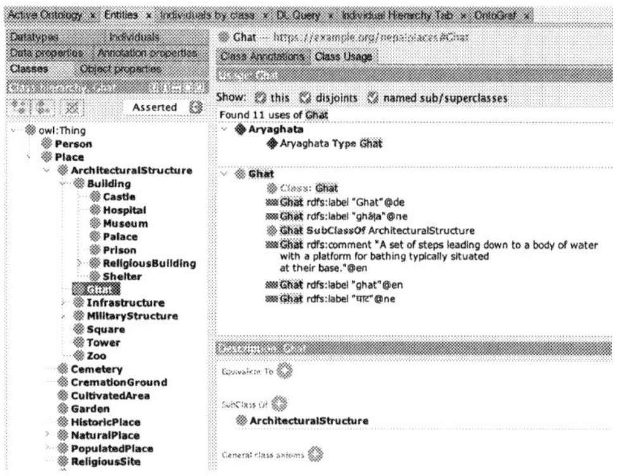

Figure 3: Newly added class `Ghat` (Protégé).

Concepts behind Classes. For the classification of each individual, we closely look at a pre-existing class that seems suitable at first sight. E.g., for the modeling of the toponym Bhadrakali, an open air shrine of the goddess Bhadrakālī east of Tundikhel in Kathmandu, we turn to the class `Shrine`, in the DBpedia ontology labeled as Engl. "shrine" and placed within the hierarchy < `ReligiousBuilding` < `Building` < `ArchitecturalStructure`.[22] A closer look at the concept behind `Shrine` reveals a problem: Engl. *shrine* [< lt. SCRĪNIUM "case or chest for books or papers", (von Wartburg, since 1922, 11,337b)] is attested since ca. 1000 (Ælfric of Eynsham) and seems strongly connected to the Christian Occident, typically suggesting a container with physical remains of a religiously venerated person, cf. the senses registered by OED SHRINE n. with sense n°1 "A box, coffer [...]", n°2 "The box [...] in which the relics of a saint are preserved [...]", etc., and sense n°5a defines a more generic concept that, however, still refers to an architectural structure: "A place where worship is offered or devotions are paid to a saint or deity; a temple, church".[23] It becomes clear that the class `Shrine` is not adequate for a mapping of Nepalese shrines that are often open-air places of worship. Thus, we include a generic concept represented by `ReligiousSite` that is not related to `ArchitecturalStructure`, accompanied by the comment "A natural site where religious rituals and activities, e.g., prayer and sacrifice, are carried out.".

Class and Property Labeling. When defining the classes and properties, our aim is to include labels in English, German, and Nepali (alongside English comments). There, we experience a noticeable impact on the ontology engineering by the translation process of the labeling, unveiling shortcomings within the class structure adopted from DBpedia with respect to Nepalese reality. E.g., there is no adequate Nepali term for a monastery in a generic sense: the Nepalese language differentiates *bahāla / vihāra*, a Buddhist monastery, from *maṭha*, a monastery of Hindu ascetics, and from *girjāghara*, a Christian monastery.[24] This results in adding three sub-classes to the pre-existing `Monastery`: `MonasteryChristian`, `MonasteryBuddhist` and `MonasteryHindu`, cf. the individual Bhinchẽ Bāhāla as an example:

```
1  :Bhinche_Bahala rdf:type owl:NamedIndividual ,
2                           :MonasteryBuddhist ;
3      :isLocatedIn         :Patan ;
4      rdfs:label           "Bhinchẽ Bāhāla"@ne ,
5                           "Bhiṃkṣe Bāhāla"@ne ;
6      rdfs:comment "Buddhist monastery in Patan
7      and the city quarter surrounding it."@en ;
8      rdfs:seeAlso <https://danam.cats.uni-
9      heidelberg.de/report/711b19a4-ec10-
10     11e9-b125-0242ac130002> ,
11     <https://nepalica.hadw-bw.de/nepal/
12     ontologies/viewitem/821> .
```

Listing 4: The Buddhist monastery Bhinchẽ Bāhāla.

Note the linking (through `rdfs:seeAlso`, l. 8-10) to the respective entry in the *Nepal Heritage Documentation Project* (NHDP; Heidelberg Centre for Transcultural Studies, Heidelberg University).

[22] Cf. `http://mappings.dbpedia.org/server/ontology/classes//Shrine`.

[23] *Oxford English Dictionary* – OED Online. March 2022. Oxford University Press. `www.oed.com`.

[24] This term being rarely used and replaced by Nep. *carca* designating the church.

The examples described reveal a Western-centric cultural bias within the encyclopedic resource of DBpedia. This results in an information imbalance in the direction of the reality of non-western cultures such as the Nepalese. This flaw can be counteracted, e.g., by ontological work such as NEPALPLACES, and we hope that our efforts foster more endeavors in this regard.

4.4.2. Ambiguity within the Entries of the Documenta Nepalica

The entries of the named entities register show ambiguities that need to be resolved while integrating them into the ontology. See, e.g., Fig. 4, where the entry misses the distinction between the historical district of Deukhurī and the valley of Deukhurī. The entry for the place name of Dang is yet more complex: "a valley located in the Inner Tarai in midwest Nepal (north of Deukhurī valley) that was prior to the conquest by the Gorkha troops in 1786 divided among small principalities belonging to the Bāīse Rājya: Dang and Chilli in the valley itself, and Salyan and Phalabang in the hills [...]; a district in Western Nepal, part of the Lumbini Province; until 1961 together with Deukhurī one of the 32 districts formed in the Rana period", `https://nepalica.hadw-bw.de/nepal/ontologies/viewitem/389`: The entry describes both the Dang valley and the Dang district that, in turn, must be differentiated into a modern administrative unit and a historic administrative unit of the Rana period. Thus, for the content of these entries, different instances must be introduced to the ontology (e.g., `Deukhuri_District` and `Deukhuri_Valley` for the entry Deukhurī), explicitly defined as different individuals. This has so far been done manually. For future automatic processing, ways of an automatized information identification and entity recognition must be evaluated.

4.4.3. Geographical Names Entangled with Offices and People

The Documenta Nepalica include a great amount of information on administrative, religious and social offices and roles together with persons holding the office or role during a particular time and at a particular place. This empirical information is very valuable for a nuanced interpretation of responsibilities, dependencies, interacting, and structural developments within Nepalese society from a diachronic and a spatial perspective. To model the manifold relations of a place presents a challenge to the development of the ontology. The following gives an example of such relations: The Degutalejyū Temple located at the Hanumānḍhokā palace in Kathmandu is the place of activity of a particular *nagarcī*, a drummer who is a musician playing an important social and religious-ritual role. This role is connected to land endowments for financing the religious and charitable functions of the *nagarcī*, as witnessed in different documents. One such document is a royal deed from King Gīrvāṇayuddha in Vikram Samvat 1864 (= CE 1807[25]). The deed grants plots of land (with rice fields, gardens, lots, etc.) to a person called Bandhuvā Damāī (Badhuvā Nagārci, resp.) for conducting rituals (providing the necessary material, e.g., buffalo, goats, cloth, etc.), for the upkeep of two large religious banners and three long trumpets offered to Degutalejyū, and, also, for military services.[26]

Since we want to keep NEPALPLACES focused on toponymy and not populate it with aspects related to anthroponymy and prosopography, we establish a connection of NEPALPLACES to a sister ontology called NEPALPEOPLE. This sister ontology models persons within the Documenta Nepalica, including their proper names, life events and genealogical aspects, professions, societal roles, and more. In NEPALPEOPLE, Bandhuvā Damāī and all other persons with the same position (of *nagarcī*) are modeled as individuals connected (via a specific NEPALPEOPLE property `hasPosition`) to a position defined through the class `Nagarci`; this position is, in turn, enriched with temporal information and, through a property `hasPlace`, with the individual 'Degutalejyū Temple in Kathmandu' of NEPALPLACES.[27]

4.5. Integration of chronological aspects

The ontology provides classes representing historical concepts: `HistoricalPlace`, `HistoricalAreaOfAuthority`, `HistoricalSettlement`, and `HistoricalDistrict`, the latter classifying, e.g., former districts of the Rana period until 1961 such as said Deukhurī and Dang districts. However, these classes do not inform us about a precise date and, thus, the dimension of time needs to be integrated: When was, e.g., a district created, and when did the existence come to an end or merge into another administrative area? E.g., Tanahun is a modern district in Western Nepal and part of the Gandaki Province but it has also been a kingdom, i.e., one of the Caubīsī Rājya (twenty-four sovereign and intermittently allied petty kingdoms in South Asia ruled by the Khas people and unified between 1744 [by Pṛthvīnārāyaṇa Śāha, king of Gorkha Kingdom, cp. List. 2] and 1816 to what is now present-day Nepal (van Driem, 2001, 1107). The Time Ontology in OWL (Cox and Little, 2020) provides a wide range of classes, object properties and data types to model time instances and time spans that are of particular interest for Nepalese temporal entities entangled with toponyms: Alongside the Gregorian calendar as standard time, one can define alternative calendars through the property `time:hasTRS` with the object being, e.g., a DBpedia entry. The following example

[25]The Nepalese documents show different calendars: Vikram Samvat (VS), Shaka Era (ŚS), and Nepal Sambat (NS); when not further specified, we use CE (Commen Era).

[26]Document DNA_0013_0031, `https://nepalica.hadw-bw.de/nepal/editions/show/794`.

[27]Details of NEPALPEOPLE are not subject of this paper.

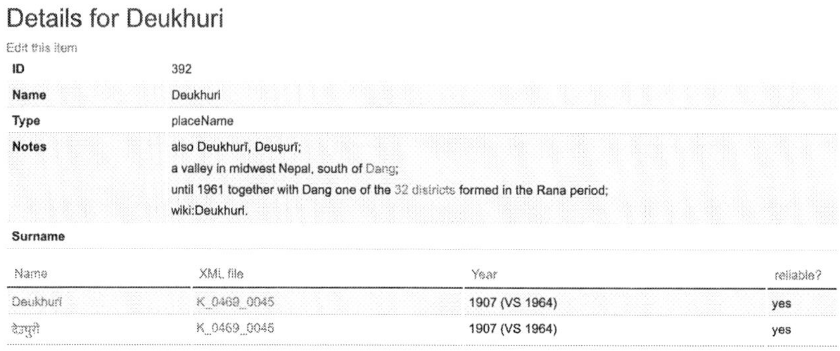

Details for Deukhuri

Edit this item

ID	392
Name	Deukhuri
Type	placeName
Notes	also Deukhurī, Deuṣurī; a valley in midwest Nepal, south of Dang; until 1961 together with Dang one of the 32 districts formed in the Rana period; wiki:Deukhuri.
Surname	

Name	XML file	Year	reliable?
Deukhurī	K_0469_0045	1907 (VS 1964)	yes
देउखुरी	K_0469_0045	1907 (VS 1964)	yes

Figure 4: Deukhurī in the named entities register of the Documenta Nepalica.

shows how to model the CE date (lines 1–3) and the VS date (lines 5–9) of the same event, i.e., the building of a shelter (nep. *pāṭī*) in a specific place, that is, in Kayatā Hiti (Kathmandu):

```
1 :Building_Kayatahiti_Pati_Gregorian
2     rdf:type time:DateTimeDescription ;
3     time:year "1796"^^xsd:gYear .
4
5 :Building_Kayatahiti_Pati_VS
6         rdf:type time:GeneralDateTimeDescription ;
7     time:hasTRS
8         <https://dbpedia.org/page/Vikram_Samvat> ;
9     time:year "1852"^^time:generalYear .
```

Listing 5: Inclusion of VS calendar with Time Ontology in OWL.

Including the Gregorian calendar parallel to the historical Nepalese calendar (VS in the given example) is important for aligning the dates with standard CE time and, thus, creating a common ground with temporal information of other resources. However, to access the data one still needs to focus on an explicit date. Therefore, we want to evaluate how to define historical periods based on the evidence in the Documenta Nepalica (backed by related research) and how to make them interoperable with PeriodO. PeriodO is a gazetteer of historical periods, initially designed for European antiquity (Rabinowitz et al., 2016).[28] Its aim is to make concepts of periods explicit through a spatio-temporal definition based on an authoritative source. This adds new, finegrained concepts to globally agreed-upon concepts. The '19th century' is one such concept. Much like the temporal borders of the 'Renaissance' differ depending on space, the 19th century also proves to be a dynamic notion: Based on its aspects of 'modernity' brought "through massive scientific and technological changes, industrialisation, overseas exploration, nationalism, new forms of administration and new media" (Cubelic et al., 2018, 1), the term of the 'Nepalese long 19th century' has become an authoritative notion of a period for Nepal, cf. Osterhammel (2011, 87–88), Michaels (2018), Zotter (2018). Hence, it could be integrated into PeriodO. Through such periods, historical geographical concepts such as former kingdoms and areas of rulership can be made comparable and interoperable with other places, be they chronologically congruent, previous, subsequent, or overlapping.

In this context, it needs to be discussed (i) when to consider a place as historical and (ii) how to classify it. Would the evidence of a continuous, legal administrative succession decide on the classification as an area of authority (cf. the hierarchy in Fig. 5)? For instance, is Punjab under Maharaja Ranjit Singh, the 'Lion of Punjab', a `HistoricalAreaOfAuthority`, a `Country` to be classified as 'historical', or even a `HistoricalPlace`?

Figure 5: Historical concepts of NEPALPLACES.

5. Conclusion

NEPALPLACES presents the first step towards the creation of LINKEDOPENNEPAL. It shows very promising results but still is a work in progress: By incrementally populating the ontology with all the toponyms registered in the Documenta Nepalica text corpus, the ability of NEPALPLACES to facilitate modeling of all relevant information will be put to the test. This is a process that will most likely necessitate repeatedly revisiting its structure. To populate NEPALPLACES in an exhaustive way is, thus, a task that cannot easily be integrated into the research project's time frame and work flow. Therefore, we consider executing this task either in the form of a satellite or, more likely, a follow-up project.

[28] Cf. https://perio.do/en/.

6. Bibliographical References

Acheson, E., De Sabbata, S., and Purves, R. (2017). A quantitative analysis of global gazetteers: Patterns of coverage for common feature types. *Computers, Environment and Urban Systems*, 64:309–320.

Aguado de Cea, G., Montiel-Ponsada, E., Kernerman, I., and Ordan, N. (2016). From Dictionaries to Cross-lingual Lexical Resources. *Kernerman DICTIONARY News*, 24:25–31.

Bajracharya, M. and Michaels, A. (2022). Introduction. In Manik Bajracharya, editor, *Slavery and Unfree Labour in Nepal. Documents from the 18th to Early 20th Century*, pages 6–36. Heidelberg University Publishing, Heidelberg.

Bechhofer, S., van Harmelen, F., Hendler, J., Horrocks, I., McGuinness, D., Patel-Schneider, P., and Stein, L. (2004). OWL Web Ontology Language. Reference. W3C Recommendation 10 February 2004. URL: https://www.w3.org/TR/2004/REC-owl-ref-20040210/ [accessed: 03-10-2022].

Bellandi, A., Giovannetti, E., and Weingart, A. (2018). Multilingual and Multiword Phenomena in a lemon Old Occitan Medico-Botanical Lexicon. *Information*, 9 (3), 52.

Berners-Lee, T. (2009). Linked Data. URL: https://www.w3.org/DesignIssues/LinkedData.html [accessed: 03-15-2022].

Bizer, C., Heath, T., and Berners-Lee, T. (2009). Linked Data – The Story So Far. *International Journal on Semantic Web and Information Systems*, 5:1–22.

Bosque-Gil, J., Gracia, J., Montiel-Ponsoda, E., and Gómez-Pérez, A. (2018). Models to represent linguistic linked data. *Natural Language Engineering*, 24(6):811–859.

Brickley, D. and Guha, R. (2014). XML Schema Part 0: Primer Second Edition. URL: https://www.w3.org/TR/rdf-schema/ [accessed: 03-14-2022].

Chiarcos, C., McCrae, J., Cimiano, P., and Fellbaum, C. (2013). Towards Open Data for Linguistics: Lexical Linked Data. In Alessandro Oltramari, et al., editors, *New Trends of Research in Ontologies and Lexical Resources: Ideas, Projects, Systems*, pages 7–25. Springer, Berlin, Heidelberg.

Cimiano, P., McCrae, J. P., and Buitelaar, P. (2016). Lexicon Model for Ontologies: Community Report. Final Community Group Report, 10 May 2016. URL: https://www.w3.org/2016/05/ontolex/ [accessed: 03-15-2022].

Cimiano, P., Chiarcos, C., McCrae, J., and Gracia, J. (2020). *Linguistic Linked Data: Representation, Generation and Applications*. Springer, Cham.

Ciotti, F. and Tomasi, F. (2016–2017). Formal Ontologies, Linked Data, and TEI Semantics. *Journal of the Text Encoding Initiative* [Online], Issue 9.

Cox, S. and Little, C. (2020). Time Ontology in OWL. W3C Candidate Recommendation 26 March 2020. URL: https://www.w3.org/TR/owl-time/ [accessed: 03-10-2022].

Crofts, N., Doerr, M., and Gill, T. (2003). The CIDOC Conceptual Reference Model. A Standard for Communicating Cultural Contents. *Cultivate Interactive*, 9.

Cubelic, S., Michaels, A., and Zotter, A. (2018). Studying Documents of South Asia: An Introduction. In Simon Cubelic, et al., editors, *Studies in Historical Documents from Nepal and India*, pages 1–33. Heidelberg University Publishing, Heidelberg.

Cyganiak, R., Wood, D., and Lanthaler, M. (2014). RDF 1.1. concepts and abstract syntax: W3C recommendation 25 February 2014. URL: https://www.w3.org/TR/2014/REC-rdf11-concepts-20140225/ [accessed: 03-14-2022].

Declerck, T., Wandl-Vogt, E., and Mörth, K. (2015). Towards a Pan European Lexicography by Means of Linked (Open) Data. In Iztok Kosem, et al., editors, *Electronic Lexicography in the 21st Century: Linking Lexical Data in the Digital Age. Proceedings of the eLex 2015 Conference, 11-13 August 2015, Herstmonceux Castle, United Kingdom*, pages 342–355, Ljubljana/Brighton. Trojina, Institute for Applied Slovene Studies/Lexical Computing Ltd.

Diwasa, T., Bandhu, C., and Nepal, B. (2007). *The Intangible Cultural Heritage of Nepal: Future Directions*. UNESCO Kathmandu Series of Monographs and Working Papers No 14, Kathmandu.

Eide, Ø. (2014–2015). Ontologies, Data Modeling, and TEI. *Journal of the Text Encoding Initiative*, Issue 8.

Fallside, D. and Walmsley, P. (2004). RDF Schema 1.1. W3C Recommendation 25 February 2014. URL: https://www.w3.org/TR/xmlschema-0/ [accessed: 03-14-2022].

Gandon, F., Sabou, M., and Sack, H. (2017). Weaving a Web of Linked Resources. *Semantic Web Journal*, 6:1–6.

Herman, I., Aside, B., McCarron, S., and Birbeck, M. (2015). RDFa Core 1.1 – Third Edition. URL: https://www.w3.org/TR/rdfa-core [accessed: 03-14-2022].

Hutt, M. (1988). *Nepali. A National Language and its Literature*. Sterling Publishers, New Delhi.

Jarrar, M., Amayreh, H., and Mccrae, J. (2019). Representing Arabic Lexicons in Lemon – a Preliminary Study. In Thierry Declerck et al., editors, *2nd Conference on Language, Data and Knowledge (LDK 2019). Posters Track*. Birzeit University.

Khatiwoda, R., Cubelic, S., and Michaels, A. (2021). *The Mulukī Ain of 1854. Nepal's First Legal Code*. Heidelberg University Publishing, Heidelberg.

Michaels, A. (2008). *Siva in Trouble. Festivals and Rituals at the Pasupatinatha Temple of Deopatan*. OUP, New York.

Michaels, A. (2018). *Kultur und Geschichte Nepals*. Alfred Kröner Verlag, Stuttgart.

Osterhammel, J. (2011). *Die Verwandlung der Welt: Eine Geschichte des 19. Jahrhunderts*. C.H. Beck, München.

Pokharel, S., Sherif, M., and Lehmann, J. (2014). Ontology Based Data Access and Integration for Improving the Effectiveness of Farming in Nepal. In *Proceedings of the International Conference on Web Intelligence and Intelligent Agent Technologies (WI-IAT '14)*, pages 319–326.

Prud'hommeaux, E. and Carothers, G. (2014). RDF 1.1 Turtle: Terse RDF Triple Language. W3C Recommendation, 25 February 2014. URL: http://www.w3.org/TR/turtle/ [accessed: 03-10-2022].

Rabinowitz, A., Shaw, R., Buchanan, S., Golden, P., and Kansa, E. (2016). Making Sense of the Ways We Make Sense of the Past: The Periodo Project. *Bulletin of the Institute of Classical Studies*, 59(2):42–55, 12.

Riccardi, T. (2003). Nepali. In George Cardona et al., editors, *The Indo-Aryan Languages*, pages 538–580, New York. Routledge.

TEI Consortium. (2017). TEI P5: Guidelines for Electronic Text Encoding and Interchange. Version 3.2.0. Last updated on 10th July 2017. URL: http://www.tei-c.org/release/doc/tei-p5-doc/en/html/ [accessed: 03-16-2022].

Tittel, S., Bermúdez-Sabel, H., and Chiarcos, C. (2018). Using RDFa to Link Text and Dictionary Data for Medieval French. In John P. McCrae, et al., editors, *Proceedings of the Eleventh International Conference on Language Resources and Evaluation (LREC 2018). 6th Workshop on Linked Data in Linguistics (LDL-2018), 12 May 2018, Miyazaki, Japan*, pages 30–38, Paris. ELRA.

van Driem, G. (2001). *Languages of the Himalayas*. Brill, Leiden/Boston/Köln.

von Wartburg, W. (since 1922). *Französisches Etymologisches Wörterbuch. Eine darstellung des galloromanischen sprachschatzes – FEW*. ATILF. [continued by O. Jänicke, C.T. Gossen, J.-P. Chambon, J.-P. Chauveau, and Yan Greub].

Wood, D., Zaidman, M., Ruth, L., and Hausenblas, M. (2014). *Linked data: structured data on the web*. Manning Publications Co., New York.

Zotter, A. (2018). Papier ist geduldig. Digital edierte Dokumente geben Aufschluss zur Nationalstaatsbildung in Nepals "langem 19. Jahrhundert" (1768–1951). In Union der deutschen Akademien der Wissenschaften, editor, *Die Wissenschaftsakademien – Wissensspeicher für die Zukunft Forschungsprojekte im Akademienprogramm*, Berlin.

Proceedings of the EURALI Workshop @LREC2020, pages 17–21
Marseille, 20 June 2022

Semiautomatic Speech Alignment for Under-Resourced Languages

Juho Leinonen[1], Niko Partanen[2], Sami Virpioja[2], Mikko Kurimo[1]
[1]Aalto University, [2]University of Helsinki
{juho.leinonen, mikko.kurimo}@aalto.fi
{niko.partanen, sami.virpioja}@helsinki.fi

Abstract

Cross-language forced alignment is a solution for linguists who create speech corpora for very low-resource languages. However, cross-language is an additional challenge making a complex task, forced alignment, even more difficult. We study how linguists can impart domain expertise to the tasks to increase the performance of automatic forced aligners while keeping the time effort still lower than with manual forced alignment. First, we show that speech recognizers have a clear bias in starting the word later than a human annotator, which results in micro-pauses in the results that do not exist in manual alignments, and study which is the best way to automatically remove these silences. Second, we ask the linguists to simplify the task by splitting long interview audios into shorter lengths by providing some manually aligned segments and evaluating the results of this process. Finally, we study how correlated source language performance is to target language performance, since often it is an easier task to find a better source model than to adapt to the target language.

Keywords: speech recognition, cross-language forced alignment, low-resource

1. Introduction

When collecting new speech corpora, a valuable type of metadata to add is timestamps for the words in the audio. These are useful for other researchers for checking the context of the spoken word and for speech recognition and synthesis research. This matching of text to speech is called forced alignment, and it is necessary for many linguists' work. Both word and utterance-level alignments have various uses and clear benefits when compared to transcriptions that have no timestamp information available. Creating word-level alignments from utterance-level annotations can also be considered a special context of forced alignment.

Currently, many tools have automated the alignment process with speech recognizers. However, this automatic forced alignment is limited to languages with capable speech recognizers. While there are ready-made recipes to train a speech recognizer when given data, one should not underestimate the domain expertise required to accomplish this, especially if an error occurs and needs fixing. Another significant issue is the data. A large corpus can have a recognizer trained on it, and afterward, it can align the data. Nevertheless, there are languages and domains with insufficient data to train a recognizer. Especially in case of seriously under-documented languages there are no possibilities to have larger amounts of training data of any type. Here, cross-language forced alignment can help researchers quickly create good alignments with significantly less effort than manual aligning. However, cross-language recognition adds complexity to an already challenging task, so we examine what researchers might do to make this task easier.

Automatic forced alignment is not a new concept. Many of the first automatic speech recognition (ASR) systems have been used for generating alignments since it is a natural part of speech recognition workflow; speech recognition frameworks generate forced alignments of the audio and then use these as training examples for the machine learning method underneath. Forced aligners only need the first part of the process since they assume the model already exists. FAVE (Rosenfelder et al., 2011) and Munich AUtomatic Segmentation system (MAUS) (Kisler et al., 2017) work like this.

In contrast, Montreal Forced Aligner (MFA) (McAuliffe et al., 2017) allows the researcher to train a new recognizer for a new language or adapt an existing one for a new corpus. However, this does require data, recommendations being at least one hour in the optimal case (Johnson et al., 2018). In addition, if the researcher is working with a language with no speech recognizer, there usually is no pronunciation lexicon either. This is an issue since most aligners work with the conventional speech recognition framework of using a lexicon to combine the orthography with the acoustic models performing the aligning. A recent approach gaining popularity is using end-to-end framework to both recognize (Chan et al., 2015) and align speech (Li et al., 2022) without the use of lexicons. The other benefit of this approach is the ability to jointly train the whole model, which has shown great promise with very large datasets.

Cross-language forced alignment (CLFA) solves these issues because it uses a well-resourced source language to do the alignments without the researcher having to train a new acoustic model with insufficient data. However, this requires a model for a language that is related to the target language. The process is still challenging, so it would benefit from all advantages it can get.

In this paper, we examine how different types of linguistic knowledge affect cross-language forced alignment. We demonstrate the concepts first with a larger high quality Finnish corpus, and then with a real use case and try to apply them to a current Komi documentation project. We focus on word-level alignment, as it is sufficient resolution for the corpus documentation task we are trying to improve, and much easier to produce for evaluation purposes than phone-level alignment.

2. Related Research

Forced aligners are based on popular speech recognition frameworks, such as HTK (Young et al., 2002) for FAVE and Prosodylab-aligner (Gorman et al., 2011). Some of the first research on CLFA is using these frameworks for Yoloxóchitl Mixtec, an Oto-Manguean language (DiCanio et al., 2013). Currently, the most popular forced alignment toolkit is the MFA (McAuliffe et al., 2017). Based on Kaldi (Povey et al., 2011), it uses its popular speech recognition pipeline from input features to model choice using Gaussian mixture models (GMM) to model the phonemes of the speech. It provides useful features such as data validation, speaker adaptive training (SAT), and fine-tuning on new data. Tang and Bennett (2019) use it to align cross-language speech by pooling the source and target data together before training the model. Another tool based on Kaldi is Gentle[1], and in comparison to MFA, it uses deep neural networks (DNN) instead of GMMs to model phonemes. Munich AUtomatic Segmentation system (MAUS) (Kisler et al., 2017) is another tool capable of forced alignment. Its framework is based on statistical expert systems and it has been used in forced alignment and cross-language forced alignment. Strunk et al. (2014) use a language-independent version of MAUS to align many under-resourced languages with good results. Jones et al. (2019) use MAUS to align English based Kriol, comparing Italian source language to the language-independent MAUS. Surprisingly they found that Italian performed better than the independent model, showing promise for large related language source models. Promising results have also been achieved by applying Connectionist temporal classification (CTC) algorithm to align speech (Kürzinger et al., 2020).

3. Experiments

We will evaluate the effects of two methods for utilizing expert knowledge to improve the accuracy of automatic alignments. First, we eliminate artificial micropauses of different durations from end-alignments. Second, we simplify the data before alignment by segmenting it. The performance metric we use is the percentage of aligner-created word-boundaries 10ms, 25ms, 50ms, and 100ms length from the correct gold label boundary. A better model will have a higher percentage in lower millisecond ranges. Our code and models are publicly available.[2]

[1] https://github.com/lowerquality/gentle

[2] https://github.com/aalto-speech/finnish-forced-alignment

Lang	Dataset	Length	Tokens
fin	Finnish	1h7m27s	6464
kpv	Recording 1 (R1)	2m45s	179
	Recording 2 (R2)	4m11s	259
	Recording 3 (R3)	4m45s	446
	Recording 4 (R4)	4m32s	344

Table 1: The length of the speech data and number of tokens, each adding two datapoints (start and end boundary). Datasets in Komi (kpv) represent recordings from 1950 representing four subvarieties of Ižma dialect.

3.1. Datasets

Komi materials used in this experiment have been archived into the Institute for the Languages of Finland (Kotus). They were initially recorded in the 1950s and transcribed in the 1960s (Itkonen, 1958; Stipa, 1962). The whole collection represents different Komi dialects, and in this sample, four localities of the Ižma dialect were included. The recordings are available for research purposes in the Tape Archive of the Finnish Language maintained by Kotus, and the whole collection will be published when ready in the Language Bank of Finland. The manual word-level alignment was created primarily to test different forced alignment systems, and the annotations also include more extensive utterance-level segmentation. In practice, the intended goal is to align transcriptions and audio recordings at a coarser level, which would make them comparable to different contemporary language documentation corpora. Since the Komi dataset is so small, we also experiment with a Finnish dataset (Vainio, 2001; Raitio et al., 2008) of read-speech from one speaker created for speech synthesis purposes. Details of the data can be seen in Table 1.

3.2. Models

We take the Finnish Kaldi ASR model created in (Mansikkaniemi et al., 2017) and used in (Leinonen et al., 2021) as a baseline (Base). In addition, we experiment with two other Kaldi-based Finnish ASR models: Donate Speech (DS) model from a Finnish crowdsourcing project called Lahjoita Puhetta that collected over 3600 hours of speech (Moisio et al., 2022), and Conversational (Conv) model from (Moisio, 2021). For the former, a 100h manually transcribed subset of the whole data was used for training. The sizes of the acoustic models are 36.5, 16.6 and 16.5 million parameters for Base, DS and Conv. While the baseline is considerable larger, the latter two have more modern speech recognition architecture utilizing Kaldi's most recent updates and trained with a larger variety of speech data.

However, all of them are fundamentally DNN-based acoustic models trained with the lattice-free maximum mutual information (LF-MMI) criterion. They all also use the same acoustic features, 39 dimension Mel-frequency cepstral coefficients (MFCCs) and Cepstral mean and variance normalization (CMVN). For speaker adaption they employ Kaldi's i-vectors. Since these are conventional automatic speech recognition models, they need pronunciation dictionaries. We create them by assuming a direct grapheme-to-phoneme (G2P) mapping. For Finnish this is straightforward as the writing system has a clear phoneme-to-grapheme correspondence. For Komi this direct G2P assumption is also sensible so we use domain expertise to match a Komi letter to the closest Finnish phonetic equivalent. In cases where a single phoneme would be insufficient, we combine multiple Finnish phonemes to represent a single Komi phoneme.

We also experiment with a Wav2Vec2 (W2V2) model (Baevski et al., 2020) from the Lahjoita Puhetta project. The pre-trained model is based on VoxPopuli corpus (Wang et al., 2021), fine-tuned with the same subset as the DS model. We modify the code in (Hira, 2021), which is using the CTC segmentation method presented in (Kürzinger et al., 2020) to create the alignments. Wav2Vec2 maps the speech directly to text so no pronunciation dictionary is needed.

3.3. Removing Silence

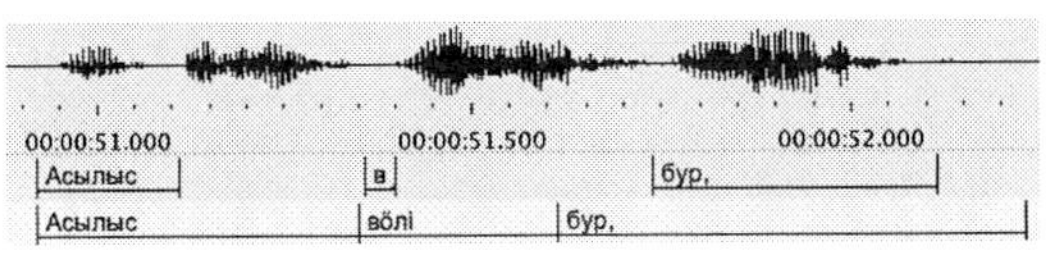

Figure 1: Difference in occurrences of small silences in automatic (upper) and manual (lower) alignments.

Figure 1 shows that automatic forced aligners leave short silences between words, while human-produced annotations for continuous speech, as in this example, have word boundaries with no silences. Current speech aligners' original purpose is to produce training material for speech recognition training. This material is optimized to contain all necessary information to differentiate between the tokens used, not to be optimal for corpus documentation in linguistic settings. This optimization can create micro-pauses as a side effect. However, to be a valuable tool for linguists, the results should serve their needs.

Therefore we experiment on the optimal way to remove the silences, testing where to split the silence before merging it to the surrounding words, extending the word boundary markings to cover the silence. We try three different values for a duration below which we consider a silence to be a splittable micro-pause. For convenience we use the same values as for the cutoffs used for errors, excluding 10ms, as that is our model's minimum resolution and therefore splitting it would be ineffective. We also compare three types of splitting: a start split merges the silence to the next word, middle divides it evenly between the words, and end split extends the word boundary of the first word to contain the silence.

3.4. Segmenting Audio

Another possible solution to make the alignment task simpler is to use segmented audio. Longer segments are challenging since errors from the beginning can propagate. Here we compare aligning the four Komi audios in full to shorter sentence-long segments of the same audio.

4. Results

Model	<10	<25	<50	<100
Base	0.21	0.55	0.84	0.98
DS	0.22	0.62	0.94	1.00
Conv	0.29	0.67	0.93	1.00
W2V2	0.12	0.29	0.59	0.91

Table 2: Accuracies of different Finnish models with the Finnish data. Percentages describe the amount of alignment deviations below the 10, 25, 50 and 100 millisecond cutoff values.

As we can see from Table 2, there was room for improvement in Finnish forced alignment. While the DS model is marginally better than Base in shorter than 10ms errors, it has 7 percentage points more of its deviations below the 25ms cutoff, and over 94% of its errors are below 50ms. Depending on the purpose of the automatic alignments, it might not need any manual correction. The Conv model is even better, with almost a third of the mistakes being less than 10ms, the resolution of Kaldi's alignments. It is also 5 percentage points better than the DS in 25ms range, however slightly worse in 50ms. This even though the data of the DS model, one person speaking uninterrupted, might be a closer match to the domain of the test data. The Wav2vec2 approach performs the poorest, being basically one error range behind the other models.

Table 3 shows the results of the silence tests. When comparing results to those shown in Table 2 we see that every conventional model gains minor improvements from the start split, with other types either not changing the results or worsening them. The most significant gains are achieved for the DS model, with 2-3% in absolute terms and 9-5% relative. As mentioned earlier, these improvements are related to that the speech recognition models start the words later than human annotators. While splitting does not change the order of the models in terms of performance, it is a simple algorithm with a consistent improvement with start split and 50ms or less micro-pause duration.

With the Wav2Vec2 algorithm, we see even larger gains with splitting silences, with absolute increases of 3-14 percentage points and 24-31% relative. Here the best improvements are again with the start split; however,

Model	Type / Duration	<10			<25			<50			<100		
		25ms	50ms	100ms	25ms	50ms	100ms	25ms	50ms	100ms	25ms	50ms	100ms
Base	start	0.22	0.22	0.22	0.56	0.56	0.56	0.86	0.86	0.86	0.98	0.98	0.98
	middle	0.21	0.21	0.21	0.55	0.54	0.54	0.84	0.84	0.84	0.98	0.98	0.98
	end	0.20	0.20	0.20	0.53	0.53	0.53	0.83	0.82	0.82	0.98	0.98	0.97
DS	start	0.24	0.24	0.24	0.64	0.65	0.65	0.95	0.95	0.95	1.00	1.00	0.99
	middle	0.23	0.22	0.22	0.62	0.62	0.61	0.95	0.95	0.94	1.00	1.00	1.00
	end	0.21	0.21	0.20	0.59	0.58	0.58	0.94	0.93	0.92	1.00	1.00	0.99
Conv	start	0.30	0.30	0.30	0.68	0.68	0.68	0.93	0.94	0.93	1.00	1.00	0.99
	middle	0.29	0.29	0.29	0.67	0.67	0.67	0.93	0.93	0.93	1.00	1.00	0.99
	end	0.28	0.28	0.28	0.67	0.66	0.66	0.93	0.93	0.92	1.00	1.00	0.99
W2V2	start	0.12	0.14	0.15	0.30	0.38	0.38	0.60	0.72	0.73	0.91	0.93	0.93
	middle	0.11	0.11	0.11	0.29	0.28	0.29	0.59	0.60	0.62	0.91	0.92	0.92
	end	0.11	0.09	0.08	0.28	0.20	0.19	0.58	0.47	0.45	0.91	0.89	0.88

Table 3: Different Finnish models with resulting alignments post-processed with different silence removal methods using the Finnish dataset. Type describes the split used, Duration tells below what length is considered a micro-pause.

the optimal micro-pause duration is longer than in conventional models, being the maximum distance measured in errors, 100ms.

When we combine the previous results with those of segmenting the Komi audio, we can see mixed results from Table 4. If the model recognizes the full audio at all, it gets better results than with the segmented pieces, but the segments allow every audio to be aligned: only failed cases are with complete audios. The splitting of silences less than 50ms helps only marginally. It may be the case that when the results are poor, a longer micro-pause duration needs to be considered, as with the Wav2Vec2 model. Interestingly, the superior model for Finnish performs worse here overall. The only cases where it surpasses the baseline are for the segmented Recordings 1 and 4, in both below 100ms errors. The baseline model seems more robust against cross-language speech recognition, something that cannot be tested on Finnish data. Unfortunately, this does not allow easy comparison of models before choosing the right one for a CLFA task.

5. Conclusion

In this paper, we evaluated expert knowledge on cross-language forced alignment in the form of segmenting audio and splitting inaccurate micro-pauses in resulting alignments.

We began experimenting with the splitting of silences due to feedback from linguists. We found that silence splitting performed well on language-specific alignment on excellent audio quality but less on cross-language tasks with poorer audio quality. Instead of finding a global parameter for this, it might be best to find ways to describe the results and allow users to set these values themselves while trying to generate metrics to warn of unsafe values.

As for segmenting audio, low-quality recordings can be aligned with segmented audio, resulting in poorer quality alignments, while the full length has a chance of failing. Segmentation helps in the case of challenging recordings, but the correct places to cut audio are not obvious. However, the speed of automatic forced alignment allows an iterative process to experiment with both methods to achieve the best results possible.

Data & Model		<10		<25		<50		<100	
		-	sil	-	sil	-	sil	-	sil
Base	R1#	0.16	0.16	0.29	0.30	0.49	0.49	0.62	0.62
	R1	0.27	0.27	0.37	0.37	0.51	0.51	0.62	0.62
	R2#	0.17	0.17	0.28	0.28	0.41	0.41	0.53	0.53
	R2	0.34	0.34	0.43	0.43	0.50	0.50	0.62	0.62
	R3#	0.00	0.00	0.00	0.00	0.01	0.01	0.03	0.03
	R3	-	-	-	-	-		-	-
	R4#	0.19	0.19	0.32	0.32	0.45	0.46	0.61	0.61
	R4	-	-	-	-	-	-	-	-
Conv	R1#	0.13	0.13	0.28	0.28	0.46	0.46	0.70	0.70
	R1	-	-	-	-	-	-	-	-
	R2#	0.14	0.14	0.29	0.30	0.46	0.46	0.62	0.62
	R2	-	-	-	-	-	-	-	-
	R3#	0.00	0.00	0.00	0.00	0.01	0.01	0.03	0.02
	R3	0.00	0.00	0.00	0.00	0.00	0.00	0.00	0.00
	R4#	0.11	0.11	0.29	0.29	0.48	0.49	0.70	0.70
	R4	-	-	-	-	-	-	-	-

Table 4: Results with full Komi audios compared to segmented audios (#). Without splitting (-), or 50ms (sil). Dash (-) in results represents failed alignment run.

6. Acknowledgements

We acknowledge the computational resources provided by both the Aalto Science-IT project and CSC – IT Center for Science, Finland. SV was supported by the FoTran project, funded by the European Research Council (ERC) under the European Union's Horizon 2020 research and innovation programme (grant agreement № 771113).

7. References

Baevski, A., Zhou, H., Mohamed, A., and Auli, M. (2020). wav2vec 2.0: A framework for self-supervised learning of speech representations.

Chan, W., Jaitly, N., Le, Q. V., and Vinyals, O. (2015). Listen, attend and spell.

DiCanio, C., Nam, H., Whalen, D. H., Timothy Bunnell, H., Amith, J. D., and García, R. C. (2013). Using automatic alignment to analyze endangered language data: Testing the viability of untrained alignment. *The Journal of the Acoustical Society of America*, 134(3):2235–2246.

Gorman, K., Howell, J., and Wagner, M. (2011). Prosodylab-aligner: A tool for forced alignment of laboratory speech. *Canadian Acoustics*, 39(3):192–193.

Hira, M. (2021). Forced alignment with wav2vec2. `https://github.com/pytorch/audio/blob/main/examples/tutorials/forced_alignment_tutorial.py`.

Itkonen, E. (1958). Komin tasavallan kielitieteeseen tutustumassa. *Virittäjä*, 62(1):66–66.

Johnson, L. M., Di Paolo, M., and Bell, A. (2018). Forced alignment for understudied language varieties: Testing prosodylab-aligner with tongan data. *Language Documentation & Conservation*, 12:80–123.

Jones, C., Li, W., Almeida, A., and German, A. (2019). Evaluating cross-linguistic forced alignment of conversational data in north australian kriol, an under-resourced language. *Language Documentation and Conservation*, pages 281–299.

Kisler, T., Reichel, U., and Schiel, F. (2017). Multilingual processing of speech via web services. *Computer Speech & Language*, 45:326 – 347.

Kürzinger, L., Winkelbauer, D., Li, L., Watzel, T., and Rigoll, G. (2020). CTC-segmentation of large corpora for german end-to-end speech recognition. In *Speech and Computer*, pages 267–278. Springer International Publishing.

Leinonen, J., Virpioja, S., and Kurimo, M. (2021). Grapheme-based cross-language forced alignment: Results with uralic languages. In *Proceedings of the 23rd Nordic Conference on Computational Linguistics (NoDaLiDa)*, pages 345–350.

Li, J., Meng, Y., Wu, Z., Meng, H., Tian, Q., Wang, Y., and Wang, Y. (2022). Neufa: Neural network based end-to-end forced alignment with bidirectional attention mechanism.

Mansikkaniemi, A., Smit, P., Kurimo, M., et al. (2017). Automatic construction of the Finnish parliament speech corpus. In *INTERSPEECH 2017–18th Annual Conference of the International Speech Communication Association.*

McAuliffe, M., Socolof, M., Mihuc, S., Wagner, M., and Sonderegger, M. (2017). Montreal forced aligner: Trainable text-speech alignment using kaldi. In *Interspeech*, volume 2017, pages 498–502.

Moisio, A., Porjazovski, D., Rouhe, A., Getman, Y., Virkkunen, A., Grósz, T., Lindén, K., and Kurimo, M. (2022). Lahjoita puhetta – a large-scale corpus of spoken finnish with some benchmarks.

Moisio, A. (2021). Speech recognition for conversational finnish. Master's thesis, Aalto University School of Electrical Engineering, Espoo.

Povey, D., Ghoshal, A., Boulianne, G., Burget, L., Glembek, O., Goel, N., Hannemann, M., Motlicek, P., Qian, Y., Schwarz, P., et al. (2011). The kaldi speech recognition toolkit. In *IEEE 2011 workshop on automatic speech recognition and understanding*, number CONF. IEEE Signal Processing Society.

Raitio, T., Suni, A., Pulakka, H., Vainio, M., and Alku, P. (2008). Hmm-based finnish text-to-speech system utilizing glottal inverse filtering. In *Ninth Annual Conference of the International Speech Communication Association.*

Rosenfelder, I., Fruehwald, J., Evanini, K., and Yuan, J. (2011). Fave (forced alignment and vowel extraction) program suite. http://fave. ling. upenn. edu.

Stipa, G. J. (1962). Käynti syrjäänien tieteen tyyssijassa. *Virittäjä*, 66(1):61–68.

Strunk, J., Schiel, F., Seifart, F., et al. (2014). Untrained forced alignment of transcriptions and audio for language documentation corpora using webmaus. In *LREC*, pages 3940–3947.

Tang, K. and Bennett, R. (2019). Unite and conquer: Bootstrapping forced alignment tools for closely-related minority languages (mayan). In *Proceedings of the 19th International Congress of Phonetic Sciences, Melbourne, Australia*, pages 1719–1723.

Vainio, M. (2001). Artificial neural network based prosody models for finnish text-to-speech synthesis.

Wang, C., Rivière, M., Lee, A., Wu, A., Talnikar, C., Haziza, D., Williamson, M., Pino, J., and Dupoux, E. (2021). Voxpopuli: A large-scale multilingual speech corpus for representation learning, semi-supervised learning and interpretation.

Young, S., Evermann, G., Gales, M., Hain, T., Kershaw, D., Liu, X., Moore, G., Odell, J., Ollason, D., Povey, D., et al. (2002). The htk book. *Cambridge university engineering department*, 3(175):12.

Proceedings of the EURALI Workshop @LREC2020, pages 22–27
Marseille, 20 June 2022

How to Digitize Completely: Interactive Geovizualization of a Sketch Map from the Kuzmina Archive

Elena Lazarenko, Aleksandr Riaposov
Universität Hamburg
Hamburg, Germany
{elena.lazarenko, aleksandr.riaposov}@uni-hamburg.de

Abstract

This paper discusses work in progress on the digitization of a sketch map of the Taz River basin – a region that is lacking highly detailed open-source cartography data. The original sketch is retrieved from the archive of Selkup materials gathered by Angelina Ivanovna Kuzmina in the 1960s and 1970s. The data quality and challenges that come with it are evaluated and a task-specific workflow is designed. The process of the turning a series of hand-drawn images with non-structured geographical and linguistic data into an interactive, geographically precise digital map is described both from linguistic and technical perspectives. Furthermore, the map objects in focus are differentiated based on the geographical type of the object and the etymology of the name. This provides an insight into the peculiarities of the linguistic history of the region and contributes to the cartography of the Uralic languages.

Keywords: Uralic languages, language maps, digitization

1. Introduction

The aim of the long-term project INEL (Grammar, Corpora, Language Technology for Indigenous Northern Eurasian Languages)[1] is sustainable documentation and analysis of the resources in highly endangered indigenous Northern Eurasian languages and their varieties (Arkhipov and Däbritz, 2018). One of the tasks pursued by the project is documentation of linguistic data in the Selkup language (Brykina et al., 2021). A significant amount of Selkup data originates from the archive collected by Angelina Ivanovna Kuzmina (1924–2002) in years 1962-1977 (Tučkova and Helimski, 2010). The collection of hand-written notes and audio recordings from the archive has been extensively digitized by INEL and an access to the written part of the archive has been provided via a Kibana Dashboard[2] that allows for the interactive exploration of the materials. The content of Kuzmina's manuscripts is scanned and stored in PDF format and alongside with the TEI P5 compliant XML catalogue ingested into the project's Elastic cluster (Lehmberg, 2020). This provides a web-based access to the manuscripts with the possibility to create complex search queries and set filters based on such criteria as keywords, place of origin, speaker, and many others. While most of the the texts from the PDFs are available not only as scans but also in markup data formats via the published versions of the INEL Selkup Corpus and via a web-based Tsakorpus platform[3], one of the archive notebooks contains data that until now has been available only as a PDF scan. It is a hand-drawn sketch map that covers the region around the river Taz and depicts toponyms and hydronyms of this region. Cartography of languages of Northern Eurasia (e.g. Uralic) is not sufficiently researched and there are blank spaces when it comes to the language distribution within this area (Koriakov, 2020). Therefore this map could be of interest for researchers but since it cannot be used for any kind of analysis in its current form, we decided to create a digital searchable version of it. It will contribute to the information about the geographic objects of the region. Moreover, we pursue a task to transform this sketch map into a language map of the region by differentiation of the objects according to their name etymology in order to visualize the distribution of different languages in this area. This paper describes the steps that have been undertaken so far and the challenges of this task. At the moment, a working version of the digitized map can be found here: https://inel.corpora.uni-hamburg.de/portal/geo/kuzmina/map.html.

2. Background

The sketch map can be found in books 3 and 4 of the first archive volume. It consists of 18 A5 format pages with the total of ca. 580 objects depicted. At least 514 objects are unique, i.e. are marked only once. Vast majority of the names on the map are hydronyms such as rivers, lakes, swamps and smaller water objects. Another big group of objects are land objects, such as settlements and islands. Moreover, there are objects of unclear origin. Each A5 list of the map has a sequential number that allows to build a single image.

[1]The project is funded by the German Federal Government and Federal States in the Academies' Programme, with funding from the Federal Ministry of Education and Research and the Free and Hanseatic City of Hamburg. The Academies' Programme is coordinated by the Union of the German Academies of Sciences and Humanities.

[2]https://inel.corpora.uni-hamburg.de/portal/kuzmina/

[3]https://inel.corpora.uni-hamburg.de/SelkupCorpus/search

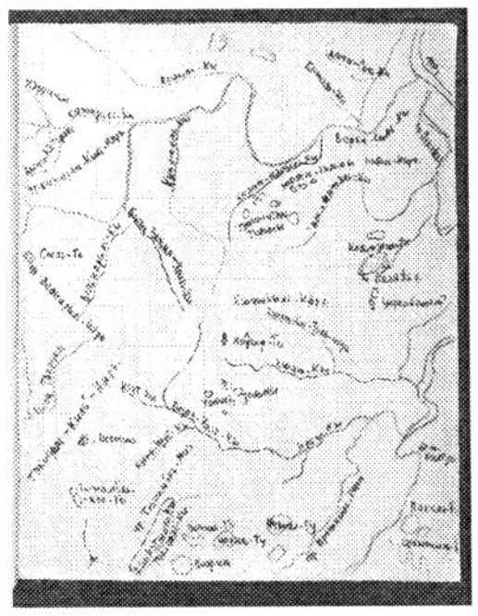

Figure 1: Example of the original sketch

2.1. Visualization challenges

At first sight it seems that the sketch depicts the geographical properties of the region with enough precision to start working with it directly, however already in the beginning we detected following challenges that created obstacles for a seamless and straightforward visualization of the map data with digital tools:

- **Absent coordinates**. No information about longitude and latitude and coordinate system is provided, which makes it impossible to use the sketch map in its original state as a reliable source of geolinguistic data.
- **Ambiguous scaling**. The distribution of the objects is arbitrary and does not follow scaling principles.
- **Inconsistent orthography and incomplete naming**. Some of the toponyms appear in unclear, hard-to-discern handwriting, for others only a part of the name is available. This makes it markedly difficult to find their direct counterparts on the modern maps of the region (see 2.2.2 for examples).
- **Poor naming convention**. A number of objects have abbreviations in front of their names, which pose problems due to the lack of a proper map legend and internal inconsistencies - e.g., о. might stand for either озеро (a lake) or остров (an island). The abbreviation ур. (for урочище) means a salient landmark of any kind, i.e. a swamp, a copse in an open field, a settlement, or some natural border; given such vagueness, we can only assume which objects were thus marked.

Together with scarce amount of precise geographical and geolinguistic data on the Taz basin, the issues listed above present an obstacle to transform the sketch map into a properly georeferenced and scaled map in a straightforward manner. Hence, we were unable to use existing GIS software packages for digitizing hand-drawn maps and had to develop a task-specific semi-structured workflow.

2.2. Workflow steps

The following workflow was developed in order to digitize the sketch:

- Merge the scattered pieces of the original sketch into a single image;
- Identify modern names of the objects represented on the sketch;
- Determine the latitude-longitude coordinate pair for each such object;
- Geovisualize the objects with known coordinates;
- Classify the objects by type and, where possible, toponyms by language of origin.

The workflow is semi-cyclic, where after the visualization step we go back to step 2 to further improve accuracy of the previously identified coordinate pairs, thus through several iterations improving the visualization itself.

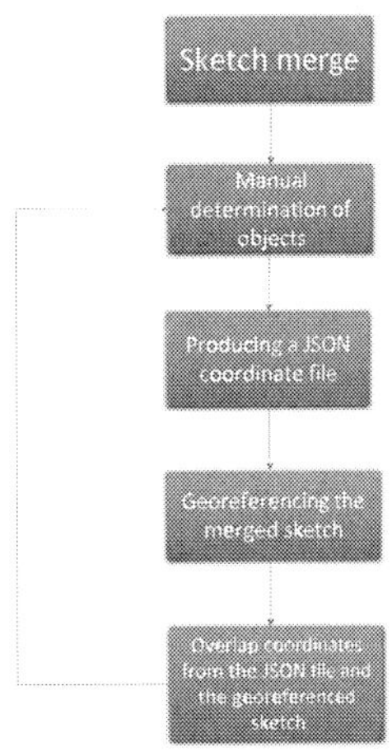

Figure 2: Workflow steps

2.2.1. Sketch merge

Due to the fact that the archive map is distributed over multiple pages, it was reasonable to merge them together for further georeferencing and scaling; moreover, it was also important for the object identification - this way we could better understand the juxtaposition of the toponyms. To do so, the archive volume pages containing the sketch were extracted from the PDF and saved as separate PNG images.

Some challenges posited themselves forthwith. Namely, there is no instruction left by Kuzmina as to how one was to put the map together; the individual pages had to be aligned with each other in a way resembling a jigsaw puzzle until it "clicked". The settlements of Tol'ka and Krasnoselkupsk (Толька and Красноселькупск respectively in the original) were taken as base points for being quite compact geographically and easily identifiable on modern maps, then the rest of the map followed suit: names of some objects, mostly rivers, were spotted on different pages, providing a reason to place these pages alongside each other; after some trial and error we could trace the flow of the Taz and its tributaries, and the composite image was complete. In retrospect, there was a method to the map's madness - the pages, once ordered, displayed a numbering pattern; in addition to that the corners of some pages have markings consisting of a number from 1 to 5 followed by a Cyrillc letter Л, С or П, the meaning of which initially was a mystery. Apparently the numbers represent the latitudinal dimension with 1 being the southernmost and 5 - its northernmost counterpart, while letters stand for "left", "center" and "right" ("Левый", "Средний" and "Правый" in Russian); unfortunately, they were not of much use when piecing the map together as some "rows" of the composite image lie four pages abreast, thus leaving some pages unmarked, and Kuzmina's notation was not consistent as to which "column" assign as leftmost, rightmost, etc.

The resulting sketch, owing to the original's somewhat arbitrary scaling and no less arbitrary borders between pages, looks quite patchy; it was very instrumental however in allowing us to disambiguate some toponyms for which there are multiple objects with matching names in the general region around the Taz, and place them correctly on the digitized map.

2.2.2. Looking for objects

Mapping the entities one may find on the sketch turned out to be quite a strenuous task, stemming from a number of facts. First, the area around the Taz basin remains relatively poorly depicted on modern go-to sources of geographical data, prompting us to cross-reference a variety of resources such as Google Maps, Yandex Maps, Wikimapia and Wikipedia. Surprising as it may seem, the most fruitful resource was the Tatar Wikipedia where we could find names for many rivers identical or almost identical to what we have on the sketch map even if these rivers have been renamed recently. Second, the names used by Kuzmina in the original sketch displayed a plethora of issues - some toponyms would have multiple spellings (e.g. Поколь-Кы/Покаль-Кы[4]), other would abruptly end in the middle (e.g. Туне... for Тунелькы-Ягарт[5]); on top of that, this lack of rigour on Kuzmina's part is further compromised by name and/or spelling changes of varying drasticity the toponyms have underwent since 1960s. All this considered, we opted for manual lookup of each object from the original sketch, as automatizing the task was not anywhere near possible.

As a preliminary step to get ahold of Kuzmina's data, we comprised a dataset containing a list of all the geographical objects on the sketch, including duplicates and misspellings. From that we started to look for the latitude-longitude coordinate pairs of items on the list via the digital maps mentioned above, beginning with easily identifiable objects (e.g. the settlements of Tol'ka, Krasnoselkupsk, and Sidorovsk), then moving on to cases where some ambiguity arose. As a means to dispel that ambiguity and prepare the data for further processing, we created a custom Google Maps view and placed coordinate markers for successfully identified objects there, settling on using only one marker per object regardless of its type; thus, for watercourses such as rivers only one coordinate pair would be set. Such visual representation of the data allowed us to check whether the placement of an object with a doubtcasting name was indeed correspondent to its position on the sketch.

Unfortunately, we were not able to identify each and every object from the sketch due to the issues mentioned above, leaving 77 of 514 in limbo for the time being. The rest we exported from Google Maps in the KML format for further processing.

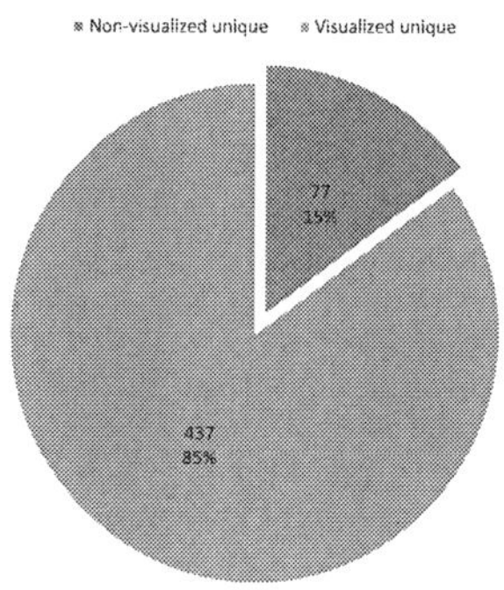

Figure 3: Distribution of identified objects

2.2.3. Technical details

No matter how convenient Google Maps were to collect the objects, it was only an intermediate step as we wanted abstain from using Google Maps services in the long-term perspective in favour of open-source solutions. Therefore for further visualization we settled to use open-source JavaScript library Leaflet[6] that works, among others, with OpenStreetMap[7] layers and is often a first-choice solution for geovisualization. Since Leaflet typically works with the JSON and GeoJSON formats, we transformed the KML data into JSON. However, the resulting JSON file was rife with irrelevant for our purposes remnants of KML data, which were manually removed. The resulting JSON file contains a FeatureCollection object where each geographical object represented as a feature with a list of attributes such as object name ("namemap",

[4] Pokol'-Ky/Pokal'-Ky

[5] Tune..., Tunel'ky-Yagart

[6] https://leafletjs.com/

[7] https://www.openstreetmap.org

"namekuz"), geographical type ("objtype") and name origin ("nameru", "namesel"). Some of the attributes (e.g. "objtype") were inherited from the original KML file, others were introduced later.[8] For testing purposes the fist version of the digitized map only showed the object distribution and the territory these objects covered. This way we could assure the quality of the JSON file, e.g. whether the latitude and longitude of points were correctly transferred from the KML structure and did not get swapped. Later we transformed it into a heatmap that colourfully depicted object clustering in order to get first impressions about the distribution of all the objects. After that we moved to classifying objects as per their type

2.2.4. Further differentiation

As soon as the quality of the JSON file was assured, we moved to more specific visualization tasks stemming from the goal to classify the objects. This was a task with gradually growing complexity. Our working hypothesis, which became a basis for further work on the data, is that geographical distribution of toponyms of different origin provides an overview of how the indigenous languages of the region were spread across the land in prerecorded history, as well as helps to determine areas of possible language contact. For that goal, we decided to group names from the sketch based on their etymology and their type - the idea behind the latter grouping being that, first, water streams such as large rivers flowing for up to 1400 km long in case of the Taz, might present a different distribution properties than compact objects such as lakes; second, we expected a different etymological outcome for settlement names since the Selkups, indigenous people of the region, preserved traditional nomadic lifestyle until well into the 20th century, at which point it is reasonable to expect local toponyms for relatively new-founded villages to display a considerable Russian influence. To begin with, as native speakers of Russian we could recognize and mark all the objects with the names of Russian origin; the respective attribute ("nameru") was also added to the JSON file. This allowed to visualize approximate distribution of the Russian versus non-Russian toponyms in the Taz basin. However, given the fact that the vast majority of the toponyms are of non-Russian origin, it did not provide us with enough information. We continued differentiating remaining toponyms by their language of origin. As the archive consists of entirely Selkup materials, it is highly likely that the source of many toponyms present on the sketch would be Selkup as well; this line of reasoning resulted in the choice of the Selkup language (provisionally omitting distinctions between its dialects) as the next direction of inquiry. To do so, we manually searched for the toponyms and their constituents in Selkup dictionaries (Bykonia et al., 2005; Kazakevič and Budianskaia, 2010), and introduced a respective attribute to the JSON file. Thus the attributes "nameru" or "namesel" would be used depending on the provenance of a toponym. Not only did we attempt to differentiate the toponyms based on their linguistic origin, but also to classify them based on the geographical type of the object. This was equally challenging due to naming convention problems specified in 2.1. To define the geographical type of the object we either evaluated its name compounds (for example, objects ending with "Кы" ("river" in Selkup) were classified as rivers), how it was depicted on the sketch map or based on the information retrieved from the modern map sources. Processing the sketch map data, the grouping we ended up settling for is presented on the Table 1.

Category	JSON "objtype"
Standing water	lake swamp
Watercourse	river creek anabranch
Land object	island settlement tract

Table 1: Types of objects

Each object then received relevant JSON attributes and each category received its own icon.

2.2.5. Putting everything together

From the technical perspective we considered it reasonable that each object type would be rendered separately in order to ensure easy map navigation. Therefore at the moment three overlays rendered from the same JSON file are loaded onto the map to display all the objects. Another layer that is also rendered from the same JSON file is the aforementioned heatmap; however, at the moment it does not appear on-load unlike other overlays and can be switched on if needed. Given the fact that many objects received only tentative coordinates and we were not fully sure about their position, to make the visualization more precise we intended to create another overlay from the sketch map. At first we needed to bring the PNG image to a state where it can be cut into layer tiles with coordinate information embedded. To do so, we used QGIS software package (long-term release version 3.22.4)[9]. One of its functions - georeferencing - allows to assign coordinate points to analogue maps, sketches, images, etc. We uploaded the PNG file to the georeferencing window and chose several objects, the coordinates of which were defined precisely. After assigning coordinates to these points, we ran a georeferencing tool with the transformation type "Thin Plate Sline" that would

[8]See 2.2.4 for further discussion of the introduced properties and types used.

[9]https://qgis.org

resample the data with the next neighbour method and use EPS:4326-WGS 84 cordinate system as the target one. We opted for Thin Plate Sline due to the fact that it can be used for images with unclear or absent scaling and no latitude-longitude information, whereas other transformation types are more suitable for analogue maps with a known coordinate system. This method requires to assign at least ten latitude-longitude pairs in order to calculate a georeferenced map. By doing so we obtained a georeferenced LZW-compressed TIFF image that was further cut into layer tiles with the maximum zoom depth of 10. Resulting tiles were overlayed on the existing Leaflet map together with the other overlays produced from the JSON file. However, the georeferncing task did not stop here. After bringing together icons from the JSON file and the sketch map tiles, we noticed several severe inconsistencies that were caused by mildly misleading orthography on the sketch map which, in turn, led us to assign coordinates to wrong objects. We updated coordinate data, purging errors from the JSON file, and afterwards introduced these points to the georeferencer and re-ran the calculations. The most up-to-date tile cut was based on 15 objects, such as lakes, islands and settlements. In order to make the map more navigable for users, we introduced features as grouped layer control where one can turn on and off each overlay separately, and on-click pop-ups displaying the name of an object in both the modern and Kuzmina's spelling. Moreover, there is a possibility to search through the whole FeatureCollection of the JSON object, allowing users to quickly find a toponym of interest.

Figure 4: Example of the digitized map.

3. Conclusion and future work

We built the first digitized variant of the sketch map from the archive of Angelina Ivanovna Kuzmina. After evaluating the quality of the source material and the challenges that come with it, we developed a data-specific workflow. The current version of the digitized map provides a good overview of the toponyms of the Taz river basin by the means of integration of modern digital maps and the original sketches. So far we have been able to assign geographical coordinates and visualize 443 objects, at least 437 of which have unique names. We have noticed that Russian toponyms is only a minor group with currently 63 visualized objects, clustering in the south-eastern and northern parts of the covered region. The differentiation of the objects of Selkup origin is still ongoing: at the moment 212 objects have been determined to emanate from Selkup. However, it is already visible that Selkup toponyms build the biggest group in the region. As the work on this visualization is still going on, we do not exclude the possibility of more changes being made to both GeoJSON and sketch map tiles. This will include deeper linguistic differentiation of the toponyms: picking out the remaining Selkup names and distinguishing them based on the dialect, as well as looking for toponyms etymologically coming from languages other than Selkup and Russian, e.g. from Evenki and Nenets. By doing so, we will turn our data into a language map and will be able to test our working hypothesis. Naturally, we also would like to bring more clarity into the remainder of the objects yet to be visualized: our task concerning these toponyms is to find coordinates and classify the objects by type. Moreover, as we find new points and double-check the existing ones, we intend to make the sketch overlay as finely-tuned and georeferenced as it can get, given irregular scaling of the original.

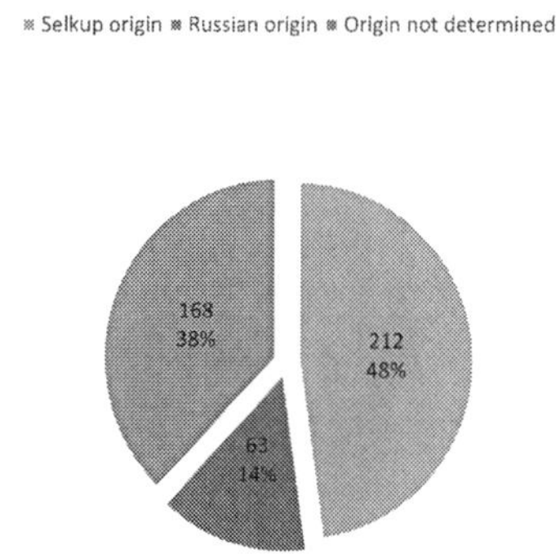

Figure 5: Etymology of the identified objects

4. Bibliographical References

Arkhipov, A. V. and Däbritz, C. L. (2018). Hamburg corpora for indigenous Northern Eurasian languages. *Tomsk Journal of Linguistics and Anthropology*, 21(3):9–18.

Bykonia, V. V., Kuznetsova, N. G., and Maksimova, N. P. (2005). *Sel'kupsko-russikii dialektnyi slovar'*. Tomsk State Pedagogical University, Tomsk.

Kazakevič, O. A. and Budianskaia, E. M. (2010). *Dialektologičeskii slovar' sel'kupskogo iazyka: Severnoe narečie*. Basko, Ekaterinburg.

Koriakov, Y. B. (2020). Kartografirovanie ural'skih yazykov. *Acta Linguistica Petropolitana. Trudy in-*

stituta lingvisticheskih issledovanii, 3(XVI):169–183.

Lehmberg, T. (2020). Digitale Edition des Kuzmina Archivs. *Finnisch-Ugrische Mitteilungen*, 44:123–130.

Tučkova, N. and Helimski, E. (2010). *Über die selkupischen Sprachmaterialien von Angelina I. Kuz'mina*, volume 5 of *Hamburger sibirische und finnougrische Materialien*. Institut fur Finnougristik/Uralistik der Universitat Hamburg, Hamburg.

5. Language Resource References

Brykina, Maria and Orlova, Svetlana and Wagner-Nagy, Beáta. (2021). *INEL Selkup Corpus*.

Proceedings of the EURALI Workshop @LREC2020, pages 28–35
Marseille, 20 June 2022

Word Class Based Language Modeling: A Case of Upper Sorbian

Isidor Konrad Maier, Johannes Ferdinand Joachim Kuhn, Frank Duckhorn
Ivan Kraljevski, Daniel Sobe, Matthias Wolff, Constanze Tschöpe
BTU Cottbus-Senftenberg, Chair of Communications Engineering, Cottbus, Germany
{isidorkonrad.maier, johannesfk.kuhn, matthias.wolff}@b-tu.de
Fraunhofer Institute for Ceramic Technologies and Systems IKTS, Dresden, Germany
{ivan.kraljevski, frank.duckhorn, constanze.tschoepe}@ikts.fraunhofer.de
Foundation for the Sorbian People, Bautzen, Germany
daniel.sobe@sorben.com

Abstract

In this paper we show how word class based language modeling can support the integration of a small language in modern applications of speech technology. The methods described in this paper can be applied for any language. We demonstrate the methods on Upper Sorbian.

The word classes model the semantic expressions of numerals, date and time of day. The implementation of the created grammars was realized in the form of finite-state-transducers (FSTs) and minimalists grammars (MGs).

We practically demonstrate the usage of the FSTs in a simple smart-home speech application, that is able to set wake-up alarms and appointments expressed in a variety of spontaneous and natural sentences.

While the created MGs are not integrated in an application for practical use yet, they provide evidence that MGs could potentially work more efficient than FSTs in built-on applications. In particular, MGs can work with a significantly smaller lexicon size, since their more complex structure lets them generate more expressions with less items, while still avoiding wrong expressions.

Keywords: word classes, minimalist grammar, language modeling, speech recognition, Upper Sorbian

1. Introduction

Recently the adoption of speech technologies, particularly speech recognition and dialogue systems has been on the rise. The tech giants (such as Google, Amazon, Microsoft, Baidu) provide speech and voice applications (personal assistants) that support mostly languages with a large population where economic interest exists.

The recent state-of-the-art automatic speech recognition (ASR) systems made a breakthrough in terms of recognition achieving "near-human" performances, however in restricted conditions, domain, and language. Also, the challenges of introducing new languages in state-of-the-art ASR systems are multi-fold, especially if they have limited electronic resources.

It is considered that if enough data for a target language exist or could be collected, then the data amount requirements for reliable speech and language modeling by using end-to-end systems and deep learning would be feasible.

In this study, we present one aspect in the development of speech technologies, namely language modeling for speech recognition in Upper Sorbian (prospectively for Lower Sorbian too) as an example of under-resourced and endangered language.

To overcome the lack of textual data necessary for reliable statistical language modeling, we adopted the word class based approach to model named entities (such as numerals, time, date). They represent reusable language resources that can be combined with both formal grammars and statistical language models in a custom speech applications. The resources including text data, grammar definitions and tools are made publicly available with an open-source license.

1.1. Sorbian Languages

The Sorbian languages are spoken in Lusatia in Eastern Germany. The Sorbian languages consist of Upper- and Lower Sorbian - which have standardized writing systems - and an intermediate dialect continuum. All Sorbian languages except Upper Sorbian are highly endangered by extinction (Moseley, 2012).

They belong to the Western Slavic languages along with Polish, Czech, Slovakian and others. They form a subbranch of the Slavic language family with high degree of mutual intelligibility (Golubović and Gooskens, 2015). Lower- and Upper Sorbian are especially similar to Polish and Czech respectively (Mětšk, 1958).

For detailed linguistic information on Upper Sorbian we recommend Anstatt et al. (2020). Overall, Upper Sorbian is described as a typical Slavic language. Its most notable peculiarities are the dual as a grammatical number and the German influence, especially on vocabulary, sentence structure and pronunciation.

1.2. State-of-the-Art

1.2.1. Speech Technology in Sorbian Languages

Due to the mutual similarity between (West) Slavic languages, cross-dialectal language technology could be employed. This approach has already showed success across Spanish dialects and across Arabic dialects, see (Elfeky et al., 2018).

Note that the division into either different languages or

just different dialects is rarely linguistically but rather politically classified (Weston and Jensen, 2000).
Just as Arabic dialects and Spanish dialects share a common standard language each, also for Slavic languages there is a constructed Interslavic language that is highly intelligible with other Slavic languages (Wierzbicki, 2019).
Specifically, Nědolužko (2019) using Czech language data for Upper Sorbian has been considered.
Sorbian language script has been standardized and integrated into various international norms, like ISO639, BCP47 and Unicode Common Locale Data Repository (CLDR) (Böhmak, 2019). Electronical Lexica for Sorbian words and for Sorbian names have been created, and a text-to-speech function for Lower Sorbian is in development (Bartels et al., 2019).
Based on the lexica an online translator was implemented. It uses a statistical MOSES decoder to translate parts of sentences. A neural system OpenNMT can form grammatically correct sentences out of the parts, see (Brězan et al., 2019). Lately, Microsoft has taken the bilingual speech corpus and added Upper Sorbian support to Bing Microsoft Translator, see (Langkabel, 2022).

1.2.2. Grammar Technology

For modelling grammars, lexical and acoustic models, we use weighted finite-state transducers (FSTs) as well as minimalist grammars (MGs).
FSTs were introduced into speech recognition technology by M. Mohri (1997). They are broadly used in current speech processing toolkits like OpenGrm (Roark et al., 2012) or the Kaldi Speech Recognition Toolkit (Povey et al., 2011). For model size reduction and efficient recognition we use an extension of FSTs for modelling context-free grammars (Duckhorn and Hoffmann, 2012; Allauzen and Riley, 2012).
There has already been detailed work by Torr (2019; Stanojević and Stabler (2018; Fowlie and Koller (2017) in realizing parsers that mimic humans internal parsing with MGs. To increase the performance of the grammars, i.a. Kobele (2018; Kobele (2021) and Ermolaeva (2020) made an effort to make the grammars of MGs more succinct. First steps are already under way, besides this work, to prepare MGs for the use in a natural language processing context (beim Graben et al., 2020; Römer et al., 2022).

1.3. Prior Work

The development of speech technologies in Upper Sorbian, particularly speech recognition, started in 2020 with a feasibility study. It encompassed speech and language resource collection and was successfully concluded in 2021. As a result, valuable resources were provided that can be employed in various speech applications.
In (Kraljevski et al., 2021b) we presented acoustic modeling in the Upper Sorbian language where an acoustic model in German was used in cross-lingual transfer learning. Here, we defined grapheme and phoneme inventories and mapped the Upper Sorbian phonemes to the most similar German equivalents. Then, phonetically balanced sentences were selected from the available textual data (HSB Common Voice project) and combined with application specific ("SmartLamp" use-case) sentences into recording prompts for speech corpus collection.
The original acoustic model in German was utilized to segment and force-align the speech corpus by the knowledge-based phoneme mappings. The quality was evaluated by the resulting confusion matrix of the free phoneme recognition and provided better derived data-driven phoneme mapping. Then, the German acoustic model was acoustically adapted to the recordings in Upper Sorbian and as such implemented in a speech recognition demonstrator for controlling smart home devices ("SmartLamp").
The studio recorded speech corpus comprises of around 11 hours of male, female, and child speakers, with the corresponding metadata, such as text corpus, lexicons, and language models. The collected resources provided the possibility for fundamental research in phonology and phonotactics of Upper Sorbian. Taking advantage of the outcomes of the feasibility study, we conducted a study for a data-driven approach for the quantitative analysis of glottal stops before word-initial vowels in Upper Sorbian (Kraljevski et al., 2021a).
However, the available resources are insufficient to employ state-of-the-art (SotA) speech recognition techniques such as hybrid Hidden-Markov-Model (HMM) combined with a deep neural network (DNN) or even end-to-end DNN, where the inputs are raw and unprocessed utterances and the outputs are the corresponding sequences of graphemes, words or semantic entities.
Therefore, in the follow-up project of the feasibility study concluded in March 2022, we improved the acoustic, lexicon and language modeling, with the aim to further develop the speech recognition in Upper Sorbian, and to extend it for Lower Sorbian.

2. Word Class Language Modeling

Depending on the intended speech application the language model can be defined either by a handcrafted formal grammar or by a statistical language model (SLM). Formal grammars are appropriate for very limited vocabulary (few hundreds to thousand words) where the spoken utterance must follow the expected order of words/morphemes. In contrast, statistical language modeling (SLM) estimates the probability of word sequences based on N-gram statistics (unigrams, bigrams, trigrams, and higher).

To train an SLM, a large amount of text data is required, which in general will never cover all the possible contexts in a given domain and the problem is even more emphasised in the case of under-resourced languages.
For instance, if a textual corpus that contains all the

numbers in the corresponding context is required; it will have a huge size and will be impossible to acquire. Instead, each occurrence of a number in the text is replaced with a label (tag) representing a word class (in this case, numerals). Consequently, training such a word class language model provides significant reduction in the complexity and the vocabulary size. Word class modeling improves the generalization in both statistical- and formal-grammar- based language models.

The concepts are demonstrated in the following sections, where word class modeling is demonstrated on numbers, time and date implemented as weighted finite-state transducer (FST) grammars and minimalist grammars (MG). Since either of the word classes are finite, they can all be generated by regular FST grammars. More powerful grammars - like MGs - can still be used in order to model the word classes with smaller model size.

2.1. Modeling with MGs

We chose to use MGs, because they are considered especially well-suited for modelling natural human language. (Torr, 2019; Stabler, 2013; Fowlie and Koller, 2017; Versley, 2016; Stanojević and Stabler, 2018) In particular, the structural operations enable MGs to draw dependencies between non-adjacent morphemes with little obstacles. However, integration of MGs into State-of-the-Art technologies is mostly still in development. For this reason, we simply present a stand-alone program that can parse a a variety of Upper Sorbian prompt sentences. In order to extend an MG, we add new items that hold a new category and use selectors to connect the new category with the present grammar. Example: In Figure 3 an integer time of day expression gets extend by selecting items of a modifier category and a daytime category.

Exceptions on the possible connections of certain items with categories via selection can be handled with the distribution of licensors and licensees. Example: In Figure 4 the pair $\pm m30$ regulates that 'januar' can form a date by connecting with 'třicety' (30th), while 'februar' cannot.

2.2. Modeling with FSTs

FSTs have a simpler structure compared to MGs and they are a lot more commonly used in State-of-the-Art language technology.

However, the simpler structure implies some limitation for the grammar:

- An FST always needs several transitions for the same morpheme, if the morpheme can appear in different positions in the construction. Hence, FSTs often require a larger model size than MGs do.
- Since dependency relation between morphemes is only controlled by (non-)adjacency of transitions, it is inefficient to model dependencies between non-adjacent morphemes.
Example: Assume we want to extend a present complex grammar - with start node S and end node E - by the option to put all final expression in brackets. Then all expression have to start with '(', if and only if they end with ')'. The only way to model this dependency is to duplicate the entire complex structure between S and E, which requires to duplicate the entire FST, see Figure 1.

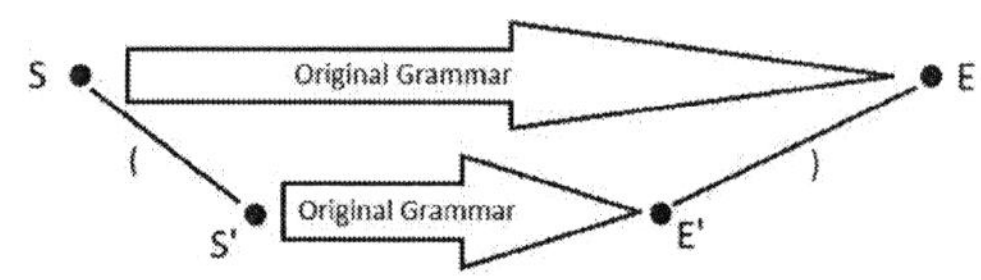

Figure 1: FST model of bracket relation

Sub-grammars can be incorporated by replacing transitions in an FST with another FST. This enables the use for the grammars from the following sub-sections in a larger handcrafted grammar or in a statistical language model.

2.3. Numbers

In either model we first we build a basic grammar of cardinal numerals $1-9$, onto which we construct a grammar for $1-99$. The smaller grammars (in MGs: categories) are used to recursively build larger grammars onto, so we gain grammars for numerals up to 999, then 10^6-1, 10^9-1, $10^{12}-1$ and $10^{15}-1$. In the MG, the rising sets of numbers are represented by distinct categories.

The constructions are not always uniform, so we have to handle exceptions. A frequent exception is that, if the two digits before a decimal power's noun - like "milion", "miliard", "bilion",... - are larger than 4, then the genitive plural "milionow"/"miliardow"/"bilionow"/... is used. On the contrary, $3*10^6$ and $4*10^6$ call the nominative plural ("tři/štyri miliony"), $2*10^6$ the nominative dual ("dwaj milionaj") and $1*10^6$ the nominative singular ("milion").

In the FST model, we handle this by introducing a special subgrammar for numerals $5-99$, while the connection of the numerals $1-4$ with $10^{6/9/12/15}$ is handled individually. The MG model handles it by the distribution of licensors and licensees.

As another exception, there are two words for 50. The expressions "pjećdźesat" (five tens) and "połsta" (half hundred) are arbitrarily interchangeable, even as subexpressions inside other numerals like of 51, 150 or 50000. It is no problem for modelling, but once it comes to generating, a decision making is needed.

For the FST model, we also built some special numeral grammars like NUM0-23 and NUM0-59, which

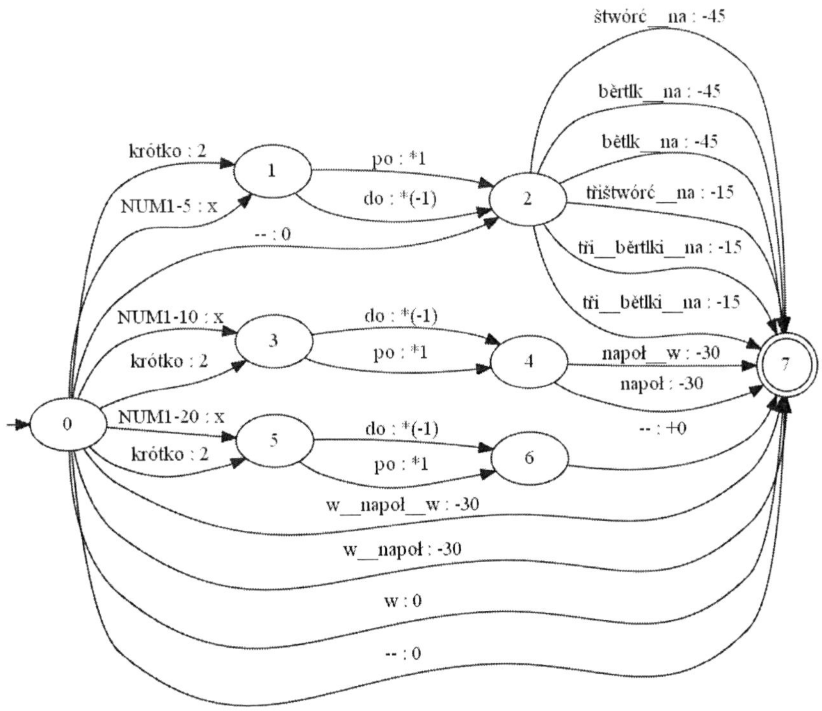

Figure 2: Sorbian hour time modifiers.
Note: NUMz-y represents a subgrammar FST for the numerals from z to y.

become incorporated in the time of day FST grammar as hour and minute counts. We also built ordinal numeral FST grammars ORD1-29, ORD1-30, ORD1-31 (all masculine gender) and a grammar for feminine ordinals ORD1-31f, which become incorporated in the date FST grammars as day counts of the months.
In the MG model, these special grammars are directly built into the time of day MG and date MG respectively.

2.4. Time of Day

The time of day grammars convert time of day expressions into a numerical representation of the time. As a representation we do not use the classical $hh : mm$ format but rather just the count of minutes after midnight. We assume that this one-dimensional representation is not just easier to compute, but also easier to work with in the post-process. For the purpose of a printout, a minute count m can easily be converted into $hh : mm$ with:

$$hh = \lfloor \frac{m}{60} \rfloor \; mod \; 24 \text{ and } mm = m \; mod \; 60. \qquad (1)$$

Note that the minute count output does not necessarily need to be between 0 and 1440, but may also be negative. Still, the mod-operator in (1) will always lead to an hour computation between $0 - 23$.
We are considering two different types of time expressions.

- One covers the accurate digital expressions, that are mostly used in official exact speech and for odd appointments of, e.g. a bus or train departure. These expressions can be simply modeled out of a numeral between $0 - 23$ as the hour count, a numeral between $0 - 59$ as the minute count and "hodźin" as a connection word between the hour and minute count.

- The second type covers the more common - but complicated - everyday expressions like "tři štwórć na pjećich" (corresponding to "quarter to five"). We modeled this type of expressions as a construction out of 3 blocks.

  - The first block can represent the daytime (morning, noon,...). It is important to include into the grammar, since it does influence the meaning. For instance, "six in the morning" has a different meaning than "six in the evening".

  - The second block consists of any modifier of the clocktime, like in English "X/quarter to/past" or "half past" or even combinations out of those. We discussed with the client - the Foundation for the Sorbian People - in order to agree on which combinations of different modifiers should be covered. We agreed on the sub-grammar presented in Figure 2

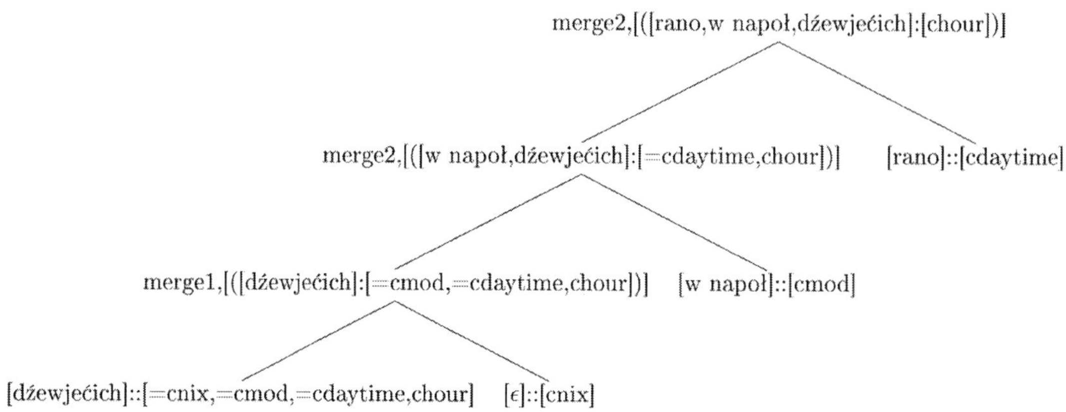

Figure 3: The integer time 'dźesaćich' (9) is extended by a modifier 'w napoł' (half to) and a daytime specifier 'rano' (morning).
'dźesaćich' first merges with a neutral item, so it becomes a derived item. As a derived item, it places the further items it merges with to the left side (Merge2). So, the last merged 'rano' ends up non-adjacent to 'dźewjećich', despite being selected by it. This way, the MG can handle non-adjacent dependencies.

- The third part numerically represents the related hour. In Upper Sorbian everyday speech a 12 hour format is used, so e.g. "dwěmaj" could either mean 2:00 or 14:00. The actual meaning can be determined based on the daytime.

The blocks of daytime and hour have a dependency. For instance, 'six' cannot be connected with 'noon'. If it could, it would even be highly ambiguous, whether it means 6 or 18.
This dependency of non-adjacent parts of the expression makes the FST model laborious. As shown in Figure 1, it requires to include several copies of the modifier grammar (Figure 2) - one for each day time - into the grammar.
An MG can handle non-adjacent dependencies as shown in Figure 3.

2.5. Dates

For the date grammars, we again decided to represent the numerical meaning in a single number - the day count after New Year's Eve. Again, we will also - and even mostly - use negative numbers. Since there are leap years, the day count after New Year's Eve is indefinite for any date from March to December. However, the day count till New Year's Eve is definite, so we use negative counts for March till December but positive counts for January and February. So, the output is always a number between -305 and 60.
Moreover, we built two different date grammars for nominative and genitive case. Both cases are needed for some significant wordings.
The date grammars are built out of an ordinal number representing the day and a name for the month. We included 3 different names for each month: A numerical name as the ordinal number of the month, a Gregorian name and an older traditional name.
In the FST model we combine the month names with the ordinal number grammars ORD1-29, ORD1-30, ORD1-31 or ORD1-31f, see 2.3, depending on the length and gender of the month (name).
In the MG model we instead handle the combinations with the license pairs as shown in Figure 4.

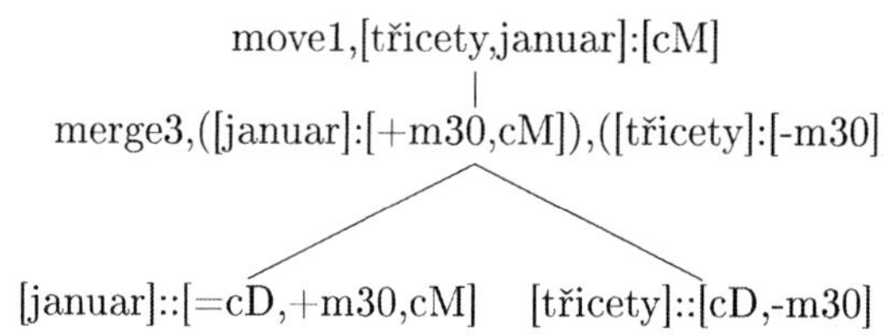

Figure 4: The licensor $+m30$ allows 'januar' to become a terminating date expression after merging with 'třicety' (30th).
'februar' would not hold this licensor. So, if 'februar' merged with 'třicety', the construction could not terminate, since 'třicety's licensee $-m30$ would never be triggered.

3. Practical Implementation

3.1. Finite-State-Transducers (FSTs)

We implemented the grammars to represent different building blocks for the numerals, time, and date. We created tools that combine FST based language models (handcrafted grammars or statistical language models) containing word class tags with the corresponding word class grammars. The resulting language model in OpenFST (Allauzen et al., 2007) format and the corresponding lexicon are included in the configuration for the dLabPro/UASR speech recognizer (Hoffmann et al., 2007). Since the OpenFST format is interchangeable, it could be easily incorporated within other speech recognition frameworks.

We developed word class grammars and combined them together with lexicon and phoneme models into an FST, which translates directly from speech frames to semantic token sequences.

During the recognition, the decoder searches all allowable sequences of tokens to find the one that matches the speech the best acoustically.

We evaluated the functionality of the grammars by speech recognition experiments on a small set of fifteen audio examples recorded by one speaker.

The output of the recognizer was analysed in terms of word error rates (WER) and character error rates (CER) for the semantic concepts and used to debug the grammars. The following example ("Make appointment Wednesday evening at seven.") shows such a recognition result:

Ref-Words: ČIN TERMIN SRJEDU WJEČOR W SEDMICH
Res-Words: ČIN TERMIN SRJEDU WJEČOR SEDMICH
Word-ER 16.7% C=5 I=0 D=1 S=0

Ref-Sematic: ČIN TERMIN
<WDAY>+3</WDAY><TIME>+720+0+420</TIME>
Res-Sematic: ČIN TERMIN
<WDAY>+3</WDAY><TIME>+720+0+420</TIME>
Char-ER 0.0% C=48 I=0 D=0 S=0

The "Ref-Words" denotes the reference transliterations, while "Res-Words" the results of the speech recognition. The error rates are calculated from the number of correctly recognized tokens (C), insertions (I), deletions (D) and substitutions (S). Similarly, the "Ref-Semantic" and the "Res-Semantic" denote the reference and the recognized semantic expressions respectively, with the corresponding tags (<WDAY>- weekday, <TIME>- time of day). The expressions were calculated as described in the Sections 2.4 and 2.5.

The semantic meaning in three of fifteen sentences were wrongly recognized, mostly due to the recognition errors because of the simple acoustic modeling and missing pronunciation variants. The errors are mostly wrongly recognized months: "WOSMEHO JUNIJA" as "WOSMO JULIJA" ("eight of Juni" as "eight of July"), "SEDMEHO SEPTEMBRA" as "SEDMEHO SEDMO" ("seventh of September" as "seventh of July").

The software tools, the guidelines and all the needed resources are published in a repository of the Foundation for the Sorbian People [1] under the MIT license.

The repository contains fully reproducible examples of both approaches (CFG and SLM) using word classes for language modelling. The resources can be used for building custom word class grammars to be used in practical and more complex speech applications, such as personal voice assistants, meeting protocol transcriptions and dictation of domain specific texts (such as in law, medicine, industry).

[1] https://github.com/ZalozbaDev/speech_recognition_language_modeling

3.2. Minimalist Grammars (MGs)

Regarding the MGs, since its integration into speech technology is still in development, their practical use nowadays is rather limited. We restrict ourselves to parsing the mentioned "Res-Words" from a written form.

Since we have no tools to search through the sentences after outputs of a minimalist (time of day/date) grammar, we build an extra MG of prompts that builds the sentences with variable inputs of times of day and dates.

Another issue for our parser are the numerous ϵ-items - items with empty phonetic part. From a phonetic point of view, any amount of them could be anywhere in the sentence. So, they create a need for greater look ahead in the structural part of the grammar than the currently used parser can manage in a reasonable amount of time. To overcome the problem, we gave all ϵ-items a virtual phonetic 'e', which was also built in the sentences at all places they virtually appear at. Still, even then our parser had to find out, which combination of the 69 ϵ-items in the grammar is needed. So, it still required hours to parse a single sentence.

After we numerated the virtual phonetics by calling them 'e1',...,'e69', the sentences could be parsed in real time.

4. Conclusions and Future Work

We have presented word class based language modeling applied in the case of Upper Sorbian. The word classes model the semantic expressions of numerals, date and time of day. The implementation of the created grammars is realized in the form of finite-state-transducers (FSTs) and minimalists grammars (MGs). The latter realization is a novelty in speech technology.

The usage of the FSTs was practically demonstrated in a use-case of a simple smart-home speech application in Upper Sorbian. It is able to set wake-up alarms and appointments with numerals, date and time of day expressed in a spontaneous and natural speech.

In order to make the speech application more widely usable, more example prompts can be added and the speech recognizer can be trained by more different speakers to improve it.

The created speech and language resources are publicly available as open-source and can be used as building blocks to develop more complex speech applications.

Our future work will be focused on developing an MG framework that is more flexible and user friendly in development and computationally more efficient in practical deployment.

We expect, that our MG parser will soon be able to generate the semantic of parsed sentences, so it could work as a translator of natural prompts into machine readable lambda expressions. An optimization of the detection of ϵ-items would greatly improve the efficiency and applicability of the program.

Generally, future applications will not be restricted to speech recognition, and in only one language, but also applicable in a wide range of language independent Natural Language Processing (NLP) applications.

5. Bibliographical References

Allauzen, C. and Riley, M. (2012). A pushdown transducer extension for the openfst library. In Nelma Moreira et al., editors, *Implementation and Application of Automata*, volume 7381 of *Lecture Notes in Computer Science*, pages 66–77. Springer, Berlin Heidelberg.

Allauzen, C., Riley, M., Schalkwyk, J., Skut, W., and Mohri, M. (2007). OpenFst: A general and efficient weighted finite-state transducer library. In *Proceedings of the Ninth International Conference on Implementation and Application of Automata, (CIAA 2007)*, volume 4783 of *Lecture Notes in Computer Science*, pages 11–23. Springer. `http://www.openfst.org`.

Anstatt, T., Clasmeier, C., and Wölke, S. (2020). *Obersorbisch. Aus der Perspektive der slavischen Interkomprehension*. Narr Francke Attempto Verlag, Tübingen.

Bartels, H., Wölke, S., Szczepańska, J., and Měškank, J. (2019). Digitalne rěcne resurse: pśeglěd - doglěd - póglěd. Presented at the "Konferenz zum Thema "Digitalstrategie & sorbische Sprache", Bautzen".

beim Graben, P., Römer, R., Meyer, W., Huber, M., and Wolff, M. (2020). Reinforcement learning of minimalist grammars. *CoRR*, abs/2005.00359.

Brězan, B., Wenk, J., and Langner, O. (2019). Online-Übersetzer deutsch-sorbisch und sorbisch-deutsch - herausforderungen und lösungen. Presented at the Konferenz zum Thema "Digitalstrategie & sorbische Sprache", Bautzen.

Böhmak, W. (2019). Unicode common locale data repository und standardisierung -für die sichtbarkeit der sorbischen sprache in der digitalen welt. Presented at the "Konferenz zum Thema "Digitalstrategie & sorbische Sprache", Bautzen".

Duckhorn, F. and Hoffmann, R. (2012). Using context-free grammars for embedded speech recognition with weighted finite-state transducers. In *Proceedings of the 13th Annual Conference of the International Speech Communication Association (Interspeech 2012)*, pages 1003–1006, Portland, OR, USA, September.

Elfeky, M. G., Moreno, P., and Soto, V. (2018). Multi-dialectical languages effect on speech recognition: Too much choice can hurt. *Procedia Computer Science*, 128:1–8. 1st International Conference on Natural Language and Speech Processing.

Ermolaeva, M. (2020). Induction of minimalist grammars over morphemes. *Proceedings of the Society for Computation in Linguistics*, 3(1):484–487.

Fowlie, M. and Koller, A. (2017). Parsing minimalist languages with interpreted regular tree grammars. In *Proceedings of the 13th International Workshop on Tree Adjoining Grammars and Related Formalisms*, pages 11–20.

Golubović, J. and Gooskens, C. (2015). Mutual intelligibility between west and south slavic languages. *Russian Linguistics*.

Hoffmann, R., Eichner, M., and Wolff, M. (2007). Analysis of verbal and nonverbal acoustic signals with the Dresden UASR system. In Anna Esposito, et al., editors, *International Workshop on Verbal and Nonverbal Communication Behaviours. COST Action 2102*, volume 4775 of *Lecture Notes in Computer Science*, pages 200–218, Vietri sul Mare, Italy, March. Springer-Verlag. ISBN 978-3-540-76441-0.

Kobele, G. M. (2018). Lexical decomposition. *Computational Syntax lecture notes*.

Kobele, G. (2021). Minimalist grammars and decomposition. *The Cambridge Handbook of Minimalism. Cambridge University Press, Cambridge, to appear*.

Kraljevski, I., Bissiri, M. P., Duckhorn, F., Tschoepe, C., and Wolff, M. (2021a). Glottal Stops in Upper Sorbian: A Data-Driven Approach. In *Proc. Interspeech 2021*, pages 1001–1005.

Kraljevski, I., Rjelka, M., Duckhorn, F., Tschöpe, C., and Wolff, M. (2021b). Cross-lingual acoustic modeling in upper sorbian – preliminary study. In Stefan Hillmann, et al., editors, *Studientexte zur Sprachkommunikation: Elektronische Sprachsignalverarbeitung 2021*, pages 43–50. TUDpress, Dresden.

Langkabel, T. (2022). Microsoft nimmt obersorbisch in den bing-translator auf. Microsoft News Center.

Mohri, M. (1997). Finite-state transducers in language and speech processing. *Computational Linguistics*, 23(2):269–311.

Moseley, C. (2012). *The UNESCO atlas of the world's languages in danger: Context and process*. World Oral Literature Project.

Mětšk, F. (1958). Serbsko-pólska rěčna hranica w 16. a 17. lětstotku. In *Lětopis, Reihe B, Band III*, pages 4–25, Budyšin [Bautzen]. Ludowe nakładnistwo Domowina.

Nědolužko, A. (2019). Maschinelles erkennen der tschechischen sprache. vorsprung für die sorben? Presented at the "Konferenz zum Thema "Digitalstrategie & sorbische Sprache", Bautzen".

Povey, D., Ghoshal, A., Boulianne, G., Burget, L., Glembek, O., Goel, N., Hannemann, M., Motlicek, P., Qian, Y., Schwarz, P., Silovsky, J., Stemmer, G., and Vesely, K. (2011). The kaldi speech recognition toolkit. In *IEEE 2011 Workshop on Automatic Speech Recognition and Understanding*. IEEE Signal Processing Society, December. IEEE Catalog No.: CFP11SRW-USB.

Roark, B., Sproat, R., Allauzen, C., Riley, M., Sorensen, J., and Tai, T. (2012). The opengrm open-source finite-state grammar software libraries. In *ACL 2012 System Demonstrations*, pages 61–66. http://www.opengrm.org.

Römer, R., beim Graben, P., Huber-Liebl, M., and Wolff, M. (2022). Unifying physical interaction, linguistic communication, and language acquisition of cognitive agents by minimalist grammars. *Frontiers in Computer Science*, 4.

Stabler, E. (2013). Two models of minimalist, incremental syntactic analysis. *Topics in cognitive science*, 5, 06.

Stanojević, M. and Stabler, E. (2018). A sound and complete left-corner parsing for minimalist grammars. In *Proceedings of the Eight Workshop on Cognitive Aspects of Computational Language Learning and Processing*, pages 65–74.

Torr, P. (2019). *Wide-coverage statistical parsing with minimalist grammars*. Ph.D. thesis, 10.

Versley, Y. (2016). Discontinuity (re) ^{2}-visited: A minimalist approach to pseudoprojective constituent parsing. In *Proceedings of the Workshop on Discontinuous Structures in Natural Language Processing*, pages 58–69.

Weston, T. B. and Jensen, L. M., (2000). *Cultural and regional diversity*. Lanham, Md, Rowman & Littlefield Publishers.

Wierzbicki, N. (2019). Interslavic language — will bulgarian, polish and croatian understand a constructed language? — #1.

Proceedings of the EURALI Workshop @LREC2020, pages 36–41
Marseille, 20 June 2022

Bringing Together Version Control and Quality Assurance of Language Data with LAMA

Aleksandr Riaposov, Elena Lazarenko, Timm Lehmberg
Universität Hamburg
Hamburg, Germany
{aleksandr.riaposov, elena.lazarenko, timm.lehmberg}@uni-hamburg.de

Abstract

This contribution reports on work in process on project specific software and digital infrastructure components used along with corpus curation workflows in the the framework of the long-term language documentation project INEL. By bringing together scientists with different levels of technical affinity in a highly interdisciplinary working environment, the project is confronted with numerous workflow related issues. Many of them result from collaborative (remote-)work on digital corpora, which, among other things, include annotation, glossing but also quality- and consistency control. In this context several steps were taken to bridge the gap between usability and the requirements of complex data curation workflows. Components of the latter such as a versioning system and semi-automated data validators on one side meet the user demands for the simplicity and minimalism on the other side. Embodying a simple shell script in an interactive graphic user interface, we augment the efficacy of the data versioning and the integration of Java-based quality control and validation tools.

Keywords: corpus curation, quality assurance, workflow management

1. Introduction

Having started in 2016, the long-term project INEL (Grammar, Corpora, Language Technology for Indigenous Northern Eurasian Languages)[1], spanning 18 years, aims at a broad and comprehensive empirical analysis of language data coming from endangered languages and varieties of the Northern Eurasian Area[2]. For this purpose it generates deeply annotated digital language resources (language corpora and further accompanying resources) from existing as well as newly acquired language material. As an integral part of the project these resources are made long-term available after their finalization and also become part of on-the-fly analysis already during the process of their curation. This unique property enriches the project research by adding a dynamic momentum to the empirical work but also puts high demands on the digital workflows and tools being used along with the corpus creation.

In this paper we will first outline the corpus curation workflows that have been established in the initial six years of the project run-time by focusing on the establishment of a versioning and semi-automated quality checks. Based on this we will present the latest development steps that aim at a more user-friendly and seamless integration of both aspects into linguists everyday work.

2. Preliminary work

Up to the present day corpora in Selkup (Brykina et al., 2021), Dolgan (Däbritz et al., 2019), Kamas (Gusev et al., 2019), and Evenki (Däbritz and Gusev, 2021) languages have been finalized following strict quality and consitency criteria and published under open access conditions by the language specific sub-projects. All resources as well as multiple graphic user interfaces are available via the INEL-Portal[3]. Furthermore a comprehensive description of the project structure can be also found at (Arkhipov and Däbritz, 2018). One of the most important contributions that made this outcome possible was the adaption of *continuous integration* principles from software development projects to linguistic data curation workflows as described by (Hedeland and Ferger, 2020). Put simply, this includes the establishment of workflows and technologies, that allow for a continuous manipulation of content (in this case language data instead of programming code) whereas the data itself is kept in a state that it can be used as an empirical base for language analysis during the entire process of its creation. In the following one important core componemt of these these workflows, a versioning system, is introduced.

2.1. Version control systems

In recent years the use of version control systems (VCS) such as *Git*[4] or *Apache Subversion*[5] has established as a popular way for collaborative data management and exchange. VCS help to track down changes in the data one is working with and make snapshots

[1] https://www.slm.uni-hamburg.de/inel.html

[2] The project is funded by the German Federal Government and Federal States in the Academies' Programme, with funding from the Federal Ministry of Education and Research and the Free and Hanseatic City of Hamburg. The Academies' Program is coordinated by the Union of the German Academies of Sciences and Humanities.

[3] https://inel.corpora.uni-hamburg.de/portal/

[4] https://git-scm.com/

[5] https://subversion.apache.org/

of those changes over time; therefore, they are highly beneficial for collaborative work. Originally stemming from software development, principles of versioning have the potential for improving the quality of collaborative work on textual content like in the case of language data curation. As mentioned above, INEL places a high value on the quality and consistency of the corpus data and thus, on data curation and control. In this context versioning with the means of Git has been considered vital for the project workflows. However, this decision naturally leads to a question of how to seamlessly integrate usage of such a highly technical tool into the linguistic research routine. To do so, following aspects should be overseen:

- **Functionality:** Because Git is primarily a tool intended for software development, it encompasses by far more functions than it would be needed to synchronize the process of linguists' work. Moreover, Git commands have a tendency to transcend into being "cryptic" and hard to remember. Thus, a technically inexperienced person might find it hard to use them fully intuitively without diving into the theoretical background behind them and surrounding oneself with cheat-sheets and references. Furthermore, there is a high risk of data damage and even loss if a certain command is misused.
- **Interface.** There are two main ways to interact with Git - by the means of a command-line interface (CLI) or a graphic user interface (GUI). Following on from the functionality aspect, out-of-the-box Git GUI as well as further popular GUI solutions may seem over-saturated with various options and functions. This can lead to a more complex learning curve during the first encounters with VCSs and result into reluctance to use them. On the other hand, using Git CLI may seem to be confusing for those who have little to no previous experience with command-line shells. The confusion provoked by an unfamiliar working environment (merely a terminal window with which non tech-savvy rarely work) combined with the requirement to type in the terminal various commands, in turn, could lead to even more reluctance to learn Git CLI than the Git GUI.

Consequently, while Git could potentially bring quality control workflows on a new level, its full functionality can simultaneously become a reasonable disadvantage when users with a non-technical background are challenged to use it. To overcome this obstacle, it has been decided to develop a Git tool that fulfills several project-specific criteria. First of all, it should operate only with basic Git commands determined as necessary for the linguists' collaborative work and be easy-to-use. This would provide linguists immediate access to the tool and spare time on learning esoteric Git functionality. Secondly, its looks should be balanced and concentrated only on what is really important for the current work: not as "frightening" as the standard CLI and at the same time, not over-saturated with various buttons and working tree visualizations that do not benefit the linguist and could be potentially distracting. Finally, the tool should have a potential to be integrated into existing workflows and complement them.

2.2. LAMA - Linguistic Automation Management Assistant

To satisfy the above listed criteria, a minimalistic Git client LAMA (Linguistic Automation Management Assistant) has been developed in previous years (Ferger and Jettka, 2021a; Ferger and Jettka, 2021b). Although still being a Bash script running in a terminal window, at that point LAMA offered a simple user interface. It was no longer crucial to keep in mind all the necessary Git commands and type them manually because of a simple user menu. Moreover, since LAMA was designed to run in a Unix shell, it did not depend on further software other than Git itself. The tool was a cross-platform and ready-to-use solution, and an immediate and straightforward introduction of LAMA into the research workflows was possible.

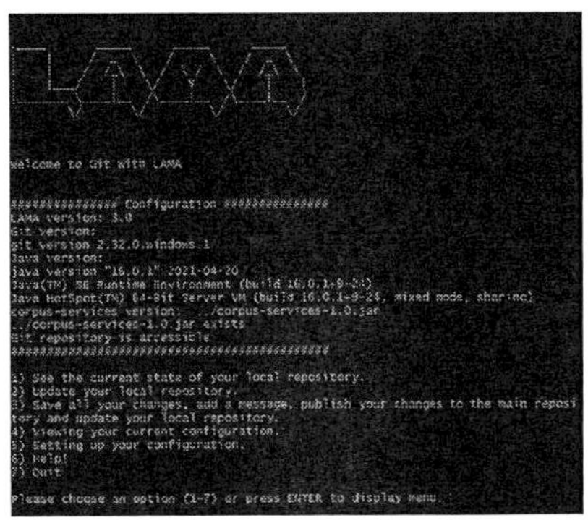

Figure 1: Previous LAMA version.

Unlike other Git clients that are aimed at broader user communities, LAMA's functionality was concentrated explicitly on what linguists need when working within INEL. This includes such basic functions as checking the status of the repository, pulling changes from the remote, staging and committing local changes and pushing them to the remote. At first, the restricted functionality of LAMA may seem rigid and and not sufficient. However, it corresponds with the established workflows and strictly follows the principles of linguistic data curation in INEL. For example, since all the linguistic data curation is done on a single Git branch, LAMA does not support branch functionality, which prevents linguists from accidental checkout of their data onto a separate branch and allows for transparent tracking of the work process. For similar reasons, various complex Git operations are not supported as well. The script is designed in such a way that one does not have to manually type any commands, but choose an option from the text-based menu. Moreover, LAMA could be easily integrated into other software used in the project:

- Messenger platforms (currently integrated within Mattermost[6] and Microsoft Teams) via API calls to webhooks in order to automatically report about errors and their origin;
- The Corpus Services framework (see section 2.3) for further quality-assurance. Earlier versions of LAMA were already able to carry out local pretty-printing of XML files before publishing the changes, moreover, there was potential to integrate other, more complex, Corpus-Services functions that was tackled at latter stages of LAMA development.

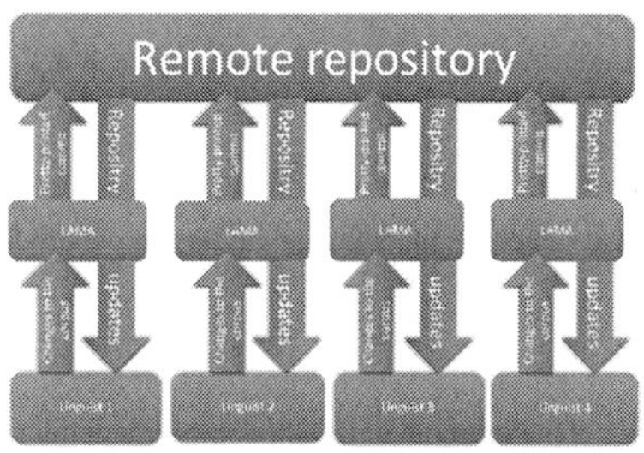

Figure 2: General LAMA workflow

Compared to the use of standardized Git clients, be it CLI or GUI, initial setup and launch of LAMA was project-specific as well. To begin with, users had to clone a corpus locally without using LAMA itself, but a default Git solution instead; afterwards they had to place the LAMA script in the respective local file structure (the script can operate only within a working directory). Another setup challenge that linguists were facing was creating a proper folder hierarchy within their working directories. This required a download (and regular updates) of Corpus Services JAR and placing it always one folder above the corpus clone to ensure the functionality of the Corpus Services pretty-printing function (see 2.3). Upon the first LAMA launch it was required to provide user credentials and afterwards the LAMA setup was ready to use, however, certain steps like repository cloning could have been repeated multiple times if work with several corpora was done simultaneously. Although initially such a setup was not considered a obstacle as long as LAMA nonetheless boosted up the performance and improved interaction with Git, later we could notice that this was a considerable shortcoming of the CLI version of LAMA. We will address this in the following sections of this paper.

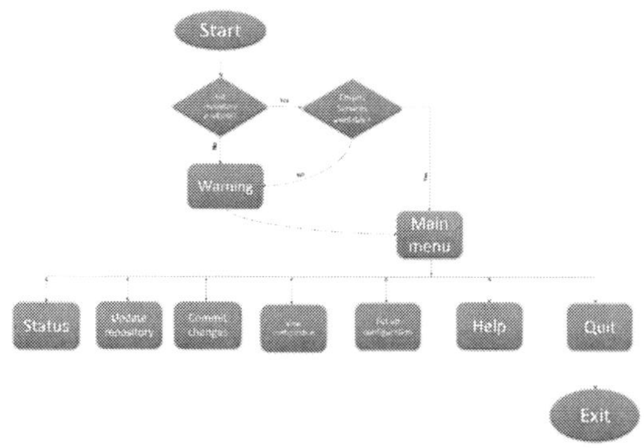

Figure 3: Algorithm of the previous LAMA version

2.3. Quality Checks

A significant part of the data curation is covered by the *Corpus Services* framework, a set of customized Java-based data validators initially developed at *Hamburg Center for Language Corpora (HZSK)*[7] as the result of longtime curation work on spoken language corpora (Ferger et al., 2020) using the EXMARaLDA System[8] (Schmidt and K., 2014) and its XML-based data formats. In the following the framework has been utilized and further developed by several projects; whereas in the infrastructure initiatives CLARIAH-DE[9], CLARIN-D[10] and the project QUEST[11] rather generic application scenarios were in the centre, development work in INEL followed project-specific tasks. The result of this effort (see https://gitlab.rrz.uni-hamburg.de/corpus-services/corpus-services) can be grouped as follows:

- Whenever a linguist working on data pushes local changes to on of the projects Git repository via LAMA, the data is automatically being pretty printed to assure unified formatting between different local copies (see Figure 2).
- Being a part of the automated INEL workflows (see Figure 4), every night a battery of scripted checks is performed on each corpus via cronjob; as a result, an updated report containing errors to be fixed and warnings to be watched out for is created. About a third of the checks in the battery are relatively simple cleanup and replacement tasks, and we run those in fully automated fixing mode,

[6] https://mattermost.com/

[7] https://corpora.uni-hamburg.de/

[8] https://exmaralda.org

[9] https://www.clariah.de

[10] https://www.clarin-d.net

[11] https://www.slm.uni-hamburg.de/ifuu/forschung/forschungsprojekte/quest.html

meaning that such a check would not only spot an error in the data, but also repair it on the fly.

- Some other Corpus Services functions are meant to be run sparsely, and are used as a part of our corpus publication workflow, e.g. a converter of EXMARaLDA EXS files to the *ISO/TEI standard "Transcription of Spoken Language"* (ISO, 2016)[12].

- From time to time a need to perform some manual task arises (e.g., conversion of corpus data between different formats such as FLEX[13], ELAN(Sloetjes and Wittenburg, 2008) and EXMARaLDA, or replacement of a certain grammatical or lexical gloss in the whole corpus).

Figure 4: Infrastructure of the automated workflows

As mentioned above, although LAMA and Corpus Services until now have been contributing to the same workflows, they have not yet been integrated into one another and the coordination of the use of both components had to be coordinated separately by the technical staff of the project. Therefore, a potential of bringing the two tools closer to each other was considered beneficial for the further improvement of the project road map.

3. Putting workflows to a new level

A simple, lightweight, cross-platform Bash script allowing non-technical users to enjoy the basic functionality of Git without delving deep inside the intricacies of version control systems was a welcome addition to the project's workflow, however, after considering the feedback from the users, it became clear that some particularities of its implementation left us room for considerable improvement. First, we underestimated how cautious some people are about working with CLI as a tool, as it subjectively feels dangerous, looks impenetrable and thus falls outside their comfortable limits of control. Second, we ran into issues caused by the output produced in the command line in case something went wrong: instead of simply pointing out to the user what the problem was, the script returned what essentially was a log with the lifespan of a CLI window; unfortunately, in some cases it managed to confuse less tech-savvy users possessing pauce log-reading competence, which in turn resulted in avoidable data loss, exacerbated by the fact that the log was not actually stored anywhere. Third, the initial version was hindered by its rigid "choose a stock option" design, which effectively prohibited the user from interacting with the script in a more complex way – e.g., it was not quite up to the task of automatizing common quality control scenarios. Here is how we addressed each of the development challenges specified above:

3.1. The challenge of usability: providing a GUI

An intuitive clickable GUI alleviates many worries about the use of command line. Having in mind that we would like to keep our GUI simple to use and easy to develop while staying cross-platform, we surveyed some options as to the implementation of said interface such as the popular framework *Electron*[14] or *Swing Application Framework* in Java, but eventually settled on *Zenity*[15], a toolkit built-in in many current Linux distributions that creates GTK dialogue boxes for shell scripts. While not sophisticated enough to provide a list of features common in fully-fledged applications, it satisfies our simplicity criterion and does the job nonetheless.

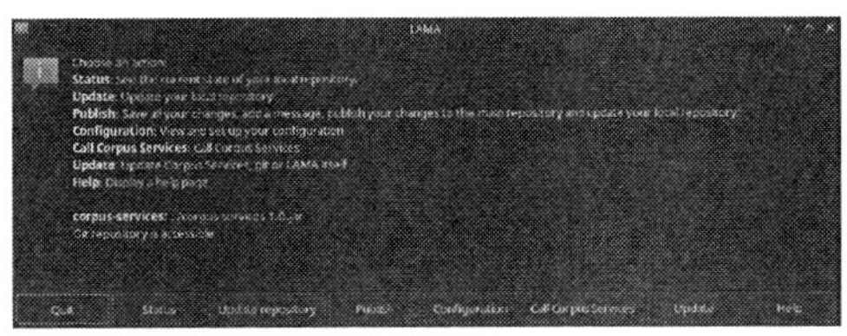

Figure 5: The main dialogue box.

Another usability goal was to eliminate the needlessly abstruse installation procedure one had to go through before launching the script for the first time. Among the requirements were the need to have a working clone of one of our corpora and an up-to-date JAR package file containing Corpus Services; then on the first launch the user had to remember to provide their credentials (in the INEL case - GitLab) without a script prompt to do so. Seeing how the users - quite rightfully - struggled to complete the installation on their own, we decided to automatize the process where possible, striving to provide a solution that would work "out of the box". Since Zenity, not available natively on Windows and MacOS, is now required to run the script, a step where Zenity is downloaded and installed was added as well. The result is that the matured script walks the user through its installation, and is able to clone

[12]http://www.iso.org/iso/cataloguedetail.htm?csnumber=37338

[13]https://software.sil.org/fieldworks/

[14]https://www.electronjs.org/

[15]https://help.gnome.org/users/zenity/stable/

a repository or fetch the JAR file on its own, thus making this once-esoteric procedure, which often required guidance, as smooth as possible. In addition to that, LAMA acquired the ability to update its core dependencies, Git and Corpus Services, as well as LAMA itself, within the script. Our users were happy to see that they gained an ability perform the operations described above by themselves, without having to ask a member of the technical team.

3.2. The challenge of output: logging

Since LAMA logging was not ideal in the previous version, our users ran into issues, e.g. they would mishandle a Git merge conflict, snowballing it into something pernicious and data-damaging. Having that in mind, we modified the way LAMA keeps track of its past activities: in case of an error the user will be presented with a concise message saying what the error was about, while the complete log is now being collected in the background. That simple feature allowed us to deal with problems more efficiently.

3.3. The challenge of quality control: Corpus Services implementation

In older versions of LAMA, only the first part of our workflow delineated in 2.3 was implemented in the script; anyone wishing to run Corpus Services for other tasks had no options but to call it from the command line using specific syntax which is not immediately clear to a linguist. That in turn severely hindered wider-scale propagation of Corpus Services as a quality control tool in non-INEL environments. In other words, we needed a user-friendly interface for it. A web interface for Corpus Services is in the works, but it has some downsides rendering it unfit to use with our corpora, namely a) it is not possible to run checks in fixing mode via the web interface; and b) there is an upper limit of 2 GB on the amount of data one can upload to be checked there, and the INEL corpora sit well outside that limit (e.g., the INEL Selkup Corpus has nearly 12 GB of files). However, Zenity-powered LAMA proved to be the solution we were looking for in the first place, as the script has already had basic Corpus Services support with none of the web interface downsides, and simply needed a GUI to let a user navigate quality control tasks gracefully.
In order to facilitate the use of the interface, we identified three large groups of tasks one might want to perform there:

- Common tasks, which include pretty printing and the ability to manually run automated checks and fixes specified in our workflow above;
- Simple tasks, or Corpus Services functions which do not require any parameter;
- Complex tasks, on the other hand, require at least one parameter such as a tier name.

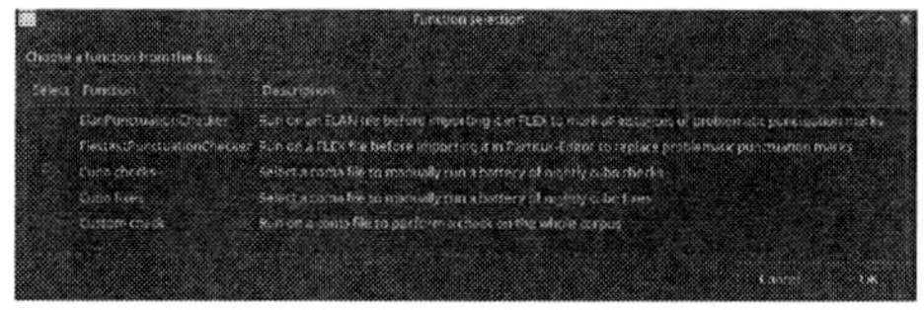

Figure 6: Quality control functions.

To run simple and complex tasks the user is asked to select a desired Corpus Services function and parameters if necessary. Common tasks are meant to be run much more often than the other tasks - hence the name; each such task comes with a description of what it does, and has some of the parameters filled in by default. The list of common tasks is curated by our technical team based on feedback received from linguists.
All in all, a GUI solution, however simple, helped us reduce overhead efforts incurred by substantial impregnability of the previous version of our toolset, thus bridging the gap between the tools we develop and the people actively using them: hence the positive feedback received from our users, who are now able to perform quality control operations on their own. Automatizing existing quality control and data manipulation procedures in the GUI allows us to focus our future development on new, as-yet-untrodden ways to improve and enrich the quality of linguistic data produced in the project.

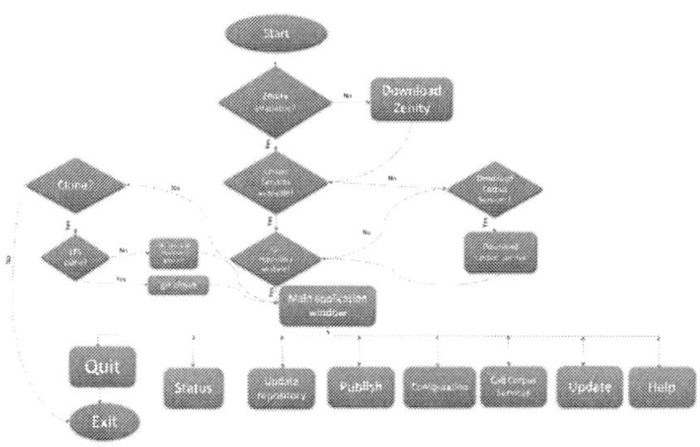

Figure 7: Algorithm of the current LAMA version

4. Conclusion and future work

In our paper we outlined technical workflows and presented internal tools used in the INEL project to process transcribed spoken language data, described the challenges we have met, and the solutions we have implemented to achieve and maintain continuous quality control of language resources being created in the project.
When devising best practices for language data-oriented tools, intended both for in-house use and the

wider scientific community, it is prudent to know what the users need and build the tools according to their needs and technical competences. An unnecessarily difficult to use tool, no matter how good, is unfortunately doomed to be rejected by some prospective users simply because the learning curve was too steep. Implementing GUI is a surefire step to flatten the curve, thus widely improving usability of the tool for many a user. We stand however by the "easy to use, easy to develop" motto for simple tools such as LAMA, where allocating extra resources to make it into a full-fledged application would not increase its usability and functionality proportionally to the efforts required.

Corpus Services finally getting a GUI, along with a web-based interface underway, is a welcome development that we hope would further increase its applicability beyond the INEL context. That being said, wider rates of community uptake require Corpus Services to evolve from a project-oriented quality control tool to something wider as well; absorbing both the availability to conform to commonly used "generic" standards of data quality as well as looking for implementations for other kinds of language data, i.e. audiovisual corpora. The development is continuously ongoing and both INEL and outside researchers are always welcome to test new tools functionality as soon as it becomes available. However, an extensive UX study on how newer LAMA versions improve the workflows is still required, after which we will be able to support our results with quantitative data.

5. Bibliographical References

Arkhipov, A. V. and Däbritz, C. L. (2018). Hamburg corpora for indigenous northern eurasian languages. *Tomsk Journal of Linguistics and Anthropology*, 21(3):9–18.

Ferger, A. and Jettka, D. (2021a). Fun with VCS - more with less: A Tool for Facilitating the Use of Git in Linguistic Research Data Management. Zenodo, September.

Ferger, A. and Jettka, D. (2021b). LAMA - your friendly and easy git script.

Ferger, A., Hedeland, H., Jettka, D., and Pirinen, T. (2020). Corpus services.

Hedeland, H. and Ferger, A. (2020). Towards continuous quality control for spoken language corpora. *Quality Control for Spoken Language Corpora.*, 15(1).

ISO. (2016). Language resource management — transcription of spoken language. Standard, International Organization for Standardization, Geneva, CH, August.

Schmidt, T. and K., W. (2014). Exmaralda. In Ulrike Gut Jacques Durand et al., editors, *Handbook on Corpus Phonology*, pages 402–419. Oxford University Press.

Sloetjes, H. and Wittenburg, P. (2008). Annotation by category-elan and iso dcr. In *6th international Conference on Language Resources and Evaluation (LREC 2008)*. Max Planck Institute for Psycholinguistics, The Language Archive, Nijmegen, The Netherlands.

6. Language Resource References

Brykina, Maria and Orlova, Svetlana and Wagner-Nagy, Beáta. (2021). *INEL Selkup Corpus (Version 2.0)*.

Däbritz, Chris Lasse and Gusev, Valentin. (2021). *INEL Evenki Corpus (Version 1.0)*.

Däbritz, Chris Lasse and Kudryakova, Nina and Stapert, Eugénie. (2019). *INEL Dolgan Corpus (Version 1.0)*.

Gusev, Valentin and Klooster, Tiina and Wagner-Nagy, Beáta. (2019). *INEL Kamas Corpus (Version 1.0)*.

Proceedings of the EURALI Workshop @LREC2020, pages 42–50
Marseille, 20 June 2022

Automatic Verb Classifier for Abui (AVC-abz)

František Kratochvíl, George Saad, Jiří Vomlel, Václav Kratochvíl
Department of Asian Studies, Palacký University Olomouc, Czech Republic,
Institute of Information Theory and Automation, Academy of Sciences of the Czech Republic
{frantisek.kratochvil, george.saad}@upol.cz, {vomlel, velorex}@utia.cas.cz

Abstract

We present an automatic verb classifier system that identifies inflectional classes in Abui (AVC-abz), a Papuan language of the Timor-Alor-Pantar family. The system combines manually annotated language data (the learning set) with the output of a morphological precision grammar (corpus data). The morphological precision grammar is trained on a fully glossed smaller corpus and applied to a larger corpus. Using the k-means algorithm, the system clusters inflectional classes discovered in the learning set. In the second step, Naive Bayes algorithm assigns the verbs found in the corpus data to the best-fitting cluster. AVC-abz serves to advance and refine the grammatical analysis of Abui as well as to monitor corpus coverage and its gradual improvement.

Keywords: automatic verb classifier, endangered languages, head-marking languages, Papuan

1. Analytical problem: Abui verb classes

Across languages, verbs are known to be sensitive to their syntactic context in various ways. Their meaning may remain constant (a paraphrase) or it may differ (e.g. number and type of arguments and their role). Their distribution across varying contexts is used to identify verbal classes that capture the meaning of the verb. Levin (2015) is an excellent overview of the various approaches to verb alternations that have been developed over the last 50+ years, starting with the work on case alternations (Fillmore, 1970), through valence databases, such as FrameNet or the Proposition Bank (Baker et al., 1998; Palmer et al., 2005) to recent typological studies, such as ValPal (Hartmann et al., 2013). Such investigations are very labour-intensive and take years to complete for well-resourced language but are rarely undertaken for low-resourced languages. The workflow described here offers a significant acceleration to this endeavour by combining a learning set with the output of corpus data.

Abui is a head-marking language which records the argument configuration of the verb in its morphology; the verbal complements are indexed on the verb (their type, person and number).[1] Therefore, the morphological indexing offers a formal means of classification, where verb stems can be classified according to their indexing of arguments analogously to the dependent-marking languages where such information can be extracted from the syntactically annotated corpus and where significant advances have indeed been made. In particular, we follow the work on automatic verb classification undertaken on well-resourced languages in using an abstract feature space that is the input for mathematical clustering tools (Merlo and Stevenson, 2001; Kipper et al., 2008; Sun and Korhonen, 2009).

In the remainder of this section we give a brief overview of the Abui verbal morphology. Abui is notable for its argument realisation, which has been argued to be sensitive to semantic rather than syntactic features where the verbal stems show a low degree of lexical stipulation, i.e. the verb stems are compatible with a large number of morphological devices and their meaning is sometimes adjusted during this process (Kratochvíl, 2007; Kratochvíl, 2011). This issue has been discussed and elaborated in other publications (Fedden et al., 2014; Kratochvíl, 2014; Kratochvíl and Delpada, 2015; Saad, 2020a; Kratochvíl et al., 2021).

1.1. Abui verbal morphology and argument indexing

Verbs are at the heart of morphological complexity in Abui. Table 1 presents a schematic morphological template of the Abui verb, where the first line indicates the slot numbers, the second line the categories marked in each slot, and the subsequent lines the values attested in each slot. The table shows that (i) the root may be preceded by up to three person-number prefixes indexing various types of undergoer arguments or an incorporated noun (slots -1 to -3) and/or (ii) by the causative or applicative prefixes (slot -4).[2] Many roots mutate to distinguish two stems (perfective and imperfective) and sometimes three (+ inceptive). Roots may be followed by (iii) up to three aspectual slots (+1 to +3) and two mood slots (+4 to +5). The table records the values attested in each slot, represented here just by their glosses. For more details on the root mutation and aspectual suffixation, see (Kratochvíl et al., 2021).

[1] Abui [abz] is a Timor-Alor-Pantar language of Eastern Indonesia. Over the last almost two decades, we have collected a corpus of roughly 22,500 sentences, of which about 6,200 have been glossed (Kratochvíl, 2022). The corpus consists of various genres and includes also elicited data.

[2] According to Siewierska (2013), systems marking undergoers alone (leaving actors unmarked) are rare, constituting only about 7% of her sample. In the Alor-Pantar family, undergoer marking is a common trait.

-4	-3	-2	-1	0	+1	+2	+3	+4	+5
EXT	EXT/U_3	U_2	U_1	$root_{mutation}$	ASP_1	ASP_2	ASP_3	$MOOD_1$	$MOOD_2$
CAUS	BEN	LOC	PAT	$root_{pfv}$	INCP	INCH	STAT	PRIOR	HORT
APPL	GOAL	REC	N	$root_{ipfv}$	STAT	PFV	PROG	REAL	PROH
				$root_{incp}$		PRF			

Table 1: Morphological template of the Abui verb

1.2. Person-number prefixes

The prefixal slots of the Abui verb index objects, applicatives, and causatives. Objects are primarily indexed by a collection of five person-number prefix series, which are given in Table 2.[3] To a large extent, each series is phonologically distinct (e.g. series PAT singular prefixes tend to end in *a*); but some plural forms are syncretic (e.g. series PAT and LOC). The person-number prefixes occur in slots -3, -2, and -1, where slot -1 is reserved to series PAT series (listed in the second column) or incorporated nouns.

PERSON	PAT	REC	LOC	GOAL	BEN
1SG	*na-*	*no-*	*ne-*	*noo-*	*nee-*
2SG	*a-*	*o-*	*e-*	*oo-*	*ee-*
1PL.EXCL	*ni-*	*nu-*	*ni-*	*nuu-*	*nii-*
1PL.INCL	*pi-*	*pu-/po-*	*pi-*	*puu-/poo-*	*pii-*
2PL	*ri-*	*ro-/ru-*	*ri-*	*ruu-/roo-*	*rii-*
3	*ha-*	*ho-*	*he-*	*hoo-*	*hee-*
3.REFL	*da-*	*do-*	*de-*	*doo-*	*dee-*
DISTR	*ta-*	*to-*	*te-*	*too-*	*tee-*

Table 2: Abui person-number indexing paradigm

Some Abui verbs may combine with multiple prefix series, as shown in (1) where several prefix combinations of the verb *wik* 'carry' are listed. The PAT series-indexed form *ha-wik* in (1a) is used when an animate object, *kaai* 'dog', is involved. In (1b), the LOC series-indexed *he-wik* indexes a definite inanimate object, while the BEN series-indexed *hee-wike* involves a human benefactor for whom an object is carried (implied or contextually available). In (1c), the GOAL series-indexed *hoo-wik* is a type of causative construction, where the first person singular agent passes firewood to another person to carry; the secondary agent is indexed with the GOAL prefix. Finally, in (1d), the plain form *wik* is used when the object *sura foqa do* 'this big book' is topicalised and the information about the argument structure is contextual (i.e. the speaker assumes their responsibility for carrying the book). To sum up, the various combinations of person indexes and the verb *wik* 'carry (in arms)' distinguish object types, modify argument structure, and are sensitive to discourse structure.

(1) a. Bui kaai **ha**-wik.
name dog 3.I-carry.IPFV
'Bui is carrying her dog in her arms.' [N2011.9]

b. A-táng do mi **he**-wik,
2SG.INAL-hand PROX take 3.III-carry.IPFV
hee-wik-e!
3.V-carryIPFV-PROG
'Carry it in your hands, carry it for him!' [N2011.3]

c. Na ara mi **hoo**-wik.
1SG.AGT firewood take 3.IV-carry.IPFV
'I give him firewood to carry.' [N2011.6]

d. Sura foqa do baai wik-e?
book big PROX ADD carry.IPFV-PROG
'This big book too, (should I) carry?' [EVY.1238]

The person-number combinations of the verb *wik* 'carry' are not generalisable to other verbs and as we will show in section 2.1, verbs show various gaps in their compatibility with the affixes.

When more than one person-number prefixes co-occur, the patientive prefix (PAT) must occur in slot -1 (U_1). This is shown in (2), where the verb *minang* 'remember' combines with two person-number prefixes in slots -1 (PAT) indexing the experiencer and in slot -2 (LOC) indexing the medicine (stimulus).

(2) Ata di he-daweng
name 3.AGT 3.AL-medicine
he-da-minang-di.
3.LOC-3.REFL.PAT-remember-INCH
'Ata remembered his medicine.'

1.3. Light verbs

The second part of the argument-marking system consists of a set of light verbs which attach before the lexical verb and may take their own person-number indexes. The main function of the light verbs is to adjust the valency of the verb in a manner similar to adpositions (prepositions and postpositions) in other languages.[4] Table 3 lists the most common light verbs that modify the argument frame of the main verb by highlighting human objects or by adding human goals or companions. All five light verbs are used to refine the marking of human participants affected by the event described by the main verb and have been analysed as differential argument marking devices (Kratochvíl, 2014).

[3] The DISTR prefixes index reciprocals and distributives.

[4] Some of the multiple prefix series in Alor-Pantar languages (including the Abui prefixes in Table 3) have their origin in complex verbs (Klamer and Kratochvíl, 2018).

category	morphology
human undergoer	U.V-**GIVE**=main.verb
experiencer	U.IV-**INSIDE**=main.verb
human goal (proximal)	U.IV-**TOUCH**=main.verb
human goal (remote)	U.IV-**THROW**=main.verb
companion	U.I-**JOIN**=main.verb

Table 3: Abui light verbs attested in complex verbs

An example of the light verb use is shown in (3), where the verb *he-fikang* 'guard, look after s.t.' combines with the light verb clitic *hee-l*. The light verb differentiates the human object *ama* 'person'. The meaning of the main verb *he-fikang* 'guard, look after s.t.' shifts due to the light verb *hee-l=* addition to 'respect s.o., pay attention to s.o.'.

(3) Deri di ama
name 3.AGT person
hee-l=he-fikang, hare
3.BEN-GIVE=3.LOC-respect.IPFV so
do-wa tanga naha
3REFL.REC-participate speak.IPFV not
'Deri respects people, so she does not talk (much)' [NB9.103]

1.4. Applicative and causative prefixes

The third part of the argument marking system is formed by applicative prefixes (*lang-*, *ming-*) and the causative prefix *ong-* (attaching in slot -4) which extend the valency of the verb but do not index number or gender features of the added arguments. An example of the applicative prefix *lang-* can be seen in (4) where the reduplicated verb *mara* 'go up, climb' combines with *lang-* to add the nominal *dieng-pe* 'kitchen' to the argument structure of the intransitive motion verb.

(4) kaai de-tamai dieng-pe
dog 3.REFL.III-keep.doing.IPFV kitchen
lang-mara~mara
APPL-RED~go.up.IPFV
'The dog is entering kitchen all the time.' [EBD.047]

Complex predicates consisting of a light verb and a main verb are also compatible with applicatives, as shown in 5. The complex verb *na-da=sama* 'be with me' combines with the applicative *ming-* to include the time description into the argument structure of the verb.

(5) tung-ai loohu **ming-na-da**=sama
year-root be.long APPL-1SG.I-JOIN=be.with
'may I have a long life!' (lit. 'may long years be with me!') [EBD.7.15.7c]

The above examples illustrate that undergoer prefix series, light verbs, and applicative/causative prefixes constitute a complex argument marking system. Through detailed examination of the combinatorics of verb stems and the undergoer-marking material we can arrive at a classification of verb stem and at a better understanding of the semantic contribution of the prefixes. In the following sections we will describe the workflow that we have designed for this purpose.

2. System design

The Automatic Verb Classifier for Abui processes two types of data through three analytical modules. The data constituting the *learning set* is manually compiled and its structure is described in section 2.1. The *learning set* is analysed with the k-means clustering technique which groups the data into a pre-specified number of clusters, as described further in section 2.2.
The next step is to include the pre-processed *corpus data* and examine the fit with the k-means based clustering. The pre-processing of the *corpus data* was described in a separate publication (Zamaraeva et al., 2017). We offer a brief summary of this work in section 2.3. In section 2.4 we describe how the comparison of the clustering based on the learning set is implemented for the *corpus data*. The final part of the module will be a Bayesian network analysis whose intended purpose is briefly discussed in section 3. The workflow of the AVC-abz system is visualised in Figure 1. It processes a manually curated and complete training data to train a classifier system whose outputs (clustering, visualisation, membership lists) aid the linguistic analysis. The Bayesian Network Analysis Module is not yet finished.

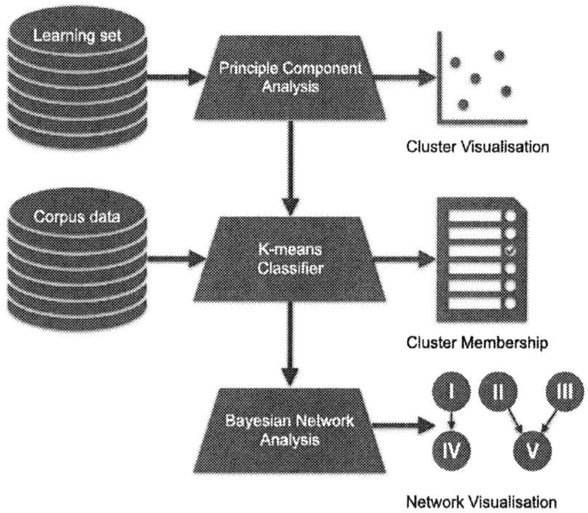

Figure 1: The components of the Automatic verb classifier for Abui (AVC-abz)

The system is implemented in an online interface available at `http://gogo.utia.cas.cz/abui/`. The four data sets (2 learning sets, 2 corpus data sets) and the source code in R are available at `https://github.com/fanacek/AVC-abz`.

2.1. Learning set structure

The *learning set* is a manually built database that maps the inflectional profiles of selected verb stems. It was

Form	Gloss	Feature
Ø-	stem alone	A
Ca-	patient (PAT)	B
Ce-	location (LOC)	C
Cee-	benefactive (BEN)	D
Co-	recipient (REC)	E
Coo-	goal (GOAL)	F
Cee-l=	human undergoer	G
Coo-q=	animate goal I	H
Coo-pang=	animate goal II	I
Ca-da=	companion (JOIN)	J
Coo-mi=	inward goal	K
ming-	applicative I (APPL)	L
lang-	applicative II (APPL)	M
ong-	causative (CAUS)	N

Table 4: Inflectional features in the learning sets

designed by the authors in close collaboration with a team of Abui speakers who are responsible for the accuracy of the grammatical information.[5]

Currently, the *AVC-abz* interface includes two learning sets counting 150 and 356 verb profiles respectively, tracking the compatibility of the verbs with 26 inflectional features. Table 4 lists fourteen of these features. The values of seven features are exemplified for six verbs in Table 5.

Table 4 lists possible morphological features of the Abui verb. Feature A is stem attested bare. Features B-F refer to person-number prefixes listed in Table 2, where the *C-* symbol is used as a shorthand for the various consonants distinguishing the person-number.[6] Features G-K combine light verbs and person-number prefixes, as listed in Table 3. Finally, forms L-K are applicative and causative prefixes. The morphological forms are accompanied by a short semantic characterisation (and a gloss).[7]

In Table 5, we exemplify the structure of the learning set (columns listing conditions A-G only). The full dataset can be viewed using the *Data* tab of the *AVC-abz* interface.

[5]While we are aware of the typical drawbacks of elicitation data that relies on a small number of speakers, such as accidental mistakes, gaps, or false negatives (forms that may sound unnatural in isolation may be fine in natural speech), we continue expanding the learning set, refining it with new verbs and information. Given the low-resourced status of Abui, it is unreasonable to expect that the corpus will reach the size where we could rely on it alone as a source of morphological information.

[6]For the ease of exposition we ignore the plural forms here. The characteristic vowel patterns in singular appear to have much higher frequency in the corpus anyway.

[7]While the gloss labels are suggestive of semantic roles, their exact semantic contribution is more complex and ultimately one of the puzzles we are working towards solving. The labels should therefore be interpreted as preliminary place-holders.

Stem	A	B	C	D	E	F	G
wik 'carry'	+	+	+	+	+	+	+
fanga 'say'	+	+	+	+	+	+	+
aquta 'blind'	+	+	-	+	+	+	+
took 'pour'	+	-	+	+	+	-	-
yaa 'go'	+	-	+	+	+	+	-
bai 'angry'	-	-	+	-	-	-	-

Table 5: Examples of Abui verb feature profiles

2.2. Principle component analysis and cluster visualisation

Using automatic clustering methods we find clusters of verbs that share a similar feature profile, i.e. the verbs occur in the same or similar morphological environments. We use the k-means clustering technique, which groups the data into a pre-specified number of clusters (k), while minimising the inter-cluster distance (d), which is defined as the total sum-of-squares distance of cluster members to the cluster mean.

The optimal number of clusters is not known in advance. The k-means technique allows us to employ expert human judgement and experiment with the optimal cluster number. To aid the human judgment we use a visualisation technique that plots the inter-cluster distance for each number of clusters. The idea here is that typically there is an elbow-like shape in the plot that enables us to identify the optimal number of clusters. The threshold for the optimal number for clusters is set so that the inter-cluster distance (d) decreases slowly after the threshold.

An example of the inter-cluster distance plot is given in Figure 2 where the plot shows an elbow-like dip in the inter-cluster distance. The inter-cluster distance decreases rapidly until 24 clusters, but starts to decrease gradually after 25 clusters. Therefore we set the threshold at 25 clusters.

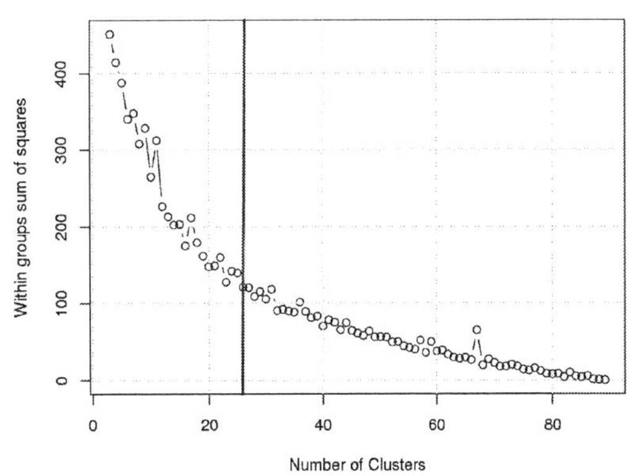

Figure 2: The inter-cluster distance plot for the learning set *Abui verbs (356) v. 2020.*

For comparison, when we examine an older and smaller learning set of 150 verbs, we can see in the inter-cluster distance plot, shown in Figure 3, that the threshold value is lower. The inter-cluster distance decreases rapidly until 17 clusters, but starts to decrease gradually after 18 clusters but the characteristic elbow-shape is less obvious.

We conjecture that the size of the learning set influences still the threshold value and therefore the learning set should be further expanded with new verbs until the threshold remains stable. This is a very useful information to guide the laborious construction of the learning set which requires a lot of time of highly-trained native speakers.

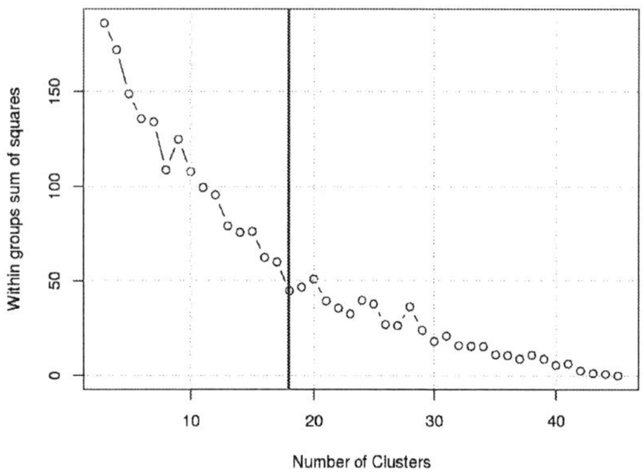

Figure 3: The inter-cluster distance plot for the learning set *Abui verbs (150) v. 2020.*

We have built a visual interface, which allows us to examine the clusters in 3D space using the first three principal components as vectors. The visual interface represents each verb by a sphere. In case there are more than one verbs in one position, the diameter of the sphere is increased proportionally to the number of verbs in that position.[8]

The interface allows the 3D space to be rotated to examine whether the cluster members are not too far apart allowing a visual inspection of the clusters. Thanks to the rotation feature, we can see the shape of the cluster, for example, whether its members are aligned along a line, lie within a sphere, are scattered far apart without an obvious geometric relation, etc.

A screenshot of the visualisation of the *Abui verbs (356) v. 2020* learning set can be seen in Figure 4. The number of clusters is set here at 25 and clusters are numbered and coloured.

The content of each cluster is listed in a separate window called *Cluster Membership* under the same number as used in the 3D plot. We use the data point closest to the mean value to characterise each cluster; i.e. the verb nearest to the mean value becomes the cluster label in the *Cluster membership* window (see section 2.4).

The cluster visualisation interface includes a version control, so that we can load newer versions of learning sets and check the differences in analysis. Similarly, the gradually improving coverage of our corpus data is also stored, as described in the next section.

2.3. Corpus data harvesting

Presently, the Abui corpus is managed using the SIL Toolbox (SIL International, 2015) and SIL Fieldworks (SIL International, 2017). Both tools support simple concordance functions but lack more powerful distributional analysis tools needed to tackle the present problem. We therefore rely on a workflow, described in (Zamaraeva et al., 2017), where a morphological grammar of Abui is inferred from interlinear glossed text (IGT) extracted from the glossed part of the Abui corpus and applied on the entire corpus following a workflow described in (Bender et al., 2014).

The workflow is built on the precision grammar architecture known as the Grammar Matrix project (Bender et al., 2002; Bender et al., 2010) which supports the creation of starter-kit precision grammars on the basis of the lexical and typological language profile and allows for specification of position classes and lexical rules (O'Hara, 2008; Goodman, 2013). In addition, the precision grammar is enhanced by the information retrieved from existing collections of IGT, using methods developed by Lewis and Xia (2008) and Georgi (2016). The system is implemented as Matrix-ODIN Morphology or 'MOM' (Wax, 2014; Zamaraeva, 2016). It extracts from a corpus of IGT information such as (i) sets of affixes grouped in position classes; (ii) for each affix also its gloss; (iii) input for each position class. The MOM system can generate a feature matrix of the same structure as the learning set.

Affixes can be expressed as a graph whose nodes represent the input relations. This can be illustrated using the example sentence in (6).

(6) he-ha-luol tila bataa ha-tang
3.LOC-3.PAT-follow rope tree 3.PAT-branch
he-tilaka mai neng nuku di mii
3.LOC-hang REAL man one 3.AGT take.PFV
ya ho-puna ba natea.
SEQ 3.REC-hold.IPFV SIM stand
'in the next one, there was a rope hanging on the tree branch when a man came and took it and remained standing there holding it.'

Classifying verbal stems is approached as a co-occurrence problem: given segmented and glossed IGT, we determine which stems co-occur with which types of affixes. Using the data in example (6), we see that (i) the verbs *mii* 'take' and *natea* 'stand' can occur freely (Feature I); (ii) the verb *tilaka* 'hang' with the prefix *he-* (Feature III); (iii) the verb *luol* 'follow' can combine with the prefixes *he-* and *ha-* (Feature II and III); and (iv) the verb *puna* 'hold' with the prefix *ho-* (Feature V).

The resulting co-occurrences can be explored visually, as described in (Lepp et al., 2019) or listed (as input

[8]Please note that in Figure 4 the largest sphere contains 164 verbs.

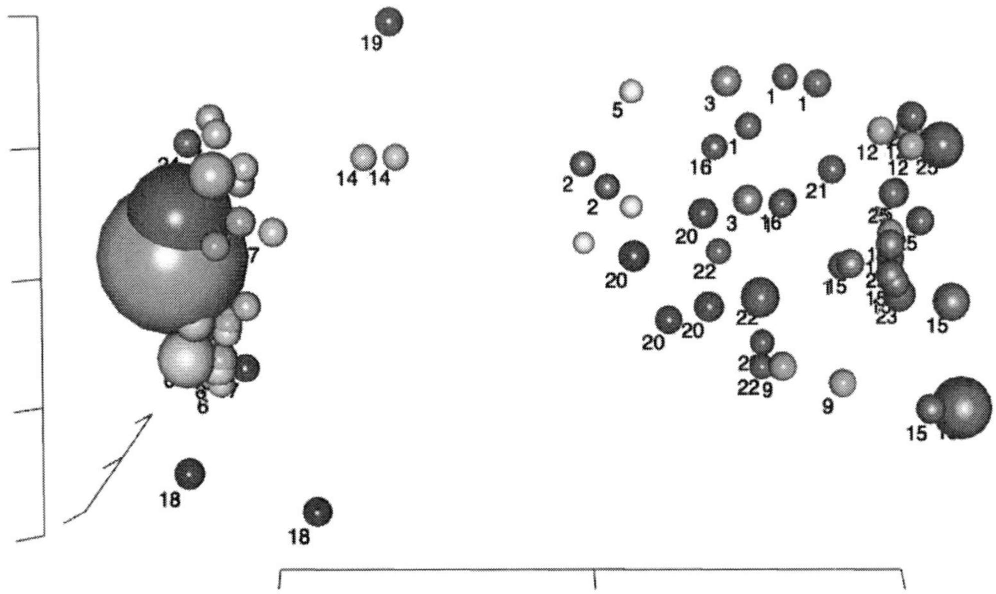

Figure 4: The visualisation of the structure of the learning set *Abui verbs (356) v. 2020.*

for the *AVC-abz*). The process is outlined in Figure 5, presented in (Zamaraeva et al., 2017), and explained briefly below.

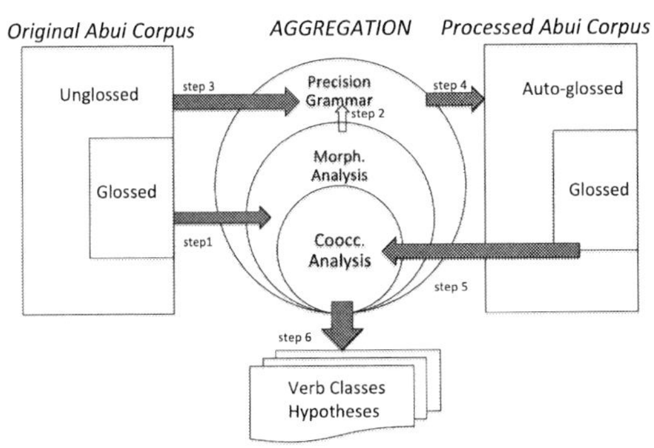

Figure 5: The components of the corpus-processing (from Zamaraeva et al., 2017).

The AGGREGATION workflow allows bootstrapping the morphological information in the glossed part of the corpus which can be used to automatically analyse words that have not been manually glossed. In this way we can process much more data and verify the validity of the clustering proposed based on the learning set, as described in section 2.2.

2.4. Cluster lists comparison

The fourth component of the system is a *Cluster list* feature, which is built on a Naive Bayes clasiffier. Naive Bayes is a simple technique that assumes independence among features. Using the *learning set* features a naive Bayes classifier considers the features of each verb in the *corpus set* and assigns each verb to the most probable cluster.

The output of the Naive Bayes is listed as a table, as shown in Figure 6. The verb stems that are assigned by the Naive Bayes to the same cluster as they were by the k-means classifier are listed in bold face. Stems found only in one of the two datasets are listed in regular plain face. Finally, stems that are assigned differently by both classifiers are listed in italics. The typographic distinction aids the human expert to quickly evaluate the classification, check the data values by clicking the listed verb stem to examine their features.

The verb profiles can be examined using the *Data* tab shown in Figure 7. Thus mismatches between the curated and automatically derived data sets do not necessarily indicate system errors. Instead, they represent cases in which corpus analysis can further our understanding of the language at hand.

Given the small size of descriptive corpora, the generated feature array will have properties of a sparse matrix, where most elements are zero, not because the combination is impossible, but because the target morpheme sequence is not attested in the corpus. The sparsity of the feature matrix is *de facto* a metric of the corpus coverage of the selected phenomena. Mathematical methods exist to solve sparse matrixes so that they can serve as a reliable input for machine learning and clustering algorithms, whose output in turn aids linguistic analysis. For example, Fisher Information evaluation (which feature(s) predicts the class membership the best) informs the fieldwork practice (i.e. which constructions should be elicited and in what sequence). The clustering analysis helps detect morphemes with similar distributional properties. The analysis can be

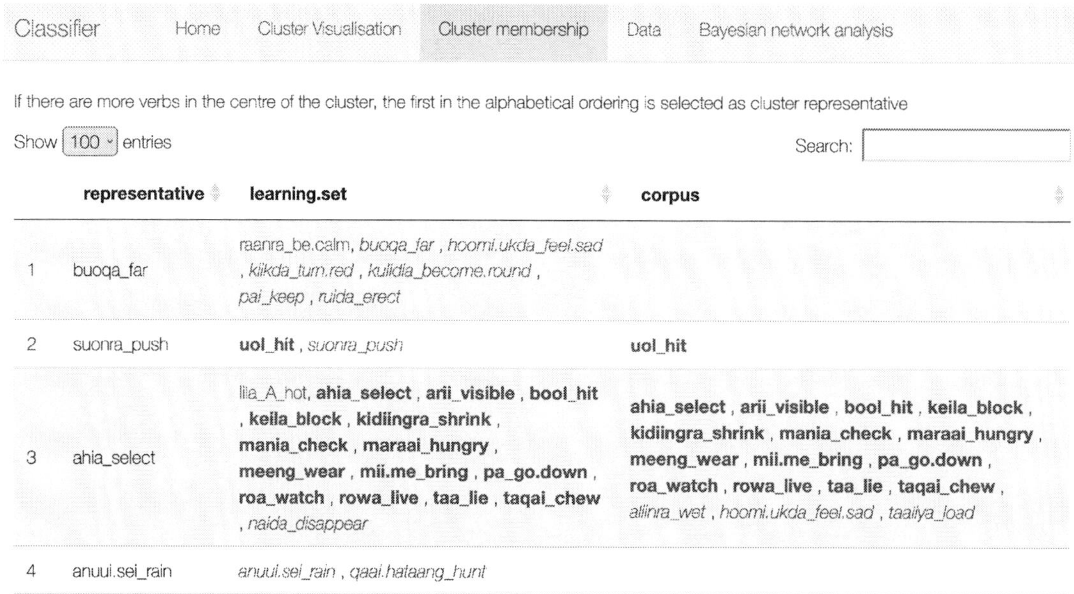

Figure 6: The cluster list comparison. The left column lists the cluster membership as suggested by the k-means algorithm. The right column is the output of a Naive Bayes algorithm.

Figure 7: The data list comparison. This overview can be searched for individual verbs in either the *Learning set* or *Corpus data*, viewed in its entirety or navigated from the *Cluster Membership* tab.

aided by visualisation methods.

Because the corpus is not phonologically normalised, we are expanding the list of alternate forms. For example the verb *aquta* 'be blind' is also attested as *akuta* in the unglossed part of the corpus. In the first two versions there was also no explicit linking for mutating stems such as *meeng* 'wear (imperfective)' and as *meen* 'wear (perfective)'. The *Cluster list* allows us to discover further such candidates in the data and update the list of alternate forms.

3. Conclusion and future work

This paper presents an integrated workflow to support automatic verb classification in Abui, based on the morphological profile of the verb stem. The system is designed to support the advanced analysis of this complex grammatical feature of Abui that has been subject of a number of detailed investigations and continues to attract interest, especially in the context of the ongoing language shift and the growing influence of Alor Malay, which have been shown to lead to a gradual overhaul of the verb inflection system (Klamer and Saad, 2020; Saad, 2020b). In particular the *AVC-abz* system has got the following properties:

- Integrated native judgment and corpus data: Both types of data are handled as distinct types (*learning set* and *corpus data*. The learning set is manually curated with the assistance of native speakers and used as input for automated classifier.
- Corpus linguistics tool for extracting corpus information: The corpus is harvested for morphosyntactic information of verb stems following the methodology described in (Zamaraeva et al., 2017). The output is distributed into clusters.
- Mathematical tools for classification and feature relations: K-means and Naive Bayes are used to analyse the *learning set* and to assign the *corpus set* data to the clusters with the best fit.
- Version control: It is typical for documentation projects that the work is ongoing and the analysis is changing. The system is designed to work with different versions of the *learning set* and *corpus data* in order to compare the coverage of the corpus and the gradual improvement of the analysis.
- Interface supporting data interpretation by the expert: The interface will serve as an open-data platform to support future publications on the Abui verb class system. It enables the expert to investigate the detailed properties of the various verbs as well as the entire class system.

The system is also relevant to the *data coverage* question put forth by Nikolaus Himmelmann as: 'the aim of a language documentation is to provide a comprehensive record of the linguistic practices characteristic of a given speech community' (Himmelmann, 1998).

There are no standards to report corpus coverage cross-linguistically except simple metrics such as number of words or sentences, or to ascertain whether the aggregated corpus 'large enough' and presents a 'comprehensive record' of the language, speaking in Himmelmann's terms. While the question of 'large enough' may be a rhetorical distraction, it is practical to develop tools that can measure the corpus coverage of specific phenomena, whose aggregation can eventually answer the 'large enough' question. The AVC-abz addresses the question of corpus coverage locally; it measures the fit between the *learning set* and the *corpus data*. We can expect that at some point most verbs from the *corpus data* will always fit in the optimal number of clusters determined by the *learning set* whose size does not need to be increased anymore.

Our future work will focus on implementing a Bayesian Network to investigate the relationships between various inflectional categories. It hedges for the possibility that some features do correlate or are dependent. This information can be for example fed into the settings of the Naive Bayes classifier which can treat dependent or correlating features as one.

Another line of further improvement concerns the orthographic variation. The Abui corpus is partly sourced within the community and therefore contains multiple orthography standards and some dialectal variation. Abui speakers do not agree on a single orthography regarding velar and uvular stops (*k*~ *q* vs. *k* only), long vowels (e.g. *a*~ *aa* vs. *a* only), and tones (not written at all or written with accents). They also do not make a strict distinction between the single stem predicates and complex predicates containing light verbs, because in both cases the predicate (simple or complex) forms a single phonological word. The resulting variation in the unglossed part of the corpus is responsible for some noise in the classification, but the presented tool enables us to find such instances and to amend the orthographic profile of the given verb.

Acknowledgments

This article reports research carried out with the generous support of the Czech Science Foundation grant 20-18407S *Verb Class Analysis Accelerator for Low-Resource Languages - RoboCorp* (PI F Kratochvíl).

4. Bibliographical References

Baker, C. F., Fillmore, C. J., and Lowe, J. B. (1998). The Berkeley FrameNet Project. In *Proceedings of COLING/ACL*, pages 86–90, Montreal. ACL.

Bender, E. M., Flickinger, D., and Oepen, S. (2002). The Grammar Matrix: An Open-Source Starter-Kit for the Rapid Development of Cross-Linguistically Consistent Broad-Coverage Precision Grammars. In John Carroll, et al., editors, *Proceedings of the Workshop on Grammar Engineering and Evaluation at the 19th International Conference on Computational Linguistics*, pages 8–14, Taipei, Taiwan.

Bender, E. M., Drellishak, S., Fokkens, A., Poulson, L., and Saleem, S. (2010). Grammar Customization. *Research on Language & Computation*, pages 1–50. 10.1007/s11168-010-9070-1.

Bender, E. M., Crowgey, J., Goodman, M. W., and Xia, F. (2014). Learning grammar specifications from IGT: A case study of Chintang. In *Proceedings of the 2014 Workshop on the Use of Computational Methods in the Study of Endangered Languages*, pages 43–53, Baltimore, Maryland, USA, June. Association for Computational Linguistics.

Fedden, S., Brown, D., Kratochvíl, F., Robinson, L. C., and Schapper, A. (2014). Variation in Pronominal Indexing: Lexical Stipulation vs. Referential Properties in Alor-Pantar Languages. *Studies in Language*, 38(1):44–79.

Fillmore, C. J. (1970). The grammar of hitting and breaking. In Roderick A. Jacobs et al., editors, *Readings in English Transformational Grammar*, pages 120–133. Waltham, MA: Ginn.

Georgi, R. (2016). *From Aari to Zulu: Massively Multilingual Creation of Language Tools using Interlin-*

ear Glossed Text. Ph.D. thesis, University of Washington.

Goodman, M. W. (2013). Generation of machine-readable morphological rules with human readable input. *UW Working Papers in Linguistics*, 30.

Iren Hartmann, et al., editors. (2013). *Valency Patterns Leipzig*. Max Planck Institute for Evolutionary Anthropology, Leipzig.

Himmelmann, N. P. (1998). Documentary and descriptive linguistics. *Linguistics*, 36(1):161–196.

Kipper, K., Korhonen, A., Ryant, N., and Palmer, M. (2008). A large-scale classification of English verbs. *Language Resources and Evaluation*, 42(1):21–40.

Klamer, M. and Kratochvíl, F. (2018). The evolution of Differential Object Marking in Alor-Pantar languages. In Ilja Seržant et al., editors, *The Diachronic Typology of Differential Argument Marking*, Studies in Diversity Linguistics, pages 69–95. Language Science Press, Berlin.

Klamer, M. and Saad, G. (2020). Reduplication in Abui: A case of pattern extension. *Morphology*, 30:311–346.

Kratochvíl, F. and Delpada, B. (2015). Degrees of affectedness and verbal prefixation in Abui (Papuan). In Stefan Müller, editor, *Proceedings of the 22nd International Conference on Head-Driven Phrase Structure Grammar, Nanyang Technological University (NTU), Singapore*, pages 216–233, Stanford, CA. CSLI Publications.

Kratochvíl, F., Moeljadi, D., Delpada, B., Kratochvíl, V., and Vomlel, J. (2021). Aspectual pairing and aspectual classes in Abui. *STUF - Language Typology and Universals*, 74(3-4):621–657.

Kratochvíl, F. (2007). *A grammar of Abui: a Papuan language of Alor*. LOT, Utrecht.

Kratochvíl, F. (2011). Transitivity in Abui. *Studies in Language*, 35(3):588–635.

Kratochvíl, F. (2014). Differential argument realization in Abui. *Linguistics*, 52(2):543–602.

Kratochvíl, F. (2022). Abui Corpus. Electronic Database: 162,000 words of natural speech, and 37,500 words of elicited material (February 2022). Palacký University Olomouc, Czech Republic.

Lepp, H., Zamaraeva, O., and Bender, E. M. (2019). Visualizing inferred morphotactic systems. In *Proceedings of the 2019 Conference of the North American Chapter of the Association for Computational Linguistics (Demonstrations)*, pages 127–131.

Levin, B. (2015). Semantics and pragmatics of argument alternations. *Annual Review of Linguistics*, 1(1):63–83.

Lewis, W. D. and Xia, F. (2008). Automatically identifying computationally relevant typological features. In *Proceedings of the Third International Joint Conference on Natural Language Processing*, pages 685–690, Hyderabad, India.

Merlo, P. and Stevenson, S. (2001). Automatic verb classification based on statistical distributions of argument structure. *Computational Linguistics*, 27(3):373–408.

O'Hara, K. (2008). A morphotactic infrastructure for a grammar customization system. Master's thesis, University of Washington.

Palmer, M., Gildea, D., and Kingsbury, P. (2005). The proposition bank: An annotated corpus of semantic roles. *Computational linguistics*, 31(1):71–106.

Saad, G. (2020a). Abui. In Antoinette Schapper, editor, *The Papuan Languages of Timor, Alor and Pantar*, volume 3 of *Sketch Grammars*, chapter 5, pages 267–345. De Gruyter Mouton, Berlin.

Saad, G. M. (2020b). *Variation and change in Abui: The impact of Alor Malay on an indigenous language of Indonesia*. LOT, Amsterdam.

Siewierska, A. (2013). Verbal person marking. In Matthew S. Dryer et al., editors, *The World Atlas of Language Structures Online*. Max Planck Institute for Evolutionary Anthropology, Leipzig.

SIL International. (2015). Field Linguist's Toolbox. Lexicon and corpus management system with a parser and concordancer; URL: http://www-01.sil.org/computing/toolbox/documentation.htm.

SIL International. (2017). Sil Fieldworks. Lexicon and corpus management system with a parser and concordancer, URL: http://software.sil.org/fieldworks/.

Sun, L. and Korhonen, A. (2009). Improving verb clustering with automatically acquired selectional preferences. In *Proceedings of the 2009 Conference on Empirical Methods in Natural Language Processing*, pages 638–647.

Wax, D. (2014). Automated grammar engineering for verbal morphology. Master's thesis, University of Washington.

Zamaraeva, O., Kratochvíl, F., Bender, E. M., Xia, F., and Howell, K. (2017). Computational Support for Finding Word Classes: A Case Study of Abui. In *Proceedings of ComputEL-2: 2nd Workshop on Computational Methods for Endangered Languages, Honolulu, Hawaii, March 6-7, 2017*. Association for Computational Linguistics (ACL).

Zamaraeva, O. (2016). Inferring Morphotactics from Interlinear Glossed Text: Combining Clustering and Precision Grammars. In *Proceedings of the 14th SIGMORPHON Workshop on Computational Research in Phonetics, Phonology, and Morphology*, pages 141–150, Berlin, Germany, August. Association for Computational Linguistics.

Proceedings of the EURALI Workshop @LREC2020, pages 51–60
Marseille, 20 June 2022

Dialogue Act and Slot Recognition in Italian Complex Dialogues

Irene Sucameli*, Michele De Quattro*, Arash Eshghi, Alessandro Suglia**, Maria Simi***
*Department of Computer Science, University of Pisa
*School of Mathematical and Computer Sciences, Heriot-Watt University
irene.sucameli@phd.unipi.it, m.dequattro@studenti.unipi.it,
a.eshghi@hw.ac.uk, as247@hw.ac.uk, simi@di.unipi.it

Abstract

Since the advent of Transformer-based, pretrained language models (LM) such as BERT, Natural Language Understanding (NLU) components in the form of Dialogue Act Recognition (DAR) and Slot Recognition (SR) for dialogue systems have become both more accurate and easier to create for specific application domains. Unsurprisingly however, much of this progress has been limited to the English language, due to the existence of very large datasets in both dialogue and written form, while only few corpora are available for lower resourced languages like Italian. In this paper, we present JILDA 2.0, an enhanced version of a Italian task-oriented dialogue dataset, using it to realise a Italian NLU baseline by evaluating three of the most recent pretrained LMs: Italian BERT, Multilingual BERT, and AlBERTo for the DAR and SR tasks. Thus, this paper not only presents an updated version of a dataset characterised by complex dialogues, but it also highlights the challenges that still remain in creating effective NLU components for lower resourced languages, constituting a first step in improving NLU for Italian dialogue.

Keywords: Dialogue systems, Italian dataset, NLU

1. Introduction

The field of Natural Language Processing (NLP) was transformed when Vaswani et al. (2017) presented their self-attention-based, Transformer model for representation or embedding of Natural Language strings, with Devlin et al. (2019) then releasing BERT, a large scale pretrained LM, showing that new state of the art results could be obtained in many canonical NLP tasks just by fine-tuning with one additional task-specific output layer. This *transfer learning* methodology forms the basis of the most important component in dialogue systems today: Natural Language Understanding (NLU). Moreover, it has also been applied to our problem of interest in this paper: that of Dialogue Act Recognition (DAR, e.g. Chakravarty et al. (2019)) combined with Slot Recognition (SR), tasks which aim to evaluate how well a system classifies the dialogue acts (i.e the goal of the speaker's utterance) and the slots (i.e the informative elements which have to be extracted in order to understand and fulfil the speaker's goal) of a sentence.

Much of the progress above has, however, been limited to the English language due largely to the unavailability of high quantities of language corpora in other languages. For example, in comparison to English, Italian stands as a lower resourced language and, with few exceptions (Mana et al., 2004; Castellucci et al., 2019; Sucameli et al., 2020), there is currently a paucity of dialogue datasets available with appropriate Dialogue Act & Slot annotations for training effective NLU models. Large scale multilingual models do exist (e.g. Multilingual BERT), but it is as yet unclear how these models *transfer* to the NLU tasks of DAR & SR. One important reason for this uncertainty is that nearly all existing, large-scale LMs have been trained on open domain, written language, whereas dialogue is known to be very different from text or written language: dialogue is highly context-dependent, is replete with fragments (Fernández and Ginzburg, 2002; Purver et al., 2009), ellipsis (Colman et al., 2008) & disfluencies (Shriberg, 1996; Hough, 2015), and is highly domain-specific (Eshghi et al., 2017). Noble and Maraev (2021) provide evidence for this, showing that pretrained BERT does not transfer well for the DAR task without being fine-tuned on the target dialogues. In this paper, we focus on NLU for dialogue systems in Italian. We present and use an enhanced version of the JILDA corpus (Sucameli et al., 2020) – one of the very few Italian dialogue datasets in the public domain – to evaluate three of the most recent pretrained LMs on the DAR & SR tasks: Multilingual BERT (Devlin et al., 2019), Italian BERT (Schweter, 2020), and AlBERTo (Polignano et al., 2019).

2. Related work

2.1. BERT for dialogue NLU

Ever since the advent of the Transformer model, BERT (Devlin et al., 2019) has become the de facto standard for the DAR and SR tasks, and has seen success in many dialogue domains in the English language (Mehri et al., 2019; Ribeiro et al., 2019; Chakravarty et al., 2019; Bao et al., 2020). For these tasks, a *transfer learning* method is employed using BERT, which uses a multi-layer bidirectional transformer to embed the input text. In such approaches, BERT is used as the pretrained encoder, whose one or more hidden layers are fed to additional output layer(s) or classifiers and fine-tuned on specific in-domain NLU datasets. Considering the effectiveness of such a transfer learning approach for dialogue, Noble and Maraev (2021) show, interestingly, that the pretrained model isn't of much use without fine-tuning on target dialogue data.

In this paper, we study the usefulness of three different versions of BERT as the pretrained language model, and evaluate their performance in the DAR & SR tasks on the JILDA 2.0 dataset, a new updated version of the collection of mixed-initiative, human-human dialogues in Italian, and in the 'job offer' domain originally presented in Sucameli et al. (2020).

2.2. Dialogue Datasets

Annotated dialogue corpora are at the core of the capacity to learn dialogue models. Among human-human corpora, it is certainly worth citing the **ReDial dataset** (Li et al., 2018), which includes 10,000 human-human recommendation dialogues collected via Amazon Mechanical Turk.

The **Twitter Corpus** (Ritter et al., 2010) also belongs to this category, with 1.3 million post-reply pairs extracted from Twitter; **The Ubuntu Dialogue Corpus** (Lowe et al., 2015) is another with a large amount of unstructured dialogues used to train dialogue systems without any NLU annotations (see e.g. Lowe et al. (2017)). There is also a number of human-machine dialogue corpora: this includes the **DSTC1** dataset (Williams et al., 2013), a popular task-oriented dataset released in conjunction with the Dialog State Tracking Challenge; and the **Frames** dataset (Asri et al., 2017), which studies user's decision-making behaviour. Finally, belongs to this category MultiWOZ, a collection of dialogues built with a Wizard of Oz (WoZ) approach. **MultiWoZ** (Budzianowski et al., 2018) is one of the most influential dialogue datasets with a recent 2.3 version released (Han et al., 2021) which addresses some annotation errors of the original. MultiWoZ 2.0 contains 10,438 dialogues collected using the WoZ approach and which cover various domains, such as restaurant and hotel search, taxi and hospitals. Thanks to the frequent updates of the dataset, MultiWoZ constitutes an important benchmark for Natural Language Understanding.

2.3. Italian Dialogue Datasets

In comparison to English, in which there are numerous dialogue datasets available (see Li et al. (2018; Lowe et al. (2017; Budzianowski et al. (2018; Liu et al. (2021) among many others), Italian is a lower resourced language: more specifically, there is currently a paucity of dialogue datasets available with appropriate Dialogue Act and Slot/Named Entity annotations for training effective NLU models. Among the few collections available are the **NESPOLE** dataset (Mana et al., 2004) in the tourism domain; the **SNIPS** dataset (Castellucci et al., 2019) – derived through translation from English; and the newly released **JILDA** dataset (Sucameli et al., 2020) which we use for our experiments in this paper.

3. The JILDA dataset

JILDA (Sucameli et al., 2020) is a collection of complex human-human dialogues realised in Italian, and in the 'job offer' domain. This dataset includes 745 mixed-initiative dialogues collected in an experiment which involved 50 Italian native speakers and was inspired by the Map-task methodology (Brown et al., 1984), in which two participants collaborate to achieve a common purpose (in this case, the realization of a task-oriented dialogue).

The produced resource consists of 17,889 utterances and a total of 263,104 tokens, characterised by great linguistic variability and syntactic complexity; indeed, the dataset presents, on average, 17 turns per dialogue with more of the 51% percentage of subordinate propositions (an example of JILDA dialogues is reported in Appendix). Furthermore, the datasets includes dialogues with linguistic phenomena that are often not contained or considered in the collections of dialogues, such as proactive and grounding phenomena. These phenomena, typical of human-human conversations, confirm, together with the evaluations made, the naturalness of the dialogues produced.


```
{"text": "Sono alla ricerca di un contratto a
tempo indeterminato, possibilmente in Italia",
    "turn_id": 2,
    "metadata": {
        "contract": [
            "tempo indeterminato"
        ],
        "location": [
            "Italia"
        ]
    },
    "dialog_act": {
        "usr_inform_basic": [
            [
                "contract",
                "tempo indeterminato"
            ],
            [
                "location",
                "Italia"
            ]
        ]
    },
    "span_info": [
        [
            "usr_inform_basic",
            "contract",
            "tempo indeterminato",
            7,
            8
        ],
        [
            "usr_inform_basic",
            "location",
            "Italia",
            12,
            12
        ]
    ]
}
```


Figure 1: Example of a JILDA annotated dialogue.

JILDA has been annotated with the DAs and slots reported in Table 1, using MATILDA, an open source tool created to annotate multi-turn dialogues (Cucurnia

et al., 2021), following the annotation scheme of MultiWOZ 2.0 (Budzianowski et al., 2018). Budzianowski et al. (2018) used a set of 13 Dialogue Acts (such as: inform, greet, request, reqmore, not found) and 23 slots to annotate dialogues referred to 7 domains (restaurant, hotel, attraction, taxi, train, hospital, police)[1].
JILDA annotation schema includes 12 dialogue acts (DA) and 14 slot types; Figure 1 shows an example of JILDA annotation schema, while Table 1 shows the distribution of different dialogue acts and slots in the JILDA dataset. In addition to this, the dataset enjoys high inter-annotator agreement (κ = 0.86 for DAs; κ = 0.82 for Slots)(Sucameli et al., 2021).
Together, all these data highlight the complexity of JILDA, and indicate that creating effective NLU models for this data is likely to be challenging. In what follows, we evaluate three different NLU models (DAR+SR) on these dialogue datasets.

DA	Occur.	Slots	Occur.
usr-greet	3222	age	130
usr-deny	1257	area	1472
usr-select	890	company-name	556
usr-inform-basic	8665	company-size	732
usr-inform-proac.	3335	contact	827
usr-request	2940	contract	1486
sys-greet	2918	degree	1243
sys-deny	759	duties	1741
sys-select	1868	job-description	1362
sys-inform-basic	6736	languages	1085
sys-inform-proac.	1590	location	1922
sys-request	6494	other	559
		past-experience	882
		skill	1994

Table 1: JILDA DA and Slot occurences.

4. JILDA 2.0

In order to be able to make a comparison between our Italian NLU model and the model based on MultiWOZ 2.1 (Han et al., 2021), one of the main benchmarks for English NLU, we decided to upgrade the current version of JILDA, realising **JILDA 2.0**.
JILDA 2.0, now available on Github [2], constitutes an updated version of the resource, implemented with design choices compliant with MultiWOZ 2.1. Specifically, we made some improvements to the annotations of the first version of the dataset, as illustrated below:

1. correction of inferred annotations. For example, the following sentence[3]:

```
sys: "Si tratta appunto di un
tirocinio post-laurea, nel
settore pubblicitario presso
una azienda pisana"
```

   was annotated as:

```
    "sys_inform_basic": [
        ["location","Pisa"]]
```

   In this case, "Pisa", although cannot be found in the sentence, was inferred from the adjective "pisana".

2. resolution of turns' annotations which were marked using dialogue acts and slots related to the next turn, due to an incorrect use by annotators of the MATILDA tool. For example[4]:

```
sys: "Cercano persone che
si occupino di gestire la
comunicazione pubblicitaria
del cliente attraverso il web"
    "sys_inform_basic": [
    ["duties", "gestire la
    comunicazione pubblicitaria"],
    [ "skill","abilità di
    comunicazione"]]
sys: "Questo significa che
abilità di comunicazione sono
essenziali"
```

   To resolve this error, the annotation has been referred to the correct turn and text spans have been updated.

3. adjustment of tokens boundaries. For example, the sentence[5]:

```
    sys: "Il candidato (...)
    ha inoltre il compito di
    gestire le comunicazioni
    per il cliente e le
    informazioni su richiesta
    dell'ospite"
```

   was annotated with:

```
    "sys_inform_basic": [
        ["duties","informazioni
        su richiesta dell'ospit"]]
```

[1] In MultiWOZ 2.0 not all the DAs and slots are used over all the domains.

[2] `http://github.com/IreneSucameli/JILDA`

[3] Translation: " *It is a post-graduate internship, in the advertising sector at a Pisan company.*"

[4] Translation: "*They are looking for people who manage the customer's advertising communication via web.*" and "*This means that communication skills are essential.*"

[5] Translation: "*The candidate (...) has also to manage the communications and information for the customer, if requested by the guest.*"

Here, the token "ospit" cannot be found in the utterance since the final vowel is missing. This kind of error depends on the tool used for the annotation, which initially allowed to select the words' range based on the single characters, instead of the entire token. In JILDA 2.0 these errors have been fixed by inserting the correct token in the span.

4. resolution of annotations which embed information from previous turns. In MultiWOZ 2.1 slots and dialogue acts are annotated and extracted turn by turn, disregarding information coming from previous or following turns. For this reason we decided to conform to the MultiWOZ standard by removing the occurrences of this annotation from JILDA, which instead presents a great number of annotations which relies on information referring to previous turns. In fact, together with the changes described in the second point, a total of 882 occurrences have been removed. With this change, the resource has been more aligned with our reference model. An example can help to understand better the changes made. In the conversation below[6] the word "da remoto" does not appear in the user's sentence, since the speaker is reffering to an implicit subject (here, the "remote working"). Therefore, the information annotated in the user turn derives from the system's turn:

```
sys: "Ti piacerebbe lavorare da
remoto?",
usr: "Si, potrebbe andare bene!"
    "usr_inform_basic": [
    [ "location","da remoto"]]
```

To conform to MultiWOZ 2.1, we decided to remove annotations referring to previous turns from the turn's span; still, the extracted information remained stored in the metadata. We decided to maintain the information since we think it could be interesting, in future works, to use specialised tag-sets in order to effectively capture relevant linguistic inferences, similarly to what was done by Bentivogli et al. (2010).

The updated dataset, produced as a result of the changes illustrated above, was then used to evaluate three of the most recent pretrained LMs on the Dialogue Act and Slot recognition tasks. The experimental results are reported in the next sections.

5. Experimental Setup

5.1. Models

Our experiments were conducted within ConvLab-2[7], an open-source multi-domain end-to-end dialogue system platform realised by Zhu et al. (2020).

[6]Translation: sys:"*Remote working would be ok for you?*" usr:"*Yes, it would be fine.*"

[7]https://github.com/thu-coai/ConvLab-2

We chose this tool in order to have results comparable to the ones produced by Han et al. (2021) with the ConvLab-2's BERTNLU module. This module, which was used for our experiments as well, is based on a pretrained BERT to which it adds on top two Multi-Layer Perceptrons (MLPs), one for dialogue act classification and another for slot tagging, as shown in Figure 2. Here, the Transformer model is called at different times within the same cycle. The number of layers depends on the pretrained LM used. For each sentence, it is called twice with the indicated inputs and outputs, and also produces a pooled representation of the context. Then, the Slot Classifier produces as many outputs as the words in the sentence, while the DAR returns a score on the different DA values.

In BERTNLU all those dialogue acts which appear in the utterances are converted using BIO tags, a common tagging format for tagging tokens in chunks (Ramshaw and Marcus, 1995). We used BERTNLU combined with three different language models available on Hugging Face: **bert-base-italian-xxl-cased** [8](Schweter, 2020), **bert-multilingual-cased** [9](Devlin et al., 2019) and **AlBERTo**[10](Polignano et al., 2019).

	bert-italian-xxl	bert-multil.	AlBERTo
Voc. Size	32K	119K	128K
Source	OPUS, OSCAR and Wikipedia	Wikipedia	TWITA

Table 2: Comparison of vocabulary size of the LMs.

The first one is trained on Wikipedia, on the OPUS corpus[11] (which includes - among the other data - transcripts of spoken language and subtitles) and on the Italian part of the OSCAR corpus[12], which consists of raw web pages. The second one is trained with the top 100 languages from Wikipedia, including Italian. Since the size of Wikipedia varies from language to language, and to avoid under-representation of lower resourced languages, in the multilingual version of BERT, high-resource languages (like English) are under-sampled, while lower resourced languages are over-sampled.

Finally **AlBERTo** (Polignano et al., 2019) is a BERT LM for the Italian language, trained on 200M tweets with a vocabulary size of 128k. AlBERTo replicates the BERT stack and it is trained using masked language modelling loss only since the authors remove the next sentence prediction loss because tweets don't have a notion of sequence of sentences like in documents.

[8]https://github.com/dbmdz/berts

[9]https://github.com/google-research/bert

[10]https://github.com/marcopoli/AlBERTo-it

[11]https://opus.nlpl.eu/

[12]https://oscar-corpus.com/

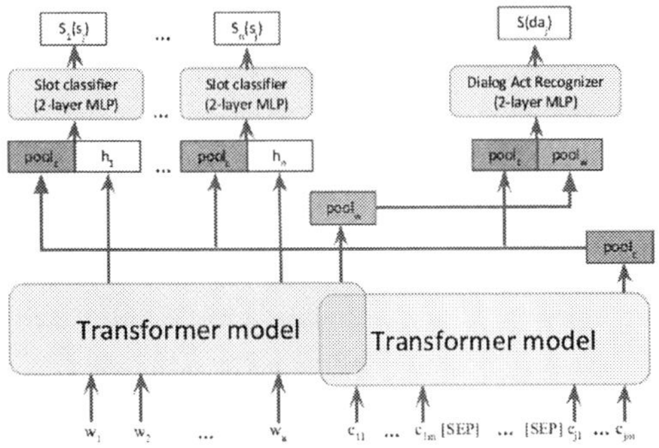

Figure 2: BERTNLU architecture. The Transformer models produce two types of pools, one for the words (w) and another for the contexts (c). These pools are sent to the Slot Classifier and the Dialogue Act Recognizer. There are as many Slot Classifiers as there are words, while for the Dialogue Act is produced a single distribution of probability on the different values.

5.2. Hyper-parameters

We used the JILDA 2.0 dataset to finetune & evaluate the above-mentioned models on the DAR & SR tasks, taking the 80% of the data for training (596 dialogues) & 20% for testing and validation (respectively, 75 and 74 dialogues). The hyper-parameter tuning procedure is described in Appendix. After fixing the hyper-parameters, we trained each model and computed average scores for Precision, Recall and F1 Score. Since JILDA used MATILDA's tokenizer, while ConvLab-2 adopts spacy and bert tokenizer, we decided to standardize the different tokenizations. Thus, it was decided to apply the spacy tokenizer [13] to JILDA 2.0 annotated data.

We also decided to unify the classification of the DA *inform-basic* and *inform-proactive*, since these two acts express the same intent, which could be expressed proactively (e.g. the speaker autonomously provided unsolicited information) or not; with a view to distinguishing the types of dialogues acts, it was therefore reasonable to consider them as a unique act. Moreover, even without this distinction, it is still feasible the comparison with the English benchmark since in MultiWOZ 2.1 there is not the difference between proactive and required dialogue acts.

In order to quantify how well each pretrained encoder – bert-base-italian, bert-multilingual & AlBERTo – encodes the target JILDA 2.0 dialogues, i.e. how well it transfers, we evaluated each model in two training conditions: 1) **end-to-end**, where the weights of the underlying encoder model were finetuned together with the task-specific DAR & SR layers; and 2) **frozen-lm** where the weights of the encoder layers were frozen with only the task-specific layers fine-tuned.

[13] `https://spacy.io/models/it`

6. Results & Discussion

6.1. The end-to-end condition

Table 3 shows the averaged results obtained for the three models in the end-to-end condition. The overall results record the cases in which both the DAs and the slots in a sentence have been correctly predicted.

		bert-ita	bert-multi	AlBERTo
Acts	Prec.	81.55	**82.85**	79.74
	Rec.	**75.36**	70.41	70.66
	F1	**78.33**	76.12	74.92
Slots	Prec.	**71.65**	68.06	70.78
	Rec.	**71.27**	66.99	65.60
	F1	**71.46**	67.52	68.09
Overall	Prec.	**74.20**	71.66	73.13
	Rec.	**72.38**	67.92	66.97
	F1	**73.28**	69.74	69.92

Table 3: Values of Precision, Recall and F1 Scores in the `end-to-end` condition.

Analysing the performance of the models reported in Table 3, it can be firstly observed that the monolingual models perform better than the multilingual one. This proves that using LM in line with the language of the training data helps to reach better results in the recognition and classification of dialogue acts and slots. Nevertheless, the F1 score difference between the multilingual and monolingual BERT models is low enough to affirm that the first model is not less effective than the monolingual ones. This shows that at least the Italian language is represented well within the multilingual BERT model.

Among the three models, the best performing one definitely appears to be **bert-ita-xxl**. Comparing the monolingual models (bert-ita-xxl vs. AlBERTo) we noticed that bert-ita shows a superior performance than AlBERTo, which, however, has a larger vocabulary than the first one; in fact, the first one is originally trained on 81GB of data and 32K terms, while the second one consists of 191GB of raw data and a vocabulary of 128K terms. This demonstrates that LMs pre-trained on data similar to dialogues are able to gain better results than those trained on textual documents, regardless of the size of their dataset. Indeed, despite its size, AlBERTo is pretrained on Italian tweets, which tend to have a simplified structure compared to that of the JILDA dialogues used in our training. On the other hand, bert-ita-xxl is based on pre-training data that includes syntactically longer and semantically richer sentences (such as data from Wikipedia and OSCAR corpus), as well as transcripts of spoken conversation and subtitles (from the OPUS corpus), which present a syntactic and semantic structure close to that of the JILDA dialogues.

The results achieved are good if we consider that they were obtained using complex training dialogues. In fact, if we compare the results obtained by bert-ita (our best model) combined with JILDA 2.0 with those obtained by bert-base trained with MultiWOZ 2.1(Eric et al., 2020), it is possible to notice that the performance achieved by the Italian model is interesting. The comparison between the two datasets is feasible, although they differ in the dialog domain and in the size of the collected data, since they use the same architecture for training the NLU model for DAR and SR tasks. In fact, MultiWOZ 2.1 (Eric et al., 2020), which deals with some annotation errors of the previous version of the dataset, introduces an additional annotation for both user's and system's side and the resulting dataset is used to train, via ConvLab-2, the BERTNLU module for the DAR and SR tasks (Han et al., 2021). The results reported in Han et al. (2021) were obtained under similar conditions to ours (e.g. the `context` and the `fine-tune` hyper-parameters were set as `true`), and were evaluated using the same metrics. For all these reasons it was possible to compare the results obtained training the models with JILDA 2.0 with those reported in Han et al. (2021).

Datasets	F1 (Slot/DA/Both)
JILDA 2.0	71.46/78.33/73.28
MultiWOZ 2.1	81.18/88.34/83.77

Table 4: Performance of BERTNLU with JILDA and MultiWOZ 2.1.

	JILDA 2.0	MultiWOZ 2.1
Dialogues	745	10.438
Tokens	263.104	1.490.615
Ontologies' entries	5.779	2.111

Table 5: Comparison of JILDA 2.0 and MultiWOZ 2.1 in terms of dataset size and lexical vocabulary.

Table 4 shows how the F1 scores achieved by JILDA, although inferior to those of MultiWOZ, are not only reasonable but also very positive, if we consider that our model was trained using a dataset which is much smaller and, at the same time, extremely rich from a lexical point of view, as shown in Table 5. In fact, JILDA has far fewer dialogues and tokens but the number of values extracted from the ontology (which includes the lexical vocabulary of each slot) is over twice, sign of the linguistic richness of the Italian dataset.
Furthermore, compared to the original JILDA data, the improvements made to the new JILDA 2.0 version and described in Sections 4 & 5.1, allowed to increase the overall F1 score of the models trained under the end-to-end condition by almost 50 scores. This shows that the changes realised actually helped the NLU models to perform better.
Therefore, from the analysis of the results obtained, it is possible to state that the NLU model trained on our dataset shows convincing performances such as to be proposed a new benchmark for the Italian NLU.

6.2. The frozen-lm condition

Table 6 shows the averaged Precision, Recall & F1 Score values obtained in the `frozen-lm` condition where the weights of the encoder stack were frozen during training and only the task-specific heads fine-tuned.

		bert-ita	bert-multi	AlBERTo
	Prec.	82.26	**96.00**	80.13
Acts	Rec.	32.01	10.57	**54.51**
	F1	46.09	19.05	**64.66**
	Prec.	70.15	63.80	**72.23**
Slots	Rec.	**55.34**	48.26	50.22
	F1	**61.87**	54.96	59.25
	Prec.	72.02	65.44	**74.34**
Overall	Rec.	49.05	38.10	**51.38**
	F1	58.35	48.16	**60.77**

Table 6: Values of Precision, Recall and F1 Score recorded for the three models without fine-tuning the language model encoder stack.

Comparing Table 3, which shows the performance of the fine-tuned models, with Table 6, it is clear that fine-tuning the weights of the encoder model together with the task-specific DAR SR layers allows to gain better values. The results above are in line with those found by (Noble and Maraev, 2021) and highlight the importance of fine-tuning pre-trained encoders. Interestingly however, comparing the performance of the three models, when the fine-tune parameter is set to false, the one which performs better is AlBERTo. We believe that this is due to the data and vocabulary size used in the original training; in the absence of fine-tuning it seems that the model with more pre-training data obtains better performances.

7. Error Analysis

Having computed the F1 scores of the three models, we conducted an error analysis in order to verify which acts and slots were recognised more easily and which with more difficulties. To this end, we calculated the accuracy for the recognition of dialogue acts and slots and for each of the models. This measure is often used to evaluate NLU models and for intent detection task (Mohamad Suhaili et al., 2021), which is similar to our DAR and SR tasks.

	bert-ita	bert-multi	AlBERTo
DA Acc.	**78.25**	76.03	74.84
Slot Acc.	**71.46**	67.57	68.08

Table 7: Averaged accuracy in DAR and SR tasks.

Table 7 reports the overall accuracy computed per each model, while Figures 3 and 4 represent the accuracy of each DA and slot and for each model.
Analysing the accuracy of each DA (Figure 3), we noticed that *inform* had the highest values, while *greet* the

lowest, probably due to the number of representation in the dataset of these acts. In fact, as illustrated in Table 1, some DAs and slots are higher represented than other; the higher is their representation in the dataset, the more accurate the models' classification is.

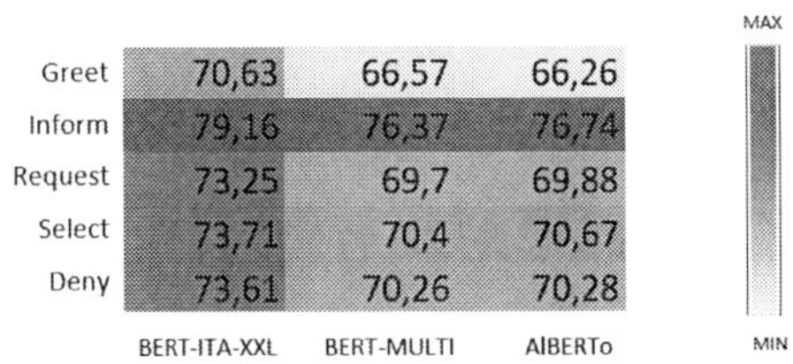

Figure 3: DAR accuracy in monolingual/multilingual BERT and AlBERTo.

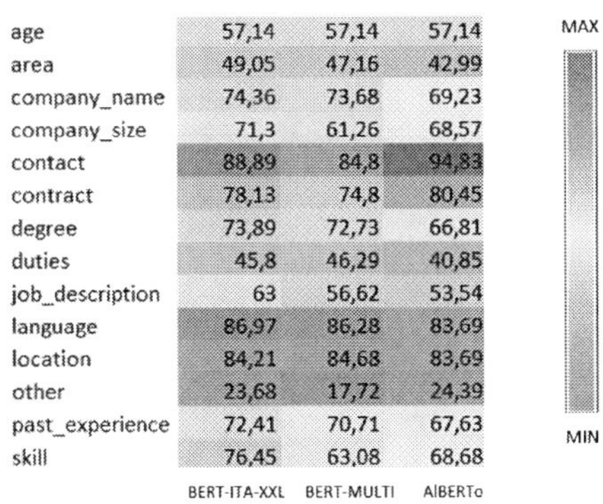

Figure 4: SR accuracy in monolingual/multilingual BERT and AlBERTo.

Regarding the classification of slots, it seems that the models had more difficulty with those slots which share lexical entries, as shown in Figure 4. When calculating slot accuracy, predicted slots were considered correct when they were used to classify the same part of text (ie the slot's value) marked by the true (ie gold) slots.

Excluding *other*, which constitutes a particular slot as it allows to mark all information which cannot be marked in another class, the slots whose recognition accuracy is less than 50.00 were only *area* and *duties*. The difficulty in recognizing these slots may be due to the fact that they presents larger and more open lexical vocabularies than those of slots such as *contract*, *contact* or *language*. In fact, for example, the lexical vocabulary of *duties* includes 985 entries, while *language* has 240 entries and *contact* less than 70.

Another aspect to take into consideration is the potential sharing of semantic contexts and syntactic structures. This means that a word, depending on the context in which it is found, could be annotated using multiple slots. Indeed, vocabulary overlapping between slots is a common phenomenon in JILDA.

For example, in the first sentence of Fig. 5[14] the text span can be annotated both with the slot *area* and with *degree*, due to the vocabulary overlap between these two slots. Similarly, in the second sentence, "insegnamento" can be considered both as a work's type or area, depending on the connotation we want to give to the term.

Cerco lavoro nel mio campo di studi. Mi sono laureato alla triennale in economia e marketing a Torino.

True label	area	economia e marketing
Predicted label	degree	economia e marketing

Al momento non abbiamo offerte di insegnamento.

True label	job_description	insegnamento
Predicted label	area	insegnamento

Figure 5: Overlap of slots' lexical vocabularies.

L'azienda ha la sua sede nella provincia di Pisa.

True label	location	provincia di Pisa
Predicted label	location	Pisa

Sono una neo-laureata in scienze sociali.

True label	degree	neo-laureata in scienze sociali
Predicted label	degree degree	neo-laureata scienze sociali

Figure 6: Text fragment selection errors. In the first example a part of the text is missing, while in the second one the relevant information is split in two slots.

Analysing the errors produced by the three models, it was also noted how, in some cases, even when the models correctly identified the relevant part of the text for the slots, they cut the informative text fragment, thus producing False Positive or False Negative. In the sentences in Figure 6 [15], for example, the model correctly recognised "Pisa", "neo-laureata" and "scienze sociali" as informative, annotating them with the correct act and slot. However, since the gold label included a larger text fragment, these predictions were considered as false by the model itself.

[14]Translation sentence n.1: " *I am looking for a job in my field of study. I graduated in Economics and marketing in Turin.*"
Sentence n.2: "*At the moment we don't have any teaching offers.*"

[15]Translation sentence n. 1: " *The company has its headquarters in the province of Pisa.*"
Sentence n.2: "*I recently graduated in social sciences*".

The analysis and the discussion conducted point out that creating effective NLU components for dialogue systems in domains grounded in data as linguistically rich & complex as JILDA remains a challenge. Therefore, starting from the values presented in Tab. 3, we propose in the future to further investigate the DAR and SR tasks for NLU Italian models, training the models with different recurring neural networks in order to achieve even a better performance.

8. Conclusion

In this paper we presented JILDA 2.0, an updated version of the Italian dataset collecting dialogues in the job application domain. In order to realise a NLU baseline trained with JILDA 2.0 that was comparable with the MultiWOZ 2.1 benchmark, we evaluated three recent pretrained LMs, namely Italian BERT, Multilingual BERT and AlBERTo. We fine-tuned and tested these models on the Dialogue Act Recognition and Slot Recognition tasks which are good proxy tasks for how well and under what training conditions these models are able to effectively encode dialogue semantics.

Our results showed that: (1) comparing the monolingual and the multilingual models, the first type resulted to be more able to obtain a better performance when specialised on an Italian dialogic dataset; (2) the size of the dataset used in the original training of the LM has less impact on the results than the type of data used in the original training; in fact, it was recorded a better performance for bert-ita-xxl, whose vocabulary is smaller than the one of AlBERTo but includes data which have linguistic features closer to those of the JILDA dialogues; (3) the multilingual BERT model performs only slightly worse than the monolingual model, highlighting the relative effectiveness of the multilingual model for the Italian language; and (4) fine-tuning the pretrained encoder is important, especially when the target data are dialogues that differ in many important ways from written data.

Furthermore, in comparison with the model trained on MultiWOZ 2.1, our NLU model presents convincing performances such as to constitute a new benchmark for the Italian NLU.

Our work demonstrates not only the issues related to the training of NLU models on lower resourced language, but, more importantly, constitutes a starting point for working on Italian models, specifically pretrained on dialogic dataset like JILDA. For future work, we will try to further refine the JILDA dataset and expand its annotation, in order to align the resource with the current version of MultiWOZ 2.3. Finally, we would like to introduce a Bidirectional LSTM in the BERTNLU architecture in order to improve the results of the current NLU module.

9. Bibliographical References

Asri, L. E., Schulz, H., Sharma, S., Zumer, J., Harris, J., Fine, E., Mehrotra, R., and Suleman, K. (2017). Frames: A corpus for adding memory to goal-oriented dialogue systems. *Proceedings of the 18th Annual SIGdial Meeting on Discourse and Dialogue*, pages 207–219.

Bao, S., He, H., Wang, F., Wu, H., and Wang, H. (2020). PLATO: Pre-trained dialogue generation model with discrete latent variable. In *Proceedings of the 58th Annual Meeting of the Association for Computational Linguistics*, pages 85–96, Online, July. Association for Computational Linguistics.

Bentivogli, L., Cabrio, E., Dagan, I., Giampiccolo, D., Lo Leggio, M., and Magnini, B. (2010). Building textual entailment specialized data sets: a methodology for isolating linguistic phenomena relevant to inference. Valletta, Malta, May 2010.

Brown, G., Anderson, Shillcock, R. A., and Yule, G. (1984). *Teaching talk: Strategies for production and assessment.* Cambridge University Press.

Budzianowski, P., Wen, T.-H., Tseng, B.-H., Casanueva, I., Ultes, S., Ramadan, O., and Gašić, M. (2018). MultiWOZ - a large-scale multi-domain wizard-of-Oz dataset for task-oriented dialogue modelling. In *Proceedings of the 2018 Conference on Empirical Methods in Natural Language Processing*, pages 5016–5026, Brussels, Belgium, October-November. Association for Computational Linguistics.

Castellucci, G., Bellomaria, V., Favalli, A., and Romagnoli, R. (2019). Multi-lingual intent detection and slot filling in a joint bert-based model. *In ArXiv abs/1907.02884.*

Chakravarty, S., Chava, R. V. S. P., and Fox, E. (2019). Dialog acts classification for question-answer corpora. In *ASAIL@ICAIL.*

Colman, M., Eshghi, A., and Healey, P. (2008). Quantifying ellipsis in dialogue: an index of mutual understanding. In *Proceedings of the 9th SIGdial Workshop on Discourse and Dialogue*, pages 96–99, Columbus, Ohio, June. Association for Computational Linguistics.

Cucurnia, D., Rozanov, N., Sucameli, I., Ciuffoletti, A., and Simi, M. (2021). Multi-annotator multi-language interactive light-weight dialogue annotator. *In EACL.*

Devlin, J., Chang, M.-W., Lee, K., and Toutanova, K. (2019). BERT: Pre-training of deep bidirectional transformers for language understanding. In *Proceedings of the 2019 Conference of the North American Chapter of the Association for Computational Linguistics: Human Language Technologies, Volume 1 (Long and Short Papers)*, pages 4171–4186, Minneapolis, Minnesota, June. Association for Computational Linguistics.

Eric, M., Goel, R., Paul, S., Sethi, A., Agarwal, S., Gao, S., Kumar, A., Goyal, A., Ku, P., and Hakkani-Tur, D. (2020). MultiWOZ 2.1: A consolidated multi-domain dialogue dataset with state corrections and state tracking baselines. In *Proceedings of The*

12th Language Resources and Evaluation Conference, pages 422–428, Marseille, France, May. European Language Resources Association.

Eshghi, A., Shalyminov, I., and Lemon, O. (2017). Interactional dynamics and the emergence of language games. *CEUR Workshop Proceedings*, 1863:17–21.

Fernández, R. and Ginzburg, J. (2002). Non-sentential utterances: A corpus-based study. *Traitement Automatique des Langues*, 43(2).

Han, T., Liu, X., Takanabu, R., Lian, Y., Huang, C., Wan, D., Peng, W., and Huang, M. (2021). Multiwoz 2.3: A multi-domain task-oriented dialogue dataset enhanced with annotation corrections and coreference annotation. In Lu Wang, et al., editors, *Natural Language Processing and Chinese Computing*, pages 206–218, Cham. Springer International Publishing.

Hough, J. (2015). *Modelling Incremental Self-Repair Processing in Dialogue*. Ph.D. thesis, Queen Mary University of London.

Li, R., Kahou, S., Schulz, H., Michalski, V., Charlin, L., and Pal, C. (2018). Towards deep conversational recommendations. *In Advances in Neural Information Processing Systems 31 (NIPS 2018)*, pages 9748–9758.

Liu, X., Eshghi, A., Swietojanski, P., and Rieser, V., (2021). *Benchmarking Natural Language Understanding Services for Building Conversational Agents*, pages 165–183. Springer Singapore, Singapore.

Lowe, R., Pow, N., Serban, I., and Pineau, J. (2015). The ubuntu dialogue corpus: A large dataset for research in unstructured multi-turn dialogue systems. *Proceedings of the SIGDIAL 2015 Conference*, pages 285–294.

Lowe, R., Pow, N., Serban, I. V., Liu, C.-W., and Pineau, J. (2017). Training end-to-end dialogue systems with the ubuntu dialogue corpus. *Dialogue and Discourse*, 8(1):31–65.

Mana, N., Cattoni, R., Pianta, E., Rossi, F., Pianesi, F., and Burger, S. (2004). The italian nespole! corpus: a multilingual database with interlingua annotation in tourism and medical domains. *In Proceedings of the Fourth International Conference on Language Resources and Evaluation (LREC'04)*.

Mehri, S., Razumovskaia, E., Zhao, T., and Eskenazi, M. (2019). Pretraining methods for dialog context representation learning. In *Proceedings of the 57th Annual Meeting of the Association for Computational Linguistics*, pages 3836–3845, Florence, Italy, July. Association for Computational Linguistics.

Mohamad Suhaili, S., Salim, N., and Jambli, M. N. (2021). Service chatbots: A systematic review. *Expert Systems with Applications*, 184:115461.

Noble, B. and Maraev, V. (2021). Large-scale text pretraining helps with dialogue act recognition, but not without fine-tuning. In *Proceedings of the 14th International Conference on Computational Semantics (IWCS)*. Association for Computational Linguistics.

Polignano, M., Basile, P., de Gemmis, M., Semeraro, G., and Basile, V. (2019). AlBERTo: Italian BERT Language Understanding Model for NLP Challenging Tasks Based on Tweets. In *Proceedings of the Sixth Italian Conference on Computational Linguistics (CLiC-it 2019)*, volume 2481. CEUR.

Purver, M., Howes, C., Gregoromichelaki, E., and Healey, P. G. T. (2009). Split utterances in dialogue: A corpus study. In *Proceedings of the 10th Annual SIGDIAL Meeting on Discourse and Dialogue (SIGDIAL 2009 Conference)*, pages 262–271, London, UK, September. Association for Computational Linguistics.

Ramshaw, L. and Marcus, M. (1995). Text chunking using transformation-based learning. In *Third Workshop on Very Large Corpora*.

Ribeiro, E., Ribeiro, R., and de Matos, D. M. (2019). Deep dialog act recognition using multiple token, segment, and context information representations. *J. Artif. Intell. Res.*, 66:861–899.

Ritter, A., Cherry, C., and Dolan, D. (2010). Unsupervised modeling of twitter conversations. *In North American Chapter of the Association for Computational Linguistics (NAACL 2010)*.

Schweter, S. (2020). Italian bert and electra models, nov.

Shriberg, E. (1996). Disfluencies in switchboard. In *In Proceedings of the International Conference on Spoken Language Processing*, volume 96, pages 3–6. Citeseer.

Sucameli, I., Lenci, A., Magnini, B., Simi, M., and Speranza, M. (2020). Becoming jilda. *In Proceedings of the Seventh Italian Conference on Computational Linguistics CLIC-it 2020*.

Sucameli, I., Lenci, A., Magnini, B., Simi, M., and Speranza, M. (2021). Toward data-driven collaborative dialogue systems: The jilda dataset. *IJCOL*.

Vaswani, A., Shazeer, N., Parmar, N., Uszkoreit, J., Jones, L., Gomez, A. N., Kaiser, u., and Polosukhin, I. (2017). Attention is all you need. In *Proceedings of the 31st International Conference on Neural Information Processing Systems*, NIPS'17, page 6000–6010, Red Hook, NY, USA. Curran Associates Inc.

Williams, J., Raux, A., Ramachandran, D., and Black, A. (2013). The dialog state tracking challenge. *In Special Interest Group on Discourse and Dialogue (SIGDIAL)*.

Zhu, Q., Zhang, Z., Fang, Y., Li, X., Takanobu, R., Li, J., Peng, B., Gao, J., Zhu, X., and Huang, M. (2020). ConvLab-2: An open-source toolkit for building, evaluating, and diagnosing dialogue systems. In *Proceedings of the 58th Annual Meeting of the Association for Computational Linguistics: System Demonstrations*, pages 142–149, Online, July. Association for Computational Linguistics.

Appendix

Appendix A

Extract from a JILDA dialogue. The reported conversation is characterised by the presence of linguistic phenomena, such as proactivity and grounding (respectively, turn 1 and turns 7 & 8), and by sentences which are syntactically complex and semantically rich.

1. Applicant: *In the meantime, should I specify my geographic preferences? They could help you target me better*
(Nel frattempo potrei specificarti le mie preferenze a livello geografico? Potrebbero aiutarti nel targetizzarmi meglio)

2. Navigator: *Yes, perfect! Thank you*
(Sì, perfetto! Grazie)

3. Applicant: *At the moment I live in Tuscany: I'm available to move to other regions and even abroad I don't have mobility problems or limitations from this point of view*
(Attualmente vivo in Toscana: sono disponibile a trasferirmi in altre regioni ma anche all'estero non ho problemi di mobilità o limiti da questo punto di vista)

4. Navigator: *I may have two offers that I would like to propose to you. Both involve post-graduate internships, one as an assistant prime contractor in a construction company in Pistoia, and the other as a junior director in Milan. I think they could be ok for you because both jobs involve management assignments and your degree could be very useful in these contexts.*
(Potrei avere due offerte che mi piacerebbe proporti. Entrambe riguardano tirocini post-laurea, uno come assistente capocommessa in una azienda edile a Pistoia, e l'altra come allievo direttore a Milano.)

5. Navigator: *Does one of them seem more appealing and do you want me to describe it first?*
(Uno dei due ti sembra più interessante e vuoi che te lo descriva per primo?)

6. Applicant: *I have to be honest: I don't think the first one is right for me. Could you describe the second job for me?*
(Devo essere sincera: il primo non penso che possa fare al caso mio. Potresti descrivermi il secondo lavoro?)

7. Applicant: *I can't quite understand what "junior director" means*
(Non riesco a capire bene che cosa significhi "allievo direttore")

8. Navigator: *Sure! The main tasks related to this job concern the planning of the budget and the income statement of the company. The area is the food sector so it's a question of filling orders and foodstuffs, as well as guaranteeing work and food safety.*
(Certo! Le principali mansioni legate a questo impiego riguardano la pianificazione del budget e del conto economico dell'azienda. Il settore è quello alimentare quindi si tratta di compilare ordini e derrate alimentari, oltre che garantire la sicurezza sul lavoro e quella alimentare.)

Appendix B

We tried 12 different hyperparameter combinations on the validation set: three batch size values (32, 64, 128) and four learning rates ($1e-4$, $2e-5$, $3e-4$, and $5e-5$). Moreover, we kept the number of steps low to prevent overfitting, with check-step: 300 and max-step: 3000. The other relevant settings include *finetune*, *context* and *context-grad*. The fist one determines if the model will be tuned or not with the BERT parameter. If *fine-tune:false*, only added classification layers will be tuned.
The context parameter defines if use context information. If context: false, the [CLS] representation of the single utterance is passed to the intent classifier while the tokens' representations are passed to the slot classifier. If true, context utterances of the last three turns are concatenated and provide context information with embedding of [CLS] for dialogue act and slot classification.
Finally, context-grad determines whether compute the gradient through context representation, and then back-propagate the loss to the context encoder.
According to the results obtained evaluating the results on the validation set, we fixed the hyper-parameters as follows:

```
"model": {
"finetune": true,
"context": true,
"context_grad": false,
"check_step":300,
"max_step":3000,
"batch_size": 64,
"learning_rate": 1e-4,
"adam_epsilon": 1e-8,
"warmup_steps": 0,
"weight_decay": 0.0,
"dropout": 0.1,
"hidden_units": 768 }
```

Proceedings of the EURALI Workshop @LREC2020, pages 61–64
Marseille, 20 June 2022

Digital Resources for the Shughni Language

Yury Makarov, Maksim Melenchenko, Dmitry Novokshanov
HSE University
105066, Moscow, Staraya Basmannaya Ulitsa, 21/4
yurmkrv@gmail.com, mgmelenchenko@edu.hse.ru, danovokshanov@edu.hse.ru

Abstract

This paper describes the Shughni Documentation Project consisting of the Online Shughni Dictionary, morphological analyzer, orthography converter, and Shughni corpus. The online dictionary has not only basic functions such as finding words but also facilitates more complex tasks. Representing a lexeme as a network of database sections makes it possible to search in particular domains (e.g., in meanings only), and the system of labels facilitates conditional search queries. Apart from this, users can make search queries and view entries in different orthographies of the Shughni language and send feedback in case they spot mistakes. Editors can add, modify, or delete entries without programming skills via an intuitive interface. In future, such website architecture can be applied to creating a lexical database of Iranian languages. The morphological analyzer performs automatic analysis of Shughni texts, which is useful for linguistic research and documentation. Once the analysis is complete, homonymy resolution must be conducted so that the annotated texts are ready to be uploaded to the corpus. The analyzer makes use of the orthographic converter, which helps to tackle the problem of spelling variability in Shughni, a language with no standard literary tradition.

Keywords: Shughni, online dictionary, morphological analyzer

1. The Shughni Language

1.1 General Information

Shughni is one of the Pamir languages, which belong to the Iranian branch of the Indo-European family. As estimated by (Edelman and Dodykhudoeva, 2009), it is spoken by circa 100,000 people in the Mountainous Badakhshan Autonomous Region of Tajikistan and in the neighbouring Badakhshan Province of Afghanistan. Our project revolves around the Shughni-Rushani subgroup of the Pamir languages. This subgroup consists of the following closely related idioms: Shughni (with Bajuwi), Rushani (with Khufi), Bartangi (with Roshorvi), and Sarikoli. The resources described below are focused on the Shughni language, especially on its variety spoken in Tajikistan.

Tajik is the official language of Tajikistan, taught in schools and exerting strong influence on Shughni, resulting in numerous loanwords and metatypic changes in the latter. A considerable part of Shughni speakers in Tajikistan also know Russian.

1.2 Writing System

Shughni has no official status in contemporary Tajikistan and there is no common writing tradition for it. Before the 20th century Arabic script was used sporadically. In the 1930s the Soviet authorities introduced a Latin-based Shughni alphabet but a decade later switched to a Cyrillic-based script. However, due to political reasons writing in Shughni was not welcomed until the 1980s, and no stable orthography was established. In the 1990s there appeared a few other writing systems. Scholars of various fields of study use different orthographies or even continue to create their own. Despite the absence of established orthography, there is a non-negligible written literature in Shughni (poetry, prose fiction, journalistic articles).

2. Online Shughni Dictionary

2.1 Benefits of Having an Online Dictionary

2.1.1 Online Dictionary as Research Tool

There is a number of reasons why online dictionary is instrumental in linguistic work. First, it facilitates creating a corpus by providing a fast interface for finding word meanings and hence making glossing an easier task. Moreover, building a lexical database is required for automatic analyzers (see 3 below), which also contribute to annotating texts for corpora, and other NLP tools. Second, if a dictionary contains a lot of examples of word usage, for some purposes it can be used as a corpus itself. Third, using existing dictionaries as a basis, researchers can update and expand them, and even turn them into a detailed lexical database by establishing an elaborate label system. Forth, while usually dictionaries of lesser-resourced languages are unidirectional (i.e., English-French and not vice versa), after digitalizing they become available for searching in both languages. Lastly, using website means that groups of researchers from different parts of the world can work on the same project cooperatively.

2.1.2 Online Dictionary for Local Communities

Online dictionary serves as an essential resource for language learning and revitalization, especially in the context of multilingualism. Speaking of teaching at schools, it is hard to imagine the codification of a language in the absence of an accessible dictionary. Available on the Internet through an easy-to-use interface, it is likely to become popular among a wider audience. This is also supposed to help those interested in developing literature in that language, and in reading existing texts.

2.2 The Case of the Shughni Language

2.2.1 Existing Dictionaries

During the 20th century two main dictionaries of the Shughni languages were published: one by Ivan Zarubin (1960), another by Dodkhudo Karamshoev (1988–1999). Both were written in Russian. While the former cannot be called comprehensive, the latter has three volumes totaling about 16,000 lexemes and contains massive illustrative material (based on high-quality field records made in the 1960–1970s in different Shughni-speaking areas). This played a decisive part in using that dictionary as a basis for the project and also in using Russian as the main language for the interface of the website[1].

2.2.2 Digitalization of the Karamshoev's dictionary

The digitalization of the Karamshoev's Shughni-Russian dictionary came in several steps. First, we scanned the volumes and used automatic recognition software to get text files. The dictionary uses two Cyrillic writing systems (for Russian and for Shughni) with a few diacritics and supplementary symbols from Greek script (see 4.1 below). This made proofreading an essential part of the process. At the same time entries were annotated, so that it would be possible to transfer every part of an entry to the corresponding section in the database.

2.3 Website Architecture

2.3.1 Searching and Database Structure

Online Shughni Dictionary is supposed to be useful both for linguists and general public (be it native speakers, language activists or language learners). This means that apart from basic functions such as finding a particular lexeme in the dictionary and giving a link to it in the output, there have to be more search options.

In our database every lexeme is represented as a network: it has different forms (spelling and phonetic variants, different grammar forms), meanings and idiomatic units (for Shughni, compound verbs and idioms are discriminated). Further, every idiomatic unit has its own set of meanings, and every meaning (both of lexemes and idiomatic units) can be illustrated with examples.

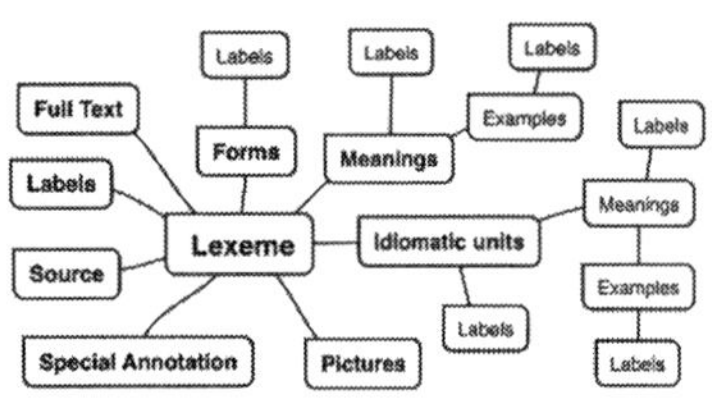

Figure 1: Representation of a lexeme in the database

Labels have different scope and hence can be applied to the lexeme in general (e.g., when it belongs to a certain dialect) or to a particular form, meaning or example. A lexeme may have multiple labels, but they will be arranged in a way that is not random but rather logical. There is also room for special annotation, be it comments about word usage or etymology. Every lexeme can be illustrated with some pictures. The online dictionary can aggregate different sources, so for each lexeme there is information about the dictionary from which it was taken.

Such database architecture makes it possible to search in particular domains, e.g., in meanings only. It is useful when one looks up 'iron' to find out what this metal is called in Shughni but gets a word for 'shirt' instead because in this entry there is an example saying, 'They *iron* their shirts every day.' Nevertheless, full texts of entries are also available as a search domain. The system of labels allows one to make conditional search queries, e.g., to find all obsolete verbs of falling in a certain dialect (provided that there are labels 'obsolete', 'verb of falling' and 'dialect X').

2.3.2 Search Engine and User Interface

In Shughni, there is no standard orthography. Some of the writing systems exploit symbols not easily accessible through every keyboard. That is why we provide users with the virtual keyboard. Despite that, one can choose not to discriminate between similar special symbols, and query with an ambiguous symbol will be parsed as having a set of analogous symbols in one place, e.g., 'wин' will be considered having either 'и' or 'ӣ', and the output will include both entries for 'wин' and 'wӣн.' Another handy function is looking up parts of words. It is possible to enter sequence 'wин' and get entries 'wин' and 'парwӣн' in the output.

Apart from the Cyrillic script illustrated above there is a Latin orthography used by some Iranists. We support both systems, so it is possible to search and view the entries using the two of them.

Another feature of the Online Shughni Dictionary is adaptive design, so it is comfortable to access the website through practically every kind of device.

2.3.3 Editing the Online Dictionary

Online Shughni Dictionary allows editors to change the database via web interface. The editing interface is intuitive and can be used by those who do not have programming skills. Every part of a lexeme (see 1.3.1 above) can be modified, e.g., it is possible to add new grammar forms, edit existing meanings, add new idiomatic units, etc. Editors are allowed to add new and delete existing entries or hide the latter from users.

While using the online dictionary users often notice typos or even mistakes. From our perspective, collecting such feedback is of vital importance. That is why there is an option to report a mistake while viewing entries. Such messages are sent to the special section of the editor's interface on the website.

2.4 Future Development

Such website architecture is suitable not only for the dictionaries of the Shughni language and its dialects but at least for other languages of Pamir as well. Digitalizing other sources in the same manner as with the Karamshoev's dictionary makes it feasible to develop a lexical database for multiple Iranian languages. Such database will be instrumental in typological studies as well as in comparative linguistics. Some of the most obvious functions that this database must have is the ability to form a list of cognates and compare same concepts (or lexemes) across different languages of the region.

We plan to create a new version of the dictionary where, among other things, special labels will be used for annotating the Tajik and Russian borrowings. Other dictionaries of the languages of the Shughni-Rushani group will be added to the platform. In addition to that, we will

[1] It is worth mentioning that most researchers studying the Shughni language have some knowledge of Russian since the latter is one of the languages widely spoken in the region.

use our corpus (see 4.2) to describe more lexemes. It will help minimize the effects of the problem of the dictionary size (see 3.3.1).

3. Automatic Morphological Analyzer

3.1 Principles of Automatic Analysis

Another instrument available on the website of our project is the morphological analyzer for Shughni. The algorithm is written in Python and uses the same database with the online dictionary. Once put into the analyzer, text is sentenized and tokenized using *nltk* module (Bird et al., 2009). Then, for each token the program tries to find correspondences in the *Forms* section of the database (see 2.3.1 above) so that the token contains a root from the database. If the correspondence is found, the program attempts to identify the remaining parts of the token (before and after the root); there is also an algorithm that makes sure that the chain of affixes or clitics in these parts are possible in Shughni.

The main goal of the analyzer is to identify every morpheme or clitic in the analyzed sentence. The set of affixes and clitics was collected manually using the grammar descriptions and dictionaries of the Shughni language. Every morpheme and clitic have special restrictions on the grammatical and phonetic contexts where they can appear. For example, suffix *-um*, which is used for forming ordinal numerals, is attached only to the stems of cardinal numerals. Lative suffix has several phonetically conditioned variants, one of which, *-rd*, appears only after vowels. These restrictions are ascribed to every morpheme and clitic, and the algorithm considers them in the process of analysis.

Grammar rules implemented in the analyzer are hardcoded. For example, verbs in the present tense get a person suffix, whereas in the past and perfect tenses person markers are clitics which are not necessarily attached to the verb. This means that if the analyzer suggests that a morpheme chain contains a present verb stem with no person suffix attached, such analysis is rejected.

3.2 Export to Corpus

The output of the analyzer can be presented in two ways. One is via intuitive web interface, another is a json-file which can be uploaded to the Shughni corpus (see 4.2 below). The thing is that there often are competing analyses in the output from which one has to choose, i.e., *homonymy resolution* must be performed before exporting the annotated text to the corpus. The website interface allows one to do it easily.

3.3 Problems of Automatic Analysis

3.3.1 Size of the Dictionary

The analysis that the program conducts is helpful but far from perfect. There are several obstacles that the algorithm currently faces. Some lexemes found in Shughni texts are simply absent from the online dictionary. Among them are collocations and proper names, e.g., names of settlements, rivers, and other geographical objects in the Badakhshan region. Another large group of words not found in the dictionary is Tajik borrowings, which are numerous since the Shughni language spoken in Tajikistan is heavily influenced by the state language, namely Tajik. It is often difficult to distinguish between borrowing and code switching as the Shughni speakers in Tajikistan are at least bilingual. The same is true for the Russian borrowings though they appear to be less frequent.

3.3.2 Spelling Variation

In the absence of a codified spelling system, a lot of words vary in how they are written. This is particularly acute when it comes to loanwords, e.g., *miloim* (corresponding to *miloyim* 'soft' in the dictionary), *salomati* (*salůmati* 'health'), *tavallud* (*tawallud* 'birthday'), *avtomobīli* (*aftamubīl* 'car') are not recognized by the analyzer. Sometimes variability arises from dialectal or even interspeaker variation.

3.3.3 Ignoring Diacritics and Special Symbols

The problem of spelling variation (see 3.3.2 above) can be partly solved by ignoring certain differences between special symbols with and without diacritics. For example, Shughni has a set of short and long vowels which correspond to symbols with and without diacritics in writing, cf. *i* and *ī*. Such symbols are often confused in texts (even by natives). That is why during processing tokens with confusable symbols the same algorithm as described in 2.3.2 above is by default applied. Analyzing 'winč' will result in getting the correct output despite the fact that 'wīnč' is the correct spelling for this stem.

This feature, however, can lead to the increase of incorrect analyses in the output (cf. minimal pairs with short and long vowels). To avoid such scenario one can switch off ignoring diacritics and special symbols in the setting.

4. Other Resources

4.1 Orthography Converter

As noted in 1.2 above, the Shughni language spoken in Tajikistan uses different orthographies based on Cyrillic and Latin alphabets. They often include diacritics or digraphs. Orthography converter is designed to solve this problem and automatically convert Shughni texts in various orthographies to the unified Latin-based spelling system used by our project for research and documentation.

Some of the existing orthographies use the same symbol for different phonemes. For example, letter *j* can denote phonemes /j/, /d͡ʒ/ and /d͡z/. The converter must be able to identify for what phoneme each problematic symbol stands. For example, for *Xudowandard půnd jītet at wi roh yen rost kinet* 'Prepare ye the way of the Lord, make his paths straight' in the input, the converter understands that letter *y* is used for /j/; then, letter *j* cannot stand for the same phoneme and should be interpreted as /d͡ʒ/ (the next frequent meaning) instead. The output of the looks like *Xudowandard půnd ǰītet at wi roh yen rost kinet*, where *y* is for /j/ and *ǰ* is for /d͡ʒ/.

It is presumed that, according to the law of large numbers, if the text is sufficiently big, there will be enough different symbols in it for the program to identify the phonetic meaning of them correctly. For special cases, users can manually choose the phonetic meanings of the problematic symbols in the settings.

The converter is accessible as a separate instrument. It also serves as a pre-processing tool in morphological analysis as the analyzer is supposed to work only with the texts in the unified Latin orthography of the project.

4.2 Corpus

The Shughni corpus contains oral and written texts of different genres including fairy tales, prose fiction, poetry, etc. Some of these are stories which were recorded during fieldwork and can be played. There are also parallel Shughni-Tajik texts. Annotation consists of layers for token, morphemes, glosses, part of speech and meaning. Glosses are mostly in English, whereas the translations are in Russian. Metadata contains information about the author or speaker, title, source, place and date of the recording, its genre and whether the text is annotated manually. The corpus runs on the open-source Tsakorpus platform developed by Timofey Arkhangelskiy (see https://github.com/timarkh/tsakorpus). The current volume of the corpus is circa 40,000 tokens.

5. Bibliographical References

Bird, S., Klein, E., and Loper, E. (2009). Natural Language Processing with Python. Sebastopol: O'Reilly Media Inc. https://www.nltk.org/book/

Edelman, D. I. and Dodykhudoeva, L. R. (2009). Shughni. In G. Windfuhr (Ed.), *The Iranian Languages*. London and New York: Routledge, pp. 787–852.

Karamshoev, D. (1988–1999). Shughni-Russian dictionary in 3 volumes. Moscow: Izd-vo “Nauka”.

Zarubin, I. I. (1960). Shughni dictionary and texts. Moscow-Leningrad: Izd-vo Akademii nauk SSSR.

6. Language Resource References

Online Dictionary of the Shughni-Rushani Language Group. (2022). Languages of Pamir: Online Dictionary / Памирские языки: онлайн-словарь, distributed via HSE University (Yury Makarov), 2.0, ISLRN 865-656-162-260-6. https://pamiri.online/

Shughni corpus. (2022). Shughni language corpus, distributed via HSE University, 1.0, ISLRN 728-407-900-078-8. https://linghub.ru/shughni_corpus/search

7. Acknowledgements

This work was supported by the Humanitarian Research Foundation of the Faculty of Humanities, HSE University in 2020, Project “Computational and Linguistic Resources for the Shughni Language” (Russian: Компьютерные и лингвистические ресурсы для поддержки шугнанского языка), and in 2021, Project “Computational and Corpus Instruments for Iranian Studies” (Russian: Компьютерные и корпусные инструменты для иранистических исследований).

We thank the anonymous reviewers for their useful comments and suggestions.

Proceedings of the EURALI Workshop @LREC2020, pages 65–69
Marseille, 20 June 2022

German Dialect Identification and Mapping for Preservation and Recovery

Aynalem Tesfaye Misganaw, Sabine Roller
Universität Siegen
aynalem.misganaw@uni-siegen.de, sabine.roller@uni-siegen.de

Abstract

Many linguistic projects which focus on dialects do collection of audio data, analysis, and linguistic interpretation on the data. The outcomes of such projects are good language resources because dialects are among less-resources languages as most of them are oral traditions. Our project *Dialektatlas Mittleres Westdeutschland* (DMW)[1] focuses on the study of German language varieties through collection of audio data of words and phrases which are selected by linguistic experts based on the linguistic significance of the words (and phrases) to distinguish dialects among each other. We used a total of 7,814 audio snippets of the words and phrases of eight different dialects from middle west Germany. We employed a multilabel classification approach to address the problem of dialect mapping using Support Vector Machine (SVM) algorithm. The experimental result showed a promising accuracy of 87%.

Keywords: language identification, dialects, less-resourced languages

1. Introduction

For widely used languages like English, French, German etc. the problem of language identification (LI) is addressed because language resources are available in significant amount. In contrast, finding language resources for dialects is a challenging task since they are among less-resourced languages, which makes it to be a bottleneck when it comes to employing language technologies.

In the DMW project, systematic data collection is performed both on conducting a survey to select speakers and interviewing them. The speakers are from different regions in middle west Germany which includes North Rhine-Westphalia, parts of Lower Saxony and Rhineland-Palatinate. The interview questions are designed in such a way that the various linguistic aspects like vocabulary (lexicon), word structure and word formation (morphology), sound structure (phonology) and sentence formation (syntax) could be analyzed, evaluated, and interpreted for identifying the non-standard way of speaking i.e., dialects.

The collected data contains, among other metadata descriptions, the audio snippets, their transcriptions in IPA (International Phonetic Alphabet) notation, the words in focus (in standard German), and the region which the speakers represent. The audio snippets contain the spoken utterances of the selected words, phrases, and sentences. In this paper, acoustic features are extracted from each audio snippets into a csv format.

The use of stop words, n-gram, Machine Learning (ML) and hybrid approaches are commonly used method of LI (Truica et al., 2015). All these methods require the use of a significant size of language resources. For resource-rich languages, the process of identifying a language, using either of the methods, is relatively easy as they have writing standards from which rules could easily be extracted. However, in addition to the lack of standard in writing and the scarcity of written resources, identifying the nuances of dialects is a challenging task.

The distinction among dialect is so fine unlike the most widely used languages where a list of frequently used words could be used to distinguish them. Nowadays, the web is a good source for linguistic resources making this work to have a great deal of significance in **crowd corpus collection** which is a key input for corpus-based research. In addition, for researchers in the field of linguistics, it will have a benefit of **mapping a particular dialect with the region** it is spoken.

Many Natural Language Processing (NLP) either assume the language they are dealing with or use LI in their pipeline before trying to solve the main problem. This work will benefit those researchers who are struggling to support the preservation of less-resourced language.

This paper is organized as follows. Related work is briefly reviewed in Section 2. The dataset description and the process of identifying the parameters are described in detail in section 3 and 4 respectively. Section 5 discusses the method employed in identifying and mapping dialects. Results and discussions are explained in section 6. Finally, we provide conclusion and recommendations for future works in section 7.

2. Related Work

There is a significant number of work on LI with the aim of developing a system which is able to recognize and infer a language under question (Jauhiainen et al., 2019) . In the survey they conducted, Jauhiainen et al.

[1] https://www.dmw-projekt.de/

showed that LI could be applied to any form of language; text, speech, and sign language; digital or otherwise. Although notable progress has been achieved for resource-rich languages in the last couple of decades, less-resourced languages and dialects do not yet benefit from the state-of-the art technologies (Chittaragi and Koolagudi, 2019).

Among the main methods used for language recognition are methods based on stop words, character n-grams, machine learning and hybrid (Truica et al., 2015). In addition, the commonly used features in solving the problem are spectral and prosodic features (Chittaragi and Koolagudi, 2019)(Bartz et al., 2017) (Cai et al., 2019), transcripts of speech data (Ramesh et al., 2021)(Malmasi and Zampieri, 2017), and written text (Truica et al., 2015).

Scannell (2007), Jauhiainen et al. (2020) and Jurgens et al. (2017) have applied LI with the aim of corpus construction for endangered languages. Web services like automatic translation need to first recognize the language before translating the content into a target language (Lui and Baldwin, 2012). Thus, LI is critical in most language processing problems where its low performance affects the whole pipeline as it propagates (Jauhiainen et al., 2019).

3. Description of the Data

The data used is from the DMW project where people representing different places in Middle West Germany are selected and interviewed. The data used in this work represents eight geographical locations (Wenkerort[2]) each representing different dialect varieties.

The data collection is done by directly interviewing dialect speakers. The interview is based on a questionnaire which contains 800 questions, a sample of which is shown in Table 1. The interview is conducted by asking the speakers a question, and by showing them a video or image and let the speakers describe it in their dialect. The questions are designed in a way aimed at getting the translation of names of objects, animals, and activities in a dialect.

The complex tasks of data collection and the subsequent preprocessing are done by employees of the project in four different partner Universities, among which 12 are responsible for the field work of interviewing dialect speakers. The interview takes about 3 to 5 hours and sometimes it takes three different sessions to get the complete interview.

Although the data contains the linguistic features like vocabulary (lexis), word structure and word

Question	English Translation	Note
Welches Tier ist das auf dem Bild?	Which animal is on the picture?	A picture of a goat is shown to the interviewee
Wie lautet die Mehrzahl von Ziege?	What is the plural of goat?	
Worauf kann man reiten?	What can you ride on?	
Was macht die Frau in dem Video gerade?	What is the woman in the video doing right now?	A video is shown for the interviewee.

Table 1 Sample Questions

formation (morphology), sound structure (phonology) and sentence formation (syntax), this work focused on the use of lexicons for identifying and mapping the dialects. The total number of audio snippets used in the study is 7814 representing eight distinct dialects from middle northwest Germany.

During the interviews, a tool - *SpeechRecorder* (Draxler and Jänsch, 2004) - is used. This tool enabled to store only part of the interview which is relevant.

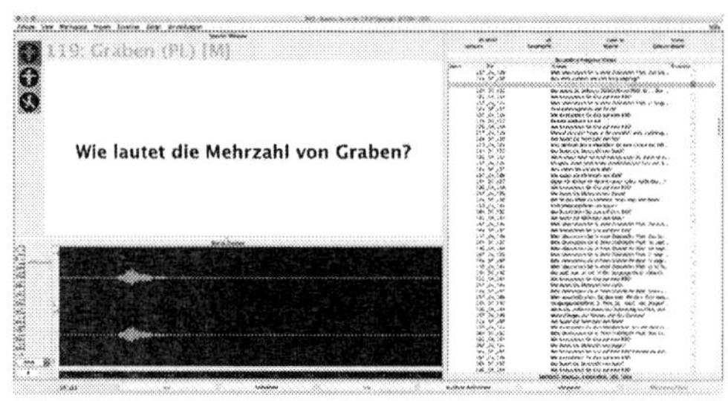

Figure 1: SpeechRecorder Software

For example, for the question text shown in Figure 1 where the question displayed means "*What is the plural of ditch?*", the speaker might utter other words before or after he speaks the answer for the question. However, using the tool the interviewer can record only the relevant part. In addition to the Speechrecorder tool, using a web-based interface further data cleaning is done in which the audio files are further cropped so that the audio exactly matches required answer.

[2] Named after the famous German linguistic researcher Georg Wenker.

Each speaker and each question are uniquely identified. The combination of these IDs is used to label the audio data. The region the speakers represent is also identified by unique ID which is used to label the dialect varieties.

Table 2 shows the distribution of audio files per dialects and the number of speakers used in each dialect region. Thus, the number of audio snippets used in this study ranges from 297 to 1303 per dialect. As presented in Table 1, except for the two dialect places, *Glehn* and *Homberg*, all the other six dialect have two speakers each.

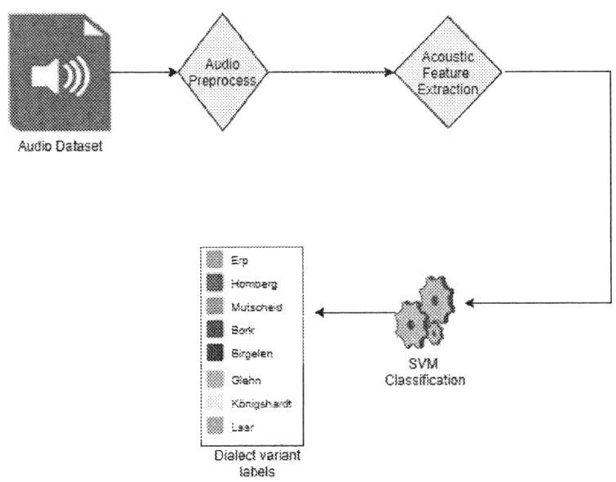

Figure 2 Block diagram for feature extraction and dialect identification

Although there are some audio snippets with longer time, the average length of the audio snippets ranges from 1sec to 5 sec.

Dialect Region	No. of Audio Snippets	No. of speakers	Total Length in min:sec
Birgelen	1301	2	19:05
Bork	1301	2	19:51
Erp	898	2	16:18
Glehn	297	1	04:14
Homberg	303	1	04:05
Königshardt	1303	2	19:49
Laar	1140	2	17:29
Mutscheid	1271	2	25:49

Table 2 Table showing the size of audio data and number of speakers for each dialect region

4. Parameter Identification/Feature extraction

Although the focus of the interview is collection of dialectal data, it is conducted in standard German. As a result, the audio files sometimes contain utterances which are unrelated to the question. This makes data cleaning an inevitable task. Thus, the audio recordings are first cropped, shown in the preprocessing step of Figure 2, to match only the utterances in dialect related to the question at hand.

After the audio preprocessing, the next process as shown in Figure 2 is acoustic feature extraction. The spectral and temporal acoustic features are extracted from the audios snippets using librosa (McFee et al., 2021). The features used in this study are shown in Table 3.

These acoustic features are used to extract audio properties like the pitch, energy, rise and fall of the frequency, and melody of the speaker.

MFCC are series of values which collectively make up an MFC (*Mel-frequency Cepstrum*). These values could range from 1 to 39, which could be generated using the audio feature extraction and manipulation module of the librosa package (McFee et al., 2021). This feature is important in that it helps identify and

Spectral Features
Chroma feature
root-mean-square (RMS)
spectral centroid
spectral bandwidth
spectral rolloff
zero crossing rate
Mel frequency cepstral coefficients (MFCC)

Table 3 List of spectral features

represent how human sounds are produced by vocal tract. The shape of the vocal tract like tongue, teeth, lips, nasal cavity, etc. determines the sound generated by humans. Correctly determining and representing this shape enables the correct representation of phonemes in the sound generated. This shows that although audio data contains utterance of words and/or phrases, the acoustic features extraction makes it possible that phoneme level properties are captured and represented in numeric format. Accordingly, in this study 20 MFCC features of each audio snippets are used.

5. Classification of Dialect Varieties

The problem of dialect identification in this work is dealt as document classification using SVM classification algorithm where the labels for documents correspond to the dialect variety and the acoustic features as documents.

The dialect varieties used in this paper are eight (*Erp, Homberg, Mutscheid, Bork, Birgelen, Glehn, Königshardt, and Laar*), where one audio snippet corresponds to one dialect. The dialect variants are named after the Wenker place the speakers represent.

The dataset shows that the number of distinct classes are the same as the number of dialects at hand. In our case, the class labels for the classification problem are eight. Accordingly, we have employed a multilabel classification method using SVM in which the dialect variants, i.e., the labels for the classification problem are converted to multi-class labels using the scikit-learn label converter.

The dataset shows that there is subtle difference among the dialects. SVM is chosen as it is capable of drawing boundary mid-way between closest points of any two classes in a dataset.

$$S = \begin{bmatrix} f_{11}f_{12}...f_{13} \cdots f_{1z} \\ f_{21}f_{22}...f_{23} \cdots f_{2z} \\ \cdots \\ f_{n1}f_{n2}...f_{n3} \cdots f_{nz} \end{bmatrix}$$

Notation 5.1

Notation 5.2 shows the acoustic features f_{iz} of the dataset of sample S of size n. In our case the number of features denoted by z, i.e., the total number of features is 26 (20 MFCC and the other six spectral features shown in Table 3).

The classification output of any given sample s_i shown in the form of Notation 5.1 is represented as a set of C values $\{c_1, c_2, c_3, \ldots c_m\}$ where c_i are labels for the given dialect region for s_i.

$$C = \{c_1, c_2, c_3, \ldots c_m\}$$

Notation 5.2

where c_i are elements in class C of size m, i.e., eight.

6. Results and discussions

The experiment is done in two phases. In the first phase only data of a single speaker per dialect is used. In the second phase, data from the second speaker is added to the dataset.

In addition, although the dataset contains 20 MFCC features, we experimented to see the difference in the accuracy of the classifier using different number of MFCC. Hence, as the number of MFCC feature used increases, the model showed improvement which is illustrated in Table 4.

The model is trained with 67% of the dataset and evaluated with the rest. Splitting the data is done in a way that the model does not do unintended classification having only one speaker as test set. The train and test are randomly selected to avoid a test set containing only one speaker. Thus, using the score metrics, we achieved a promising result of 91%.

No. of MFCC	Score
11	0.77
12	0.79
14	0.81
15	0.82
16	0.84
17	0.85
18	0.85
19	0.86
20	0.87

Table 4 List of scores based on the number of MFCC used

7. Conclusion and Future Work

This work assumes that a particular word or phrase is uttered uniquely in all the eight dialect regions. However, there are words which are pronounced the same in different dialect regions. So, we would like to recommend considering the problem as a multi-label and multi-class problem, i.e., a particular row in the dataset can assume more than one dialect variant as its label.

There are many more dialect variants in Germany, beyond the data used in this research. If the identification of German dialects includes the other varieties, it would increase the contribution to the less-resourced languages and thereby to NLP technologies in general.

Acknowledgment

The audio snippets are taken from the interviews conducted in the DMW project. For building and evaluating the model, the OMNI computing cluster of the Universität Siegen is used.

This work is Funded by the Deutsche Forschungsgemeinschaft (DFG, German Research Foundation) – Project-ID 262513311 – SFB 1187

References

Bartz, C., Herold, T., Yang, H., Meinel, C., 2017. Language identification using deep convolutional recurrent neural networks, in: Internationalconference neural information processing. pp. 880–889.

Cai, W., Cai, D., Huang, S., Li, M., 2019. Utterance-level End-to-end Language Identification Using Attention-based CNN-BLSTM, in:

ICASSP20192019IEEEInternationalConference Acoustics, SpeechSignalProcessing(ICASSP). pp. 5991–5995.
Chittaragi, N.B., Koolagudi, S.G., 2019. Automatic dialect identification system for Kannada language using single and ensemble SVM algorithms. Language Resources and Evaluation 1–33.
Draxler, C., Jänsch, K., 2004. SpeechRecorder – a Universal Platform Independent Multi-Channel Audio Recording Software, in: Proc. LREC. Lisbon, pp. 559–562.
Jauhiainen, H., Jauhiainen, T., Lindén, K., 2020. Building Web Corpora for Minority Languages, in: Proceedings 12th WebCorpusWorkshop. European Language Resources Association, Marseille, France, pp. 23–32.
Jauhiainen, T., Lui, M., Zampieri, M., Baldwin, T., Lindén, K., 2019. Automatic language identification in texts: A survey. Journal of Artificial Intelligence Research 65, 675–782.
Jurgens, D., Tsvetkov, Y., Jurafsky, D., 2017. Incorporating dialectal variability for socially equitable language identification, in: Proceedings 55th Annual MeetingAssociation Computational Linguistics (Volume 2: Short Papers). pp. 51–57.
Lui, M., Baldwin, T., 2012. langid. py: An off-the-shelf language identification tool, in: Proceedings ACL 2012 system demonstrations. pp. 25–30.
Malmasi, S., Zampieri, M., 2017. German Dialect Identification in Interview Transcriptions, in: Proceedings Fourth WorkshopNLP Similar Languages, VarietiesDialects(VarDial). Association for Computational Linguistics, Valencia, Spain, pp. 164–169.
McFee, B., Metsai, A., McVicar, M., Balke, S., Thomé, C., Raffel, C., Zalkow, F., Malek, A., Dana, Lee, K., Nieto, O., Ellis, D., Mason, J., Battenberg, E., Seyfarth, S., Yamamoto, R., viktorandreevichmorozov, Choi, K., Moore, J., Bittner, R., Hidaka, S., Wei, Z., nullmightybofo, Hereñú, D., Stöter, F.-R., Friesch, P., Weiss, A., Vollrath, M., Kim, T., Thassilo, 2021. librosa/librosa: 0.8.1rc2.
Ramesh, G., Vayyavuru, V., Rama, M.K.S., 2021. Attention-Based Phonetic Convolutional Recurrent Neural Networks for Language Identification, in: 2021NationalConference Communications (NCC). pp. 1–6.
Scannell, K.P. (Ed.), 2007. The Crúbadán Project: Corpus building for under-resourced languages.
Truica, C.-O., Velcin, J., Boicea, A., 2015. Automatic language identification for romance languages using stop words and diacritics, in: 201517thInternationalSymposium SymbolicNumericAlgorithms Scientific Computing (SYNASC). pp. 243–246.

Proceedings of the EURALI Workshop @LREC2020, pages 70–74
Marseille, 20 June 2022

Exploring Transfer Learning for Urdu Speech Synthesis

Sahar Jamal, Sadaf Abdul Rauf and Qurat-ul-ain Majid
Fatima Jinnah Women University, Pakistan,
{sahar.syed,sadaf.abdulrauf}@gmail.com,quratulain@fjwu.edu.pk

Abstract

Neural methods in Text to Speech synthesis (TTS) have demonstrated momentous advancement in terms of the naturalness and intelligibility of the synthesized speech. In this paper we present neural speech synthesis system for Urdu language, a low resource language. The main challenge faced for this study was the non-availability of any publicly available Urdu speech synthesis corpora. Urdu speech corpus was created using audio books and synthetic speech generation.To leverage the low resource scenario we adopted transfer learning for our experiments where knowledge extracted is further used to train the model using a relatively smaller Urdu training data set. The results from this model show satisfactory results, though a good margin for improvement exists and we are working to improve it further.

Keywords: Neural TTS, Urdu text to speech synthesis, Deep Neural Networks, Transfer Learning

1. Introduction

Speech tools are imperative in the current era of voice driven interfaces. Speech synthesis is one such artificial speech production technology, which transforms text into intelligible speech (Holmes, 1973). With massive progress in high resource languages in speech synthesis, development of good quality TTS systems for low resource languages leaves much to be done.

The advent of neural approaches, especially Deep Neural Networks (DNN) proved to be revolutionary in overcoming limitations of previous approaches especially the inability to represent complex contextual dependencies (Ze et al., 2013). DNNs can model speech variations like speaking style and intonation even with limited data. (Qian et al., 2014a) report Deep Neural Networks outperforming HMMs with five hours of speech corpus by especially improving prosodical features. Multitask learning also considerably enhanced the efficiency of hidden representation, which in turn made the complex mapping possible. Prosody is the main feature which improves the performance of DNN in comparison to HMM (Qian et al., 2014b). The mapping is done directly between linguistic and acoustic features for each frame of the model (Wu et al., 2015).

A neural network based parametric system (Wang et al., 2016) eliminated the need of laborious alignment procedure by integrating the text and acoustic model. Mel-frequency spectrograms were used to connect two key modules of their Neural TTS. First, a network which acted as a predictor for a sequence of mel spectrogram frames for a given input and Wavenet with a few modifications(Shen et al., 2018). The MOS obtained for this experiment came quite close to the score reported by professionally synthesized speech. Standard methods used for TTS required considerable time and effort. The Neural methods took over this task of feature engineering by the use of self operating feature learning (Mametani et al., 2019).

Deep voice (Arik et al., 2017) based on neural approaches made things simpler by minimizing human intervention while training the data. DeepVoice2 (Gibiansky et al., 2017) used less than half hour speech per speaker to provide a lot of variations in the generated synthesized speech. This was achieved by using a post-processing neural vocoder. The focus was on using less speech data compared to single speaker models while maintaining high quality output. Deepvoice 3 (Ping et al., 2017) while keeping the synthesized speech as natural as possible, reduced the training time to ten times from the standard models. On the other hand, they built up the model using about eight hundred hours of training speech data which is quite high comparative to those used in standard Neural TTS.

The language selected for this research, Urdu, is a low resourced language in field of TTS. However, it is a widely spoken language in South Asia. Presenting for DNN based approach for Hindi-Telugu language pair promising results were credited to the ability of DNN in predicting spectral parameters. The prediction causes reduction in the noise and artificiality of synthesized speech (Reddy and Rao, 2018). Using a Hindi model for text normalization, models were built for Bangla language using Long Short Term Memory RNN (Gutkin et al., 2016).

Tacotron (Wang et al., 2017) by Google is an end to end model which does automatic feature extraction. Extending it, (Jia et al., 2018) presented a multiple speaker model based on three separate modules. Speaker verification module generates a vector extracted from few seconds of speech by seen or unseen speaker. The second module maps the text to phonemes while using pre-trained speaker embeddings. Lastly, the vocoder generates the wave-forms.

We discuss in section 2, the original model architecture along with the transfer learning approach we used.

Corpus	Hours	Lines	Size	Gender	Source
Urdu					
FS1	4.5	2807	694 MB	F	Google TTS
MR1	4.6	4841	732MB	M	Youtube
MR2	11.6	11,296	1.8 GB	M	Youtube
FR1	1	631	128 MB	F	AudioBook
English					
LJ Speech	24	13,100	2.7 GB	F	Public Domain
Arabic					
Nawar	3.7	1813	1.4 GB	M	Public Domain

Table 1: Corpus description

In section 3, we briefly list the Urdu corpora and other resources used in this research along with experiments conducted with these resources and their results. Section 4 discusses the evaluation metrics used for the analysis before concluding with the future prospects in Section 5.

2. Model architecture

We used Tacotron (Wang et al., 2017) for building our systems. Tactoron is an end to end system which synthesizes speech directly from the text. We built Urdu standalone systems and transfer learned system using pre-trained models of English and Arabic as parent models. The models use a training batch size of 32 with an initial learning rate of 0.002. We used feed forward neural networks with input as a predictor for the vocoder parameters using multiple layers of hidden units (Wu et al., 2016).

The original model has three basic components. The *encoder* gives sequential representations of the input text and uses the scheme by (Lee et al., 2017) for feature extraction. A bottleneck layer is used for better generalization and convergence by using a compressed representation with reduced dimensions. The bottleneck layer is basically a pre-net with dropout mechanism. It helps to focus more on the input text. The CBHG (1-D convolution bank + highway network + bidirectional GRU) module is the building block used for feature extraction in the encoder. The *decoder* models the mel-scale spectrogram representing the relation between text and speech. The *post processor* not only fixes errors of decoder predictions but also brings it into a form which can be then converted into wave-forms. Griffin-Lim is used to generate the final outputs in form of waveform audios.

Pre-trained models for English built on LJ Speec data [1] was used to to initialize our models for transfer learning. For Arabic we built our own model using the same parameters as our Urdu models.

[1] `https://data.keithito.com/data/speech/tacotron-20180906.tar.gz`

2.1. Transfer learning

Transfer learning uses knowledge obtained from performing a task to achieve another related task. The knowledge transfer from one task to another task can contribute to learning by improving the target model, accelerating learning, increasing efficiency or decreasing required time (Torrey and Shavlik, 2009). Use of large existing data as an additional set of data was suggested by (Dai et al., 2007) to augment new smaller set of data. The boosting algorithm promised good model accuracy using only small new data set while extracting possible knowledge from parent models. We used a similar approach to train our models by using Arabic and English as the parent models.

3. Experimental Setup and Corpora

We used deep neural networks for building our text to speech synthesizer. We employed transfer learning to cater for the data scarcity and also built standalone models to establish a comparison. The details of the experiments are given in Table 1.

3.1. English Corpus

We used LJ Speech Data (Keith Ito and Linda Johnson, 2017) to build the parent model for English. It consists of 13k single speaker utterances totalling to twenty four hours of speech in female voice. The sample rate used in this corpus is 22.05 kHz.

3.2. Arabic Corpus

Nawar (Halabi, Nawar and Wald, Mike, 2016) Arabic corpus , based on 3.7 hours of professionally recorded speech was used to train the Arabic model based on transfer learning.

3.3. Urdu Corpora

There was no publicly available Urdu speech corpus for TTS research. Due to unavailability of corpora, we built our own Urdu speech corpora using audio books and synthetic speech generation. The sampling frequency was fixed at 22.05 kHz for each corpus. A brief description of these corpora is given in Table 1 and details are given as follows:

Model	Lines	Duration	MOS naturalness	MOS intelligibility
Transfer Learning English ⟶ Urdu				
M1(LJSpeech ⇒ FS1)	13,100+2807	24+4.5 hrs	3.15	3.45
M2(LJSpeech ⇒ MR1)	13,100+4841	24+4.6 hrs	3.30	3.10
M3(LJSpeech ⇒ MR2)	13,100+11,296	24+11.6 hrs	3.40	3.30
Transfer Learning Arabic ⟶ Urdu				
M4 (Nawar ⇒ FS1)	1813+2807	3.7+4.5 hrs	3.00	2.80
Urdu Standalone				
M5 (FS1)	11,296	11.6 hrs	2.90	2.60

Table 2: Model description

3.3.1. FS1-Synthetic speech corpus

FS1 Urdu corpus (Sahar Jamal, 2020) includes transcriptions collected using multiple sources which including manual annotation, news web sources and texts from some publicly available corpus. The corresponding audio data sets were generated using Google Text-to-speech system (Google, 2017). The final data set consisted of 2807 utterances on single speaker female voice.

3.3.2. MR1-Male Audio book1

This corpus (Sahar Jamal, 2021c) was made by using an Urdu audio book. It uses native Urdu speaker male voice with a duration of 4.6 hours.

3.3.3. MR2-Male Audio book2

This Urdu (Sahar Jamal, 2021a) 11.6 hours speech corpus was created by splitting multiple Urdu audio books. It is a single speaker male voice.

3.3.4. FR1-Female Audio book

This Urdu speech corpus (Sahar Jamal, 2021b) is in female voice and consists of one hour of speech data. This corpus was created using Urdu audio book.

3.4. Experiments and Results

All the models were trained until convergence following (Wang et al., 2017). We started the training using our Urdu training data `FS1`, constituting four hours of speech, the model had bad alignments (as expected). This led us to explore transfer learning techniques.

Starting with pretrained English model trained on 24 hours LJ speech corpus (Keith Ito and Linda Johnson, 2017) `M1` was built by initialising the Urdu model using the synthetic `FS1` corpus. The learned parameters of pretrained English model were used to initialize training with Urdu speech corpus `FS1`. Several learning rates were tested before setting the final learning rate to 0.02, which gave the best performance. At 477k steps, the model started to show uniform alignments.

We proceeded with using the created corpora to train the model and observe their effect on the resulting speech. `M1`, `M2` and `M3` (Table 2) were trained through the transfer learning from the English model using different Urdu Corpora for fine tuning.

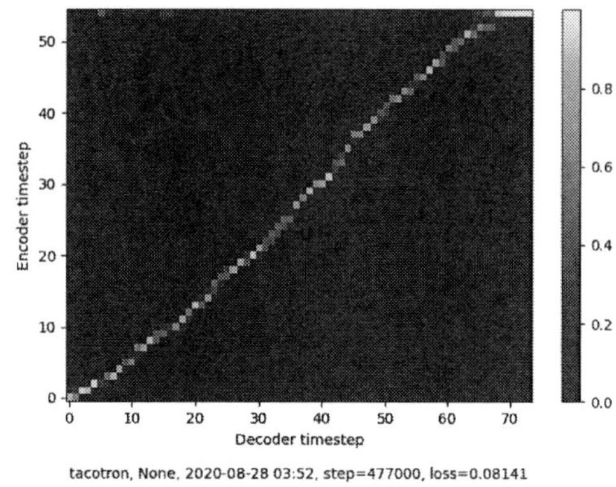

Figure 1: Attention alignment of Urdu TTS Model M1

Exploring the second language as parent, we used transfer learned from Arabic model with the synthetic `FS1` as fine-tuning corpus.

Thirdly, we built 11.6 hours Urdu stand alone TTS model `M5` following the original procedure.

4. Human Evaluation

Quality in TTS is a multidimensional term (Mariniak, 1993). The quality of synthesized speech is dependent on variable factors and parameters. The output quality is usually judged by a group of listeners (Jekosch, 1993).The evaluation is performed by observing the variation between the natural and synthesized speech.

For our study, forty subjects were selected who were native speakers of Urdu language. The subjects chosen for this experiment were provided an online form for submitting their opinions. Fifteen sentences were provided as sample and each participant was asked to listen to at-least five sentences before ranking the intelligibility and naturalness of speech. Each subject rated the synthesized speech from the rank of one to five for intelligibility and naturalness separately, these parameters are listed in table 4 with 1 being lowest and 5 being the highest quality.

Naturalness is a parameter which is hard to quantify. Different listeners participating in the experiment may have different preferences in selection of the most natural voice (Ojala, 2006). Mean opinion score (MOS) was used to asses the opinion scores . MOS is used to evaluate the quality of speech. Five categories were created for the assessment of MOS. The categories are mentioned in table 4 and results are reported in table 2.

Rank	Intelligibility Criteria
1	Very Low intelligibility, No clarity
2	Low intelligibility,few parts are comprehensible
3	Average intelligibility
4	Overall intelligible with few distortions
5	Highly Intelligible
Rank	**Naturalness Criteria**
1	Highly robotic
2	Very robotic, few instances of naturalness
3	Average naturalness
4	Overall natural with traces of robotic instances
5	Very Natural Sounding

Table 3: Assessment categories to measure naturalness and intelligibility

Figure 2 demonstrates the results of the evaluation tests performed on the TTS Model M1. Out of the forty participants more than sixty percent found the synthesized speech of M1 intelligible.
For our model M1, the naturalness factor had more margin to improve as it was considered comparatively less satisfactory than intelligibility.This is also due to the synthetic voice used in the training corpus of M1. A better and bigger corpus may provide better results with the same approach. The main advantage of using the transfer learning approach is the elimination of hand engineered feature extraction.
This study tested five different model. English was used as a parent language for the first three models. Arabic was used as the parent language for the fourth model M4. The last model M5 was a standalone Urdu Model. The results show satisfactory naturalness for all the models with parent language as English. However, the intelligibility score was much better for model M1 which had English as parent language and Urdu Synthetic Speech Corpus as the second corpus. This was the most clean and noise free corpus we used in this research.

5. Conclusion

This research work presented approaches for building an effective Urdu Text to speech system which is a zero resource language in terms of corpus availability. We explored two approaches: 1) Building and using Urdu speech corpus of different sizes to train standalone models 2) Transfer learning from English vs. Arabic. Initializing the model by a larger non-Urdu corpus and further training it on a significantly Urdu corpus, we were able to get encouraging results. Although the results seem promising , however there is room for improvement. A larger and richer Urdu corpus will significantly contribute to better results.

6. Bibliographical References

Arik, S. Ö., Chrzanowski, M., Coates, A., Diamos, G., Gibiansky, A., Kang, Y., Li, X., Miller, J., Ng, A., Raiman, J., et al. (2017). Deep voice: Real-time neural text-to-speech. In *Proceedings of the 34th International Conference on Machine Learning-Volume 70*, pages 195–204. JMLR. org.

Dai, W., Yang, Q., Xue, G.-R., and Yu, Y. (2007). Boosting for transfer learning. In *Proceedings of the 24th International Conference on Machine Learning*, ICML '07, page 193–200, New York, NY, USA. Association for Computing Machinery.

Gibiansky, A., Arik, S., Diamos, G., Miller, J., Peng, K., Ping, W., Raiman, J., and Zhou, Y. (2017). Deep voice 2: Multi-speaker neural text-to-speech. In *Advances in neural information processing systems*, pages 2962–2970.

Google. (2017). Google tts api. `https://cloud.google.com/text-to-speech/`.

Gutkin, A., Ha, L., Jansche, M., Pipatsrisawat, K., and Sproat, R. (2016). Tts for low resource languages: A bangla synthesizer. In *Proceedings of the Tenth International Conference on Language Resources and Evaluation (LREC 2016)*, pages 2005–2010.

Holmes, J. (1973). The influence of glottal waveform on the naturalness of speech from a parallel formant synthesizer. *IEEE transactions on Audio and Electroacoustics*, 21(3):298–305.

Jekosch, U. (1993). Speech quality assessment and evaluation. In *Third European Conference on Speech Communication and Technology*.

Jia, Y., Zhang, Y., Weiss, R., Wang, Q., Shen, J., Ren, F., Nguyen, P., Pang, R., Moreno, I. L., Wu, Y., et al. (2018). Transfer learning from speaker verification to multispeaker text-to-speech synthesis. In *Advances in neural information processing systems*, pages 4480–4490.

Lee, J., Cho, K., and Hofmann, T. (2017). Fully character-level neural machine translation without explicit segmentation. *Transactions of the Association for Computational Linguistics*, 5:365–378.

Mametani, K., Kato, T., and Yamamoto, S. (2019). Investigating context features hidden in end-to-end tts. In *ICASSP 2019-2019 IEEE International Conference on Acoustics, Speech and Signal Processing (ICASSP)*, pages 6920–6924. IEEE.

Mariniak, A. (1993). A global framework for the assessment of synthetic speech without subjects. In *Third European Conference on Speech Communication and Technology*.

Ojala, T. (2006). Auditory quality evaluation of present finnish text-to-speech systems. *Helsinki University of Technology*.

Ping, W., Peng, K., Gibiansky, A., Arik, S. O., Kannan, A., Narang, S., Raiman, J., and Miller, J. (2017). Deep voice 3: Scaling text-to-speech with

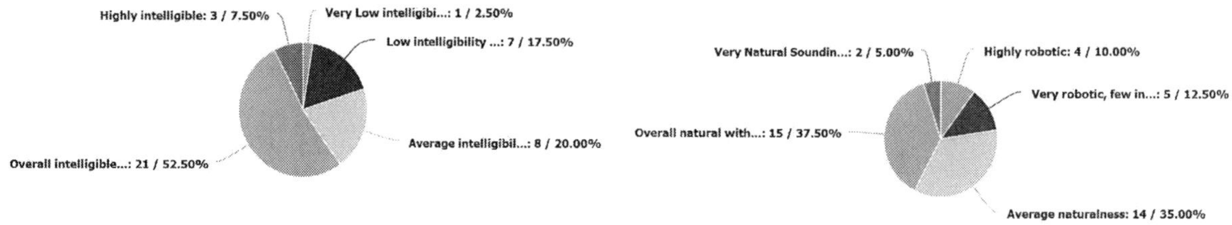

Figure 2: Left: Quality w.r.t Intelligibility for Model M1; Right: Quality w.r.t Naturalness for Model M1

convolutional sequence learning. *arXiv preprint arXiv:1710.07654*.

Qian, Y., Fan, Y., Hu, W., and Soong, F. K. (2014a). On the training aspects of deep neural network (dnn) for parametric tts synthesis. In *2014 IEEE International Conference on Acoustics, Speech and Signal Processing (ICASSP)*, pages 3829–3833. IEEE.

Qian, Y., Fan, Y., Hu, W., and Soong, F. K. (2014b). On the training aspects of deep neural network (dnn) for parametric tts synthesis. In *2014 IEEE International Conference on Acoustics, Speech and Signal Processing (ICASSP)*, pages 3829–3833. IEEE.

Reddy, M. K. and Rao, K. S. (2018). Dnn-based bilingual (telugu-hindi) polyglot speech synthesis. In *2018 International Conference on Advances in Computing, Communications and Informatics (ICACCI)*, pages 1808–1811. IEEE.

Shen, J., Pang, R., Weiss, R. J., Schuster, M., Jaitly, N., Yang, Z., Chen, Z., Zhang, Y., Wang, Y., Skerrv-Ryan, R., et al. (2018). Natural tts synthesis by conditioning wavenet on mel spectrogram predictions. In *2018 IEEE International Conference on Acoustics, Speech and Signal Processing (ICASSP)*, pages 4779–4783. IEEE.

Torrey, L. and Shavlik, J. (2009). Chapter 11 transfer learning.

Wang, W., Xu, S., Xu, B., et al. (2016). First step towards end-to-end parametric tts synthesis: Generating spectral parameters with neural attention.

Wang, Y., Skerry-Ryan, R., Stanton, D., Wu, Y., Weiss, R. J., Jaitly, N., Yang, Z., Xiao, Y., Chen, Z., Bengio, S., et al. (2017). Tacotron: Towards end-to-end speech synthesis. *arXiv preprint arXiv:1703.10135*.

Wu, Z., Valentini-Botinhao, C., Watts, O., and King, S. (2015). Deep neural networks employing multi-task learning and stacked bottleneck features for speech synthesis. In *2015 IEEE international conference on acoustics, speech and signal processing (ICASSP)*, pages 4460–4464. IEEE.

Wu, Y., Schuster, M., Chen, Z., Le, Q. V., Norouzi, M., Macherey, W., Krikun, M., Cao, Y., Gao, Q., Macherey, K., Klingner, J., Shah, A., Johnson, M., Liu, X., Kaiser, L., Gouws, S., Kato, Y., Kudo, T., Kazawa, H., Stevens, K., Kurian, G., Patil, N., Wang, W., Young, C., Smith, J., Riesa, J., Rudnick, A., Vinyals, O., Corrado, G., Hughes, M., and Dean, J. (2016). Google's neural machine translation system: Bridging the gap between human and machine translation. *CoRR*, abs/1609.08144.

Ze, H., Senior, A., and Schuster, M. (2013). Statistical parametric speech synthesis using deep neural networks. In *2013 ieee international conference on acoustics, speech and signal processing*, pages 7962–7966. IEEE.

Halabi, Nawar and Wald, Mike. (2016). *Phonetic inventory for an Arabic speech corpus*. `http://en.arabicspeechcorpus.com/`.

Keith Ito and Linda Johnson. (2017). *The LJ Speech Dataset*. `https://keithito.com/LJ-Speech-Dataset/`.

Sahar Jamal. (2020). *SJ Urdu Synthetic Corpus*. `https://github.com/saharsyed/Sj-Urdu-Synthetic-Corpus`.

Sahar Jamal. (2021a). *Kutub Urdu Speech Corpus*. `https://github.com/saharsyed/kutub-Urdu-Speech-corpus`.

Sahar Jamal. (2021b). *SJ Kahani Speech Corpus*. `https://github.com/saharsyed/SJ-Kahani-Speech-Corpus`.

Sahar Jamal. (2021c). *Urdu Adab Speech Corpus*. `https://github.com/saharsyed/Urdu-Adab-Speech-Corpus`.

Proceedings of the EURALI Workshop @LREC2020, pages 75–80
Marseille, 20 June 2022

Towards Bengali WordNet Enrichment using Knowledge Graph Completion Techniques

Sree Bhattacharyya [α], **Abhik Jana** [β]
[α]Indian Institute of Engineering Science and Technology Shibpur, India,
[β]Universität Hamburg, Germany
sreebhattacharyya.ug2018@cs.iiests.ac.in, abhik.jana@uni-hamburg.de

Abstract

WordNet serves as a very essential knowledge source for various downstream Natural Language Processing (NLP) tasks. Since this is a human-curated resource, building such a resource is very cumbersome and time-consuming. Even though for languages like English, the existing WordNet is reasonably rich in terms of coverage, for resource-poor languages like Bengali, the WordNet is far from being reasonably sufficient in terms of coverage of vocabulary and relations between them. In this paper, we investigate the usefulness of some of the existing knowledge graph completion algorithms to enrich Bengali WordNet automatically. We explore three such techniques namely DistMult, ComplEx, and HolE, and analyze their effectiveness for adding more relations between existing nodes in the WordNet. We achieve maximum Hits@1 of 0.412 and Hits@10 of 0.703, which look very promising for low resource languages like Bengali.

Keywords: Bengali WordNet, Knowledge graph, Automatic enrichment

1. Introduction

Several NLP applications use WordNet which was first introduced by Miller (1995) and is one of the important human-curated resources. WordNet has several NLP applications (Morato et al., 2004), including information retrieval (Mandala et al., 1998), query expansion (Smeaton et al., 1995; Gong et al., 2005; Pal et al., 2014), improvement of text retrieval responses (Gonzalo et al., 1998) and natural language generation (Jing, 1998), to name a few. WordNet in English is sufficiently rich in terms of vocabulary and semantic relation coverage. On the other hand, even though Bengali is one of the most widely spoken language[1], the Bengali WordNet (Bhattacharyya, 2010) is far from reaching the coverage of English WordNet. Therefore, automatic expansion of such a lexical resource for low-resource languages could be really useful. With this goal, we investigate whether it is possible to apply the existing knowledge graph completion techniques on the WordNet to accurately predict relations between different concepts. This direction could be leveraged in further enriching the WordNet by automatically predicting new relational links.

In this work, we attempt to enrich Bengali WordNet with the use of existing knowledge graph completion techniques. Towards this goal, we modify the original structure of the existing Bengali WordNet to make it suitable to be used as input to those algorithms. As a part of our investigation, we explore the applicability of three knowledge graph completion techniques namely DistMult (Yang et al., 2015), ComplEx (Trouillon et al., 2016) and HolE (Nickel et al., 2016). Note that, in this work, we pose this WordNet enrichment problem as a closed world problem where no new node gets added to the graph, only edges (signifying semantic relations) get added. We achieve three-fold cross-validation MRR of 0.504 (maximum) and Hits@1 of 0.412 (maximum) for Bengali WordNet which is really promising for such low resource languages. This investigation presents a clear view of whether these models are able to capture the semantic intricacies of this WordNet. Note that, the main challenge for these models to work accurately on the WordNet is the existence of hierarchical semantic relations. This analysis could also be significantly useful in further establishing a methodology of using larger unsupervised lexical resources to automatically increase the coverage of the WordNet, by applying knowledge graph completion techniques. We make all our code and data publicly available[2].

The rest of the paper is organised as follows: Section 2 provides a brief account of Related Work, Section 3 describes about the Bengali WordNet and the methodology of how the graph structure of Bengali WordNet is altered, Section 4 describes the experimental analysis, and Section 5 draws the conclusion.

2. Related Work

A lot of efforts have been made to deal with the problem of automatic knowledge graph completion. Additive models include TransE (Bordes et

[1]At present, there are roughly 7000 languages in the world, among which Bengali is the 7th most widely spoken [1]

[2]`https://github.com/uhh-lt/bengali-wordnet-extension`

al., 2013), TransH (Wang et al., 2014), TransM (Fan et al., 2014), TransR (Lin et al., 2015), where the relations in the knowledge graph are regarded as translation vectors, translating a head entity to a tail entity. Multiplicative models like DistMult (Yang et al., 2015), ComplEx (Trouillon et al., 2016), embed entities and relations into a unified continuous vector space, followed by defining a scoring function to measure the authenticity of the triples. There are several other neural network based models like ConvKB (Nguyen et al., 2018), ConvE (Dettmers et al., 2018), HypER (Balažević et al., 2019), CompGCN (Vashishth et al., 2020) and SACN (Shang et al., 2019) among others. Models like HAKE (Zhang et al., 2020) are also able to accurately model the hierarchical semantic relationships of knowledge graphs. Further, several different approaches for WordNet enrichment or completion have been developed in the past. Biemann et al. (2004) describes a language-independent approach for semiautomatic extension of WordNets using a bootstrapping method. Biemann et al. (2018) presents a framework for combining information from distributional semantic models with manually constructed lexical resources. The framework is applied to produce a novel hybrid resource obtained by linking a disambiguated distributional lexical network to WordNet and BabelNet. In language-specific examples of previous related work, (Lee et al., 2001), introduce a semi-automatic method to construct a Korean noun semantic hierarchy by using a monolingual (Japanese) thesaurus and Korean MRD and uses the advantage of the similarity between the two languages. Rahit et al. (2018) introduce a baseline for a Bengali WordNet (BanglaNet). It uses an approach of making semantic relations between Bengali WordNet and Princeton WordNet (Miller, 1995), which is used to derive relations between concepts. Chakravarthi et al. (2018) present an expand approach for generating and improving WordNets, which uses machine translation and applies to the Dravidian languages of Tamil, Telugu and Kannada.

3. Methodology

Since our objective is to enrich Bengali WordNet, we first discuss the WordNet itself. Then, we discuss the approach to process the WordNet such that it could be fed to knowledge graph completion techniques. Finally, we discuss the three techniques we follow for our analysis.

3.1. Bengali WordNet

For our experiment we use the Bengali WordNet from IndoWordNet (Bhattacharyya, 2010). It consists of 36346 synsets (categorized as 27281 nouns, 2804 verbs, 5815 adjectives, 445 adverbs), which

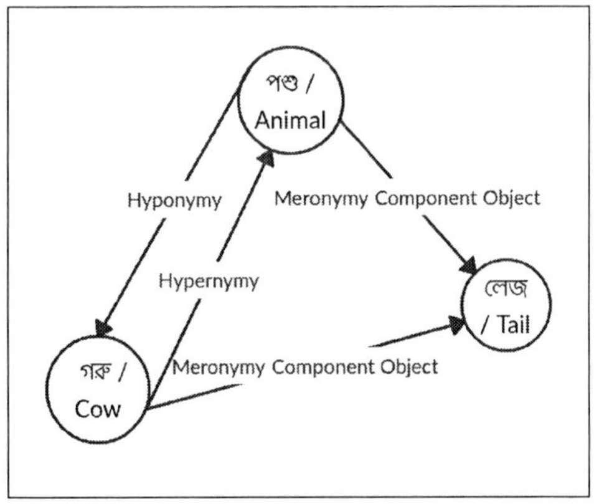

Figure 1: A snapshot of synsets as nodes and relations as edges in Bengali WordNet

are connected to other synsets through 30 different relations. The relations can be put into the following broad categories: hypernymy, hyponymy, meronymy, holonymy, ability verbs, noun attributes, verb causatives, verb entailments, function verb, and troponymy. The total number of unique words present in the Bengali WordNet is 45497. Each synset can have multiple example words (lemma names), and one head word. One word can appear in more than one synset. To obtain the data in a graphical format, the application programming interface (API) introduced by Panjwani et al. (2018) is used. As per this API, A list of edges is created - where both the nodes are synsets and the relation connecting them is the edge attribute. 72703 such edges are obtained to create a graph. In that, 36039 synsets are connected out of the total 36346 synsets of the WordNet. A snapshot is shown in Figure 1.

3.2. WordNet Structure Modification

The WordNet graph is present in the following form - synset represents a node, and different synsets are connected to each other through several relations which are represented by labeled edges. We modify the original structure to obtain a graph where each constituent word present under a Synset, becomes a node, and existing edges are replicated to connect such nodes, having relations as their attributes. To achieve this modification two things are done - First, A relation is introduced -'Synonymy' in addition to the existing 30 relations. This relation associates the words present under the same synset with each other. Edges are created connecting all possible pairs of words within the same synset, with edge attribute as the 'Synonymy' relation. Next, edges are created between every possible pair of words, which are present in two different synsets, and the edges are labelled with the same relation which is shared by the corresponding synsets that the words belong to. For any two synsets connected by an edge with

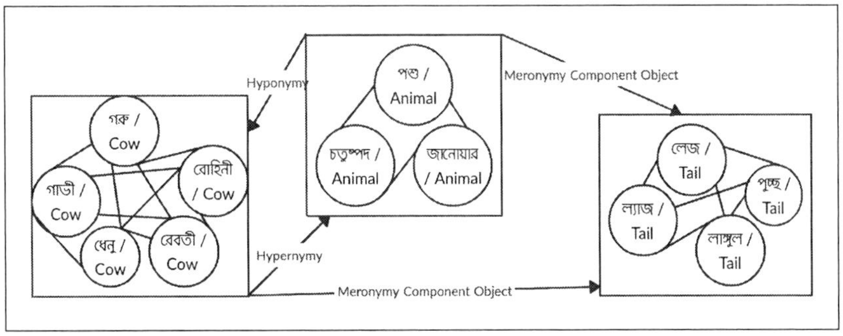

Figure 2: A snapshot of the modified WordNet graph structure. Each box is one synset. Each pair of nodes within the same box is connected to each other with the Synonymy relationship. Each pair of nodes present within two different boxes shares the relation shared between the respective boxes.

attribute 'r' (relation between synsets is 'r'), edges are created for all possible word pair combinations of the words present under both the synsets and the edge attribute assigned to the edges is also 'r'. The directionality of edges between synsets is also considered and maintained when creating edges with words as nodes. The modified structure of WordNet is presented in Figure 2. With the modified graph structure, each edge is now regarded as a triple, having subject and object entities (words), and a predicate (relation) connecting the two. The synonymy triples contain only one example of the form (head, Synonymy, tail) for two unique head and tail words. In other words, Synonymy is treated as an undirected relationship. For all the directed relationships, triples for that relationship and its inverse (if that exists in the WordNet), occur separately. For example, for two unique head and tail words, (head, Hypernymy, tail) and (tail, Hyponymy, head) both occur separately if the parent synsets of head and tail are also similarly related in the original graph.

Model	MRR	Hits@1	Hits@3	Hits@10
DistMult	0.438	0.342	0.472	0.643
ComplEx	0.492	0.382	**0.558**	0.696
HolE	**0.504**	**0.412**	0.538	**0.703**

Table 1: Three-fold cross-validated model performances.

3.3. Knowledge Graph Completion Approaches:

The three techniques used for this task are DistMult (Yang et al., 2015), HolE (Nickel et al., 2016) and ComplEx (Trouillon et al., 2016). In a nutshell, all of these models use the learned embedding vectors of the entities and relationsand use unique scoring functions to score triples (head, relation, tail). The details of these methods are described below.

DistMult: DistMult is a multiplicative model, and uses a bi-linear scoring function (Lin et al., 2018) for a triple (h, r, t) which is defined as:

$$f_r(h,t) = h^T M_r t \qquad (1)$$

M_r is a 2-D matrix operator instead of a tensor operator, and is a diagonal matrix.

ComplEx: ComplEx employs eigenvalue decomposition model to take complex valued embeddings into consideration. It uses Hermitian dot product, the complex counterpart of standard dot product between real vectors. The scoring function for a triple (h, r, t) of ComplEx is defined as:

$$f_r(h,t) = sigmoid(X_{hrt}) \qquad (2)$$

and $f_r(h,t)$ is expected to be 1 when (h,r,t) holds, otherwise -1. Here, X_{hrt} is further calculated as follows: $X_{hrt} =< Re(w_r), Re(h), Re(t) > +$ $< Re(w_r), Im(h), Im(t) >$ $- < Im(w_r), Re(h), Im(t) > -$ $< Im(w_r), Im(h), Re(t) >$ where $M_r \in R^{d \times d}$ is a weight matrix, $< a,b,c >= \sum_k a_k b_k c_k$, Im(x) indicates the the imaginary part of x and Re(x) indicates the the real part of x (Lin et al., 2018).

HolE: Holographic Embeddings (HolE) uses circular correlation to create compositional representations of entire knowledge graphs, which is related to holographic models of associative memory. The circular correlation is denoted by: (Lin et al., 2018)

$$[a * b]_k = \sum_{i=0}^{d-1} a_i b_{(i+k) mod d}$$

The score function for a triple (h, r, t) is given as (Lin et al., 2018):

$$f_r(h,t) = sigmoid(r^T (h * t))$$

For the implementation of these three algorithms, the Ampligraph framework (Costabello et al., 2019) is used[3].

[3]`https://github.com/Accenture/AmpliGraph`

	Head	Translation	Relation	Tail	Translation
DistMult	মুনি	Spiritual mentor	Hyponymy	কাশ্যপ_ঋষি	An Indian spiritual mentor
	অসুর	Demon	Synonymy	রাক্ষস	Evil Spirit
ComplEx	ব্যক্তি	Human being/person	Synonymy	বান্দা	Person
	কঠিন	Difficult	Modifies_noun	কাজ	Work
HolE	ঘরোয়া	Relating to the home	Modifies_noun	জিনিস	Tangible Object
	দমন_করা	Oppress	Hypernymy	করা	To do

Table 2: Some of the top predicted triples by each knowledge graph completion approaches

4. Experiments and Analysis

For our experiment, we fix embedding dimensions to 100, epochs to 10, negatives generated per positive to 50, and optimizer to Adagrad (Duchi et al., 2011). The search space for the learning rate is set to [0.0001, 0.001, 0.01, 0.1], the losses chosen are Pairwise Loss (Bordes et al., 2013), Absolute Margin Loss (Hamaguchi et al., 2017) and Negative Log Likelihood Loss (Trouillon et al., 2016). The search space for the margin parameter is set to [0.5, 2, 10]. The optimization search is carried out both without and with L2 regularization, and the search space for λ is set to [1e-3, 1e-4, 1e-5]. After performing the grid search, the best hyper-parameter set-up for which the results are obtained are described as follows: DistMult with a learning rate of 0.1, L2 regularization with $\lambda = 0.001$, and Negative Log Likelihood Loss. ComplEx is trained with a learning rate of 0.01, L2 regularization with $\lambda = 0.0001$, and Pairwise Loss with margin = 0.1. HolE uses a learning rate of 0.1, no regularization, and Pairwise Loss with margin = 0.5. The model performances are obtained by three-fold cross-validation, with test size being equal to 40000.

4.1. Metrics Used

The following rank-based metrics are used for evaluation:

Mean Reciprocal Rank: The Reciprocal Rank (RR) information retrieval measure calculates the reciprocal of the rank at which the first relevant document was retrieved. For a single query, the reciprocal rank is 1 where the rank is the position of the highest-ranked answer (1,2,3,...,N for N answers returned in a query). If no correct answer is returned in the query, then the reciprocal rank is 0. When averaged across queries, the measure is called the Mean Reciprocal Rank (MRR) (Craswell, 2009). It is formulated as follows:

$$MRR = \frac{1}{|Q|}\sum_{i=1}^{|Q|}\frac{1}{rank_{(s,p,o)_i}} \tag{3}$$

where Q is a set of triples and (s,p,o) is a triple $\in$ Q.

Hits@N Score: Intuitively, hits@N refers to the count of positive triples which are present in the top-N positions. Link prediction models generate a score for each of the triples, which is used to rank all the triples present. It is formally defined as:

$$Hits@N = \sum_{i=1}^{|Q|} 1\, if rank_{(s,p,o)_i} \leq N \tag{4}$$

where Q is a set of triples and (s,p,o) is a triple $\in$ Q.

4.2. Performance Analysis

The performances of the three models are presented in Table 1. HolE produces the best MRR, Hits@1, and Hits@10, whereas ComplEx produces the best Hits@3. DistMult proves to be the weakest among these three approaches. Given that, Bengali WordNet size is not that big the maximum obtained MRR of 0.504 and maximum obtained Hits@1 of 0.412 is really promising. Some of the top predicted triples by each of the three link prediction techniques are shown in Table 2. The results show that semantically close words are predicted to have almost accurate relationships between them. As a first ever attempt to enrich Bengali WordNet using knowledge graph completion techniques, we believe the results are encouraging for investigating further in this direction.

5. Conclusion

In this study, we show that off-the-shelf knowledge graph completion approaches like DistMult, ComplEx, and HolE produce promising results for predicting Bengali WordNet relations as well. This work could help largely in further enriching the WordNet using an unsupervised resource like a thesaurus. Inclusion of predicted links in the WordNet should be preceded by manual correction to ensure overall accuracy of WordNet. This work could ultimately be useful for tasks like word sense disambiguation, machine translation, etc. The immediate future work could be exploring other categories of such algorithms to be applied on WordNet for the same purpose. The broad plan is to create a framework to enrich WordNet of a range of low resource languages automatically without human intervention.

6. Bibliographical References

Balažević, I., Allen, C., and Hospedales, T. M. (2019). Hypernetwork knowledge graph embeddings. In *International Conference on Artificial Neural Networks*, pages 553–565. Springer.

Bhattacharyya, P. (2010). Indowordnet. In *Proceedings of the Seventh International Conference on Language Resources and Evaluation (LREC'10)*.

Biemann, C., Shin, S., and Choi, K.-S. (2004). Semiautomatic extension of corenet using a bootstrapping mechanism on corpus-based co-occurrences. In *COLING 2004: Proceedings of the 20th International Conference on Computational Linguistics*, pages 1227–1232.

Biemann, C., Faralli, S., Panchenko, A., and Ponzetto, S. P. (2018). A framework for enriching lexical semantic resources with distributional semantics. *Natural Language Engineering*, 24(2):265–312.

Bordes, A., Usunier, N., Garcia-Duran, A., Weston, J., and Yakhnenko, O. (2013). Translating embeddings for modeling multi-relational data. *Advances in neural information processing systems*, 26.

Chakravarthi, B. R., Arcan, M., and McCrae, J. P. (2018). Improving wordnets for under-resourced languages using machine translation. In *Proceedings of the 9th Global Wordnet Conference*, pages 77–86, Nanyang Technological University (NTU), Singapore, January. Global Wordnet Association.

Costabello, L., Pai, S., Van, C., McGrath, R., McCarthy, N., and Tabacof, P. (2019). Ampligraph: a library for representation learning on knowledge graphs. *Retrieved October*, 10:2019.

Craswell, N. (2009). Mean reciprocal rank. *Encyclopedia of database systems*, 1703.

Dettmers, T., Minervini, P., Stenetorp, P., and Riedel, S. (2018). Convolutional 2d knowledge graph embeddings. In *Thirty-second AAAI conference on artificial intelligence*.

Duchi, J., Hazan, E., and Singer, Y. (2011). Adaptive subgradient methods for online learning and stochastic optimization. *Journal of machine learning research*, 12(7).

Fan, M., Zhou, Q., Chang, E., and Zheng, F. (2014). Transition-based knowledge graph embedding with relational mapping properties. In *Proceedings of the 28th Pacific Asia conference on language, information and computing*, pages 328–337.

Gong, Z., Cheang, C. W., and Hou, U. L. (2005). Web query expansion by wordnet. In *International Conference on Database and Expert Systems Applications*, pages 166–175. Springer.

Gonzalo, J., Verdejo, F., Chugur, I., and Cigarran, J. (1998). Indexing with wordnet synsets can improve text retrieval. *arXiv preprint cmp-lg/9808002*.

Hamaguchi, T., Oiwa, H., Shimbo, M., and Matsumoto, Y. (2017). Knowledge transfer for out-of-knowledge-base entities : A graph neural network approach. In *Proceedings of the Twenty-Sixth International Joint Conference on Artificial Intelligence, IJCAI-17*, pages 1802–1808.

Jing, H. (1998). Usage of wordnet in natural language generation. In *Usage of WordNet in Natural Language Processing Systems*.

Lee, J., Un, K., Bae, H.-S., and Choi, K.-S. (2001). A korean noun semantic hierarchy (wordnet) construction. In *Proceedings of the 16th Pacific Asia Conference on Language, Information and Computation*, pages 290–295.

Lin, Y., Liu, Z., Sun, M., Liu, Y., and Zhu, X. (2015). Learning entity and relation embeddings for knowledge graph completion. In *Twenty-ninth AAAI conference on artificial intelligence*.

Lin, Y., Han, X., Xie, R., Liu, Z., and Sun, M. (2018). Knowledge representation learning: A quantitative review. *arXiv preprint arXiv:1812.10901*.

Mandala, R., Tokunaga, T., and Tanaka, H. (1998). The use of wordnet in information retrieval. In *Usage of WordNet in Natural Language Processing Systems*.

Miller, G. A. (1995). Wordnet: a lexical database for english. *Communications of the ACM*, 38(11):39–41.

Morato, J., Marzal, M. A., Lloréns, J., and Moreiro, J. (2004). Wordnet applications. In *Proceedings of GWC*, pages 20–23.

Nguyen, D. Q., Nguyen, T. D., Nguyen, D. Q., and Phung, D. (2018). A novel embedding model for knowledge base completion based on convolutional neural network. In *Proceedings of the 2018 Conference of the North American Chapter of the Association for Computational Linguistics: Human Language Technologies, Volume 2 (Short Papers)*, pages 327–333, New Orleans, Louisiana, June. Association for Computational Linguistics.

Nickel, M., Rosasco, L., and Poggio, T. (2016). Holographic embeddings of knowledge graphs. In *Proceedings of the AAAI Conference on Artificial Intelligence*, volume 30.

Pal, D., Mitra, M., and Datta, K. (2014). Improving query expansion using wordnet. *Journal of the Association for Information Science and Technology*, 65(12):2469–2478.

Panjwani, R., Kanojia, D., and Bhattacharyya, P. (2018). pyiwn: A python based api to access indian language wordnets. In *Proceedings of the 9th Global Wordnet Conference*, pages 378–383.

Rahit, K. T. H., Hasan, K. T., Al-Amin, M., and Ahmed, Z. (2018). Banglanet: Towards a wordnet for bengali language. In *Proceedings of the 9th Global Wordnet Conference*, pages 1–9.

Shang, C., Tang, Y., Huang, J., Bi, J., He, X., and Zhou, B. (2019). End-to-end structure-aware convolutional networks for knowledge base completion. In *Proceedings of the AAAI Conference on Artificial Intelligence*, volume 33, pages 3060–3067.

Smeaton, A. F., Kelledy, F., and O'Donnell, R. (1995). Trec-4 experiments at dublin city university: Thresholding posting lists, query expansion with wordnet and pos tagging of spanish. *Harman [6]*, pages 373–389.

Trouillon, T., Welbl, J., Riedel, S., Gaussier, É., and Bouchard, G. (2016). Complex embeddings for simple link prediction. In *International conference on machine learning*, pages 2071–2080. PMLR.

Vashishth, S., Sanyal, S., Nitin, V., and Talukdar, P. (2020). Composition-based multi-relational graph convolutional networks. In *International Conference on Learning Representations.*

Wang, Z., Zhang, J., Feng, J., and Chen, Z. (2014). Knowledge graph embedding by translating on hyperplanes. In *Proceedings of the AAAI Conference on Artificial Intelligence*, volume 28.

Yang, B., Yih, W., He, X., Gao, J., and Deng, L. (2015). Embedding entities and relations for learning and inference in knowledge bases. In Yoshua Bengio et al., editors, *3rd International Conference on Learning Representations, ICLR 2015, San Diego, CA, USA, May 7-9, 2015, Conference Track Proceedings.*

Zhang, Z., Cai, J., Zhang, Y., and Wang, J. (2020). Learning hierarchy-aware knowledge graph embeddings for link prediction. In *Proceedings of the AAAI Conference on Artificial Intelligence*, volume 34, pages 3065–3072.

Proceedings of the EURALI Workshop @LREC2020, pages 81–85
Marseille, 20 June 2022

Enriching Hindi WordNet Using Knowledge Graph Completion Approach

Sushil Awale, Abhik Jana
Universität Hamburg, Germany
sushil.awale@studium.uni-hamburg.de, abhik.jana@uni-hamburg.de

Abstract

Even though the use of WordNet in the Natural Language Processing domain is unquestionable, creating and maintaining WordNet is a cumbersome job and it is even difficult for low resource languages like Hindi. In this study, we aim to enrich the Hindi WordNet automatically by using state-of-the-art knowledge graph completion (KGC) approaches. We pose the automatic Hindi WordNet enrichment problem as a knowledge graph completion task and therefore we modify the Wordnet structure to make it appropriate for applying KGC approaches. Second, we attempt five KGC approaches of three different genres and compare the performances for the task. Our study shows that ConvE is the best KGC methodology for this specific task compared to other KGC approaches.

Keywords: Hindi WordNet, Knowledge Graph Completion

1. Introduction

The usability of WordNet for various Natural Language Processing tasks such as word-sense disambiguation, information retrieval, machine translation, etc. is well-known to the research community. The first-ever WordNet was created for the English language in 1985 at the Princeton University (Fellbaum and others, 1998), and over time researchers have invested efforts to develop WordNets for various languages. As WordNet is updated and maintained manually, it requires frequent revision which is an expensive and time-consuming task. Therefore there is a need for automatic enrichment of WordNet.

In this paper, we focus on the enrichment of Hindi (One of the low-resource languages from India) WordNet (Narayan et al., 2002). Formally, WordNet (Miller et al., 1990) is represented as a lexical graph database where the nodes represent synsets and the edges between them represent the type of relation. Synsets refer to a collection of synonymous words, and the relations that link the synsets include synonyms, hyponyms, meronyms, etc. On the other hand, knowledge graphs are graph structures that represent facts in the world. The facts are represented as triples (h, r, t), where h and t represent the head and tail entity, and r represents the relation between them. For example, *(Hamburg, cityIn, Germany)* is a fact in a knowledge graph. There is a genre of literature (Rossi et al., 2021), which deals with the completion of knowledge graphs where new edges or nodes are added to complete the knowledge graphs. In this work, we are considering WordNet as a type of knowledge graph with the synsets representing nodes and the lexical relations representing the edges. We explore the applicability of five knowledge graph completion techniques namely, TransE (Bordes et al., 2013), TransH (Wang et al., 2014), DistMult (Yang et al., 2014), ComplEx (Trouillon et al., 2016), and ConvE (Dettmers et al., 2018). After experimenting with all these models, we see that ConvE produces the best performance for the Hindi WordNet completion task with an MRR value of 0.294 and Hit@10 of 0.385 which is promising to move forward in this direction. In a nutshell, the main contributions of this paper are twofold-

- We pose the enrichment of Hindi WordNet as a knowledge graph completion task which is the first-ever attempt for Hindi WordNet to the best of our knowledge.
- We attempt with five KGC approaches and compare their performances and show ConvE performs better than all the four other models by a significant margin. We make all the code and data publicly available [1].

2. Related Work

Knowledge Graph Completion (KGC) is a widely researched topic in the Natural Language Processing domain. Several KGC approaches have been proposed in the domain which includes rule-based reasoning, probabilistic graph, graph calculation, and representation learning approaches. (Chen et al., 2020) In one of the earliest rule-based reasoning methods Paulheim and Bizer (2014) deduces new relational instances from existing knowledge using a first-order relational learning algorithm. Rule-based reasoning approaches are difficult to generalize and scale. Similarly, probabilistic graph-based approaches that use joint probability distribution reasoning to predict new facts are also difficult to scale due to the high complexity of the models. These models mostly use Markov Logic Networks (Lao and Cohen, 2010) and Bayesian network (Han et al., 2017). In the graph calculation approaches, new relations are predicted based on incoming and outgoing node degrees and using an adjacent matrix. Path Ranking Algorithm (Nickel et al., 2011) is one of the

[1] `https://github.com/uhh-lt/hindi-wordnet-extension`

earlier graph completion methods followed by Coupled Path Ranking Algorithm (Hayashi and Shimbo, 2017). The traditional KGC methods suffered from the problem of computational efficiency, high algorithm complexity, and poor scalability. (Chen et al., 2020) As a result, researchers have shifted towards knowledge representation learning.

A few surveys focus on representation learning (Wang et al., 2021; Rossi et al., 2021). In one such study, Rossi et al. (2021) compare different knowledge graph (KG) embedding models based on effectiveness and efficiency. The KG models are grouped into three categories by their learning methods namely, tensor decomposition models, geometric models, and deep learning models. In another recent work, Wang et al. (2021) provides a theoretical analysis of different KG models and classifies the KG models into three-main categories based on the type of scoring function used, e.g. distance-based or semantic-matching-based. This work also compares the performance of the models on two popular English KG datasets, WN18RR and FB15K-237. In our study, we follow the classification presented in this paper to select at most two KG models from each class for our study.

In addition, other approaches to enrich a WordNet have been proposed. Montoyo et al. (2001) automatically adds new categories, drawn from classification systems, to an English WordNet using Word Sense Disambiguation. Giménez and Màrquez (2006) enriches Spanish WordNet by automatic addition of synset glosses obtained from English WordNet glosses using a phrase-based English-Spanish statistical machine translation system. Other works focus on using lexical patterns to extract new relations from the unlabelled corpus. Ruiz-Casado et al. (2007) enriches the English WordNet with the addition of new relations between synsets using the edit distance-based method to generate lexical patterns from raw text. Boudabous et al. (2013) adds new semantic relations in the Arabic WordNet using expert-defined morpho-lexical patterns.

3. Methodology

As a part of our exploration, we aim to enrich the Hindi WordNet by adding the missing edges in the WordNet graph. Following the well-known direction of knowledge graph completion approaches, firstly, we embed the WordNet graph into a continuous vector space where each entity (h or t) is represented as a point in the vector space, and each relation r represents an operation (translation, rotation, etc.) in the vector space. The entity and relation representations are learned by minimizing a global loss function which involves all the entities and relations in the graph. Next, these embedding representations are used for the task of link prediction.

3.1. Link Prediction

Link prediction is the task of predicting the missing entity in a triple (h, r, t), i.e. predict h given (r, t) or predict t given (h, r). When predicting the missing entity, we replace it with all entities from the knowledge graph and rank them based on a scoring function. A higher score indicates that the triple is more likely to be true. We experiment with KGC models from different genres depending on the scoring function used.

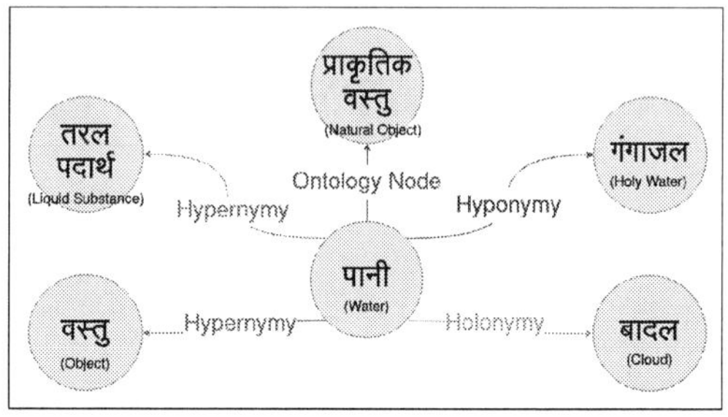

Figure 1: A snapshot of Hindi WordNet as a Knowledge Graph

3.1.1. Translation-distance-based models

The translation-distance-based models use some distance-based scoring functions for link prediction.

TransE: TransE (Bordes et al., 2013) is one of the first and simple translation-distance-based model. Given a triple (h, r, t) where $h,\ t \in E$ (set of entities) and $r \in R$ (set of relationships), TransE learns vector embeddings $\boldsymbol{h}, \boldsymbol{t}$ and $\boldsymbol{r}$ such that distance between $\boldsymbol{h} + \boldsymbol{r}$ and $\boldsymbol{t}$ is minimum. In TransE, $L1$ or $L2$ norm is used to measure the distance, $d(\boldsymbol{h}, \boldsymbol{r}, \boldsymbol{t}) = ||\boldsymbol{h} + \boldsymbol{r} - \boldsymbol{t}||$. To learn the embeddings, the following loss-function is minimized over the training set:

$$L = \sum_{(\boldsymbol{h},\boldsymbol{r},\boldsymbol{t})} \sum_{(\boldsymbol{h}',\boldsymbol{r},\boldsymbol{t}')} [\gamma + d(\boldsymbol{h} + \boldsymbol{r}, \boldsymbol{t}) - d(\boldsymbol{h}' + \boldsymbol{r}, \boldsymbol{t}')]_+ \tag{1}$$

where $[x]_+$ denotes the positive part of x, $\gamma > 0$ is a margin hyperparameter, and $d(\boldsymbol{h}, \boldsymbol{r}, \boldsymbol{t})$ is the distance of a positive sample, and $d(\boldsymbol{h}', \boldsymbol{r}, \boldsymbol{t}')$ is the distance of a negative sample.

TransH: TransH introduces two vectors for a relation $\boldsymbol{r}$, a relation-specific-specific translation vector $\boldsymbol{d_r}$ and a relation-specific hyperplane w_r. Then the embedding vectors of head $\boldsymbol{h}$ and tail $\boldsymbol{t}$ are projected to the hyperplane which gives new vectors $\boldsymbol{h}\perp$ and $\boldsymbol{t}\perp$ respectively. Then the scoring function to measure the plausibility of a triple is defined as $f_r(\boldsymbol{h}, \boldsymbol{t}) = ||\boldsymbol{h}\perp + \boldsymbol{d_r} - \boldsymbol{t}\perp||$. When $||w_r||_2 = 1$ is restricted, we get,

$$\boldsymbol{h}\perp = \boldsymbol{h} - w_r^\top \boldsymbol{h} w_r, \qquad \boldsymbol{t}\perp = \boldsymbol{t} - w_r^\top \boldsymbol{t} w_r \tag{2}$$

Then, we have the scoring function as,

$$f_r(\boldsymbol{h}, \boldsymbol{t}) = ||(\boldsymbol{h} - w_r^\top \boldsymbol{h} w_r) + \boldsymbol{d_r} - (\boldsymbol{t} - w_r^\top \boldsymbol{t} w_r)|| \tag{3}$$

Now, the model is trained over the following the loss function,

$$L = \sum_{(\boldsymbol{h},\boldsymbol{r}',\boldsymbol{t})} \sum_{(\boldsymbol{h}',\boldsymbol{r},\boldsymbol{t}')} [\gamma + f_r(\boldsymbol{h}, \boldsymbol{t}) - f_r(\boldsymbol{h}', \boldsymbol{t}')]_+ \tag{4}$$

where $[x]_+$ denotes the positive part of x, γ is the margin separating positive and negative triples.

3.1.2. Semantic-matching-based models

Semantic-matching-based models use similarity-based scoring functions or add additional information to extract more knowledge.

DistMult: DistMult (Yang et al., 2014) is a semantic-matching-based multiplicative model in which the relationship vector is enforced to be a diagonal matrix.

The head entity $\boldsymbol{h}$ and tail entity $\boldsymbol{t}$ are initialized as either a "one-hot" vector or an "n-hot" feature vector. Then the learned representations, $\boldsymbol{y_h} \in R$ and $\boldsymbol{y_t} \in R$ are given by, $\boldsymbol{y_h} = f(W\boldsymbol{h})$, and $\boldsymbol{y_t} = f(W\boldsymbol{t})$, where f can be a linear or non-linear function, and W is the parameter matrix which can be randomly initialized or initialized using pre-trained vectors.

The relation, similar to previously discussed models, is represented in the form of a scoring function. In DistMult, the function is formulated as bilinear,

$$S(\boldsymbol{y_h}, \boldsymbol{y_t}) = \boldsymbol{y_h}^T \boldsymbol{M_r} \boldsymbol{y_t} \quad (5)$$

where, $\boldsymbol{M_r} \in R^{nxn}$ is a matrix operator and is restricted to be a diagonal matrix.

$$L = \sum_{(h,r,t)} \sum_{(h',r,t')} max\{S_{(h',r,t')} - S_{(h,r,t)} + 1, 0\} \quad (6)$$

ComplEx: ComplEx (Trouillon et al., 2016) is another semantic-matching-based multiplicative model which follows the idea of forcing the relation embedding to be a diagonal matrix similar to DistMult. However, in ComplEx, the concept is extended in the complex space and as a result, the bi-linear product becomes a Hermitian product. In ComplEx, the set of entities is represented as ϵ with $|\epsilon| = n$ and the relation between two entities, head h and tail t is represented as a binary value $Y_{ht} \in \{-1, 1\}$. Its probability is given by the logistic inverse link function $P(Y_{ht} = 1) = \sigma(X_{ht})$, where $X \in R^{n \times n}$ is a latent matrix of scores, and Y the partially observed sign matrix. The scoring function used in ComplEx is given by

$$\begin{aligned} \phi(r, h, t; \theta) =&< Re(w_r), Re(h), Re(t) > + \\ &< Re(w_r), Im(h), Im(t) > + \\ &< Im(w_r), Re(h), Im(t) > - \\ &< Im(w_r), Im(h), Re(t) > \end{aligned} \quad (7)$$

where w_r in C^k is a complex vector.

An advantage of projecting the embeddings in the complex space is it disables the commutative property of the scoring function that existed in DistMult.

3.2. Neural Network based models

ConvE: ConvE (Dettmers et al., 2018) is the first neural network-based model that applies a simple convolution over the entity embeddings. The entity embedding and the relation embedding are concatenated together before passing through the convolution layer with a set $\boldsymbol{W}$ of $m \times n$ filters. The output of the convolution layer is then fed into a dense layer with a single neuron and weights $\boldsymbol{W}$, giving out a fact score. In ConvE, the scoring function is defined by a convolution over the embeddings as follows:

$$(\boldsymbol{h}, \boldsymbol{t}) = f(vec(f(\bar{\boldsymbol{h}}; \bar{\boldsymbol{r}}) * w))W)t \quad (8)$$

where w is a relation parameter, $\bar{h}$ and $\bar{r}$ denote 2D reshaping of h and r respectively.

The model is trained using logistic sigmoid function $p = \sigma(.)$ to the scores, and minimize the binary cross-entropy loss:

$$L(p, l) = -\frac{1}{N} \sum_i l_i log(p_i) + (1 - l_i) log(1 - p_i)) \quad (9)$$

where l is the label vector.

Relation	#(Synset)
ONTO_NODES	44,857
HYPERNYM	33,972
HYPONYM	30,836
MODIFIES_NOUN	9,780
ALSO_SEE	1,814

Table 1: Statistics of top five relations from Hindi Wordnet with number of synsets.

Model	MRR	H@1	H@3	H@10
TransE	0.156	0.055	0.221	0.334
TransH	0.133	0.032	0.199	0.308
DistMult	0.166	0.119	0.19	0.24
ComplEx	0.172	0.13	0.188	0.237
ConvE	**0.294**	**0.24**	**0.316**	**0.385**

Table 2: Performance of five KGC models

Relation	MRR	Hit@10
ONTO_NODES	0.267	0.418
VERB	0.239	0.436
ANTONYM	0.177	0.2
MODIFIES_NOUN	0.16	0.405
HYPERNYM	0.142	0.241

Table 3: Top 5 relations based on MRR score of ConvE model

4. Experimental Results and Analysis

Our experimental framework with all the details are mentioned below.

Hindi WordNet: For our study, we take the Hindi WordNet developed as part of the Indo WordNet at the Center For Indian Languages Technology (Narayan et al., 2002). A snapshot of the Hindi WordNet is shown in Figure 1. The Hindi WordNet consists of 39,622 synsets with a total of 59 relations. The total amount of words in the WordNet amount to 148,865 with 103,365 unique words. The top five relations based on synset count are shown in Table 1.

Model	1-1 relations		n-1 relations		n-n relations	
	MRR	**Hit@10**	**MRR**	**Hit@10**	**MRR**	**Hit@10**
TransE	0.036	0.089	0.168	0.34	0.114	0.344
TransH	0.03	0.0874	0.137	0.31	0.116	0.35
DistMult	0.007	0.009	0.16	0.24	0.103	0.262
ComplEx	0.015	0.0336	0.18	0.25	0.154	0.212
ConvE	**0.11**	**0.146**	**0.212**	**0.34**	**0.167**	**0.407**

Table 4: MRR, and Hit@10 of the models for 1-1, n-1 and n-n relations

Dataset: We convert the WordNet into RDF-style [2] triples graph fitting for the Knowledge Graph Completion task. An RDF-style triples graph consists of a triple in the form ($head$, $relation$, $tail$), where $head$ and $tail$ are synset ids and $relation$ is the relationship that exists between the two synsets. Following Dettmers et al. (2018), we remove the inverse relations from our dataset to correctly evaluate the performance of models. Therefore, we simply remove the triples with obvious inverse relations like hyponym and holonym from the dataset. In addition, we also manually remove triples (h, r, t) from the valid and test set, if (h, r', t) exists in the train set. Moreover, we also narrow the 59 relations present in the Hindi WordNet to 16 relations by grouping relations. For example, we merge all the different types (ANTONYM_SIZE, ANTONYM_TIME, ANTONYM_ACTION) of antonym relations into the relation ANTONYM. The final dataset consists 39,609 entites with 16 relations and it comprises of 86,432 train, 4,712 valid, and 4,694 test triples.

Furthermore, we follow Bordes et al. (2013) and categorize the relationships in the test dataset into four categories based on cardinalities of their head and tail arguments. The four categories include $1-1$, $1-n$, $n-1$ and $n-n$ relations. In $1-1$ relationship, a head can appear with at most one tail. For example, relationships showing capital of countries like *(paris, capital_of, france)*, *(madrid, capital_of, spain)*, etc. In $1-n$ relationship, a head can appear with many tails. For example, *(germany, has_part, dusseldorf)*, *(germany, has_part, hanover)*, etc. In $n-1$ relationship, many heads can appear with the same tail. For example, *(wintertime, hypernym, time)*, *(years, hypernym, time)*, etc. and in $n-n$ relationship, multiple heads can appear with multiple tails. For example, *(run, derivationally_related_form, atrium)*, *(run, derivationally_related_form, runner)*, etc.

Experimental Setup: We run the TransE, TransH, DistMult and ComplEx models using the OpenKE toolkit (Han et al., 2018). We run all experiments using default settings. For ConvE, we run the model published in GitHub[3]. All these models were run on a Ubuntu 20.04.2 LTS server with NVIDIA GeForce RTX 2080 Ti GPU, and 256 GB RAM.

Results and Analysis: For our experiments, we report the performance using Mean Reciprocal Rank (MRR) and Hits@(1, 3, 10) on the *filtered* setting (Bordes et al., 2013). The performance of all five models is presented in Table 2.

We evaluate the models on the metric score $Hit@k$ with $k = 1, 3$ and 10. In general, the lower values of k better indicate the performance of the models. At $k = 10$, we observe good performance from the TransE and ConvE models, whereas at $k = 3$ and $k = 1$, the ConvE models outperform all the other models significantly. In Table 3, we look at the performance of ConvE model which shows that the model does well with relations such as $onto\_nodes$, $verb$, $antonym$ which have a higher triple count in the training set. Clearly the relation class imbalance inherent in the WordNet is affecting the overall performance of the system. Some examples of induced triples from ConvE model with the rank 1 are *(दुहाना, onto_nodes, पियानो)*, *(अवसर, hypernym, समय)*, *(जन्मा, modifies_noun, जीव)* and some examples with the rank above 10 are *(रुलाई, antonym, हँसी)*, *(गुग्गुल, attributes, सुगंधित)*, *(लोकसेवा_आयोग, hypernym,समिति)*.

Further, we test the performance of the models on the different categories of the relationships discussed in Section 4. The results are shown in Table 4, with the best score marked in boldface. We do not evaluate the performance on $1-n$ relations as the test dataset contained only a few test instances.

In our results, we observe that the ConvE model outperforms the transition-distance-based models and the semantic-distance-based models. The ConvE model achieves a higher score across all relation-types signaling better generalization ability of the model.

5. Conclusion

In this study, we attempted to enrich Hindi WordNet by posing it as a knowledge graph completion task. We prepared a dataset from Hindi WordNet for evaluating such an attempt. We experimented with five Knowledge Graph Completion models of different genres and report the overall performances of all the models. We showed that the ConvE model outperforms all the other models across all relation types. However, to develop a fully automated Hindi WordNet enrichment process the evaluation results have to be improved. Hence, the next step would be to investigate approaches to mitigate relation-class imbalance in the WordNet dataset, and in future study extend WordNet enrichment for other low resource languages as well.

[2]https://www.w3.org/RDF/

[3]https://github.com/TimDettmers/ConvE

6. Bibliographical References

Bordes, A., Usunier, N., Garcia-Duran, A., Weston, J., and Yakhnenko, O. (2013). Translating embeddings for modeling multi-relational data. In C. J. C. Burges, et al., editors, *Advances in Neural Information Processing Systems*, volume 26. Curran Associates, Inc.

Boudabous, M. M., Kammoun, N. C., Khedher, N., Belguith, L. H., and Sadat, F. (2013). Arabic wordnet semantic relations enrichment through morpholexical patterns. In *2013 1st International Conference on Communications, Signal Processing, and their Applications (ICCSPA)*, pages 1–6. IEEE.

Chen, Z., Wang, Y., Zhao, B., Cheng, J., Zhao, X., and Duan, Z. (2020). Knowledge graph completion: A review. *Ieee Access*, 8:192435–192456.

Dettmers, T., Minervini, P., Stenetorp, P., and Riedel, S. (2018). Convolutional 2d knowledge graph embeddings. In *Thirty-second AAAI conference on artificial intelligence*.

Fellbaum, C. et al. (1998). Wordnet: An electronic lexical database mit press. *Cambridge, Massachusetts*.

Giménez, J. and Màrquez, L. (2006). Low-cost enrichment of spanish wordnet with automatically translated glosses: combining general and specialized models. In *Proceedings of the COLING/ACL 2006 Main Conference Poster Sessions*, pages 287–294.

Han, L., Yin, Z., Wang, Y., Hu, K., et al. (2017). Link prediction of knowledge graph based on bayesian network. *J. Frontiers Comput. Sci. Technol.*, 11(5):742–751.

Han, X., Cao, S., Xin, L., Lin, Y., Liu, Z., Sun, M., and Li, J. (2018). Openke: An open toolkit for knowledge embedding. In *Proceedings of EMNLP*.

Hayashi, K. and Shimbo, M. (2017). On the equivalence of holographic and complex embeddings for link prediction. *arXiv preprint arXiv:1702.05563*.

Lao, N. and Cohen, W. W. (2010). Relational retrieval using a combination of path-constrained random walks. *Machine learning*, 81(1):53–67.

Miller, G. A., Beckwith, R., Fellbaum, C., Gross, D., and Miller, K. J. (1990). Introduction to wordnet: An on-line lexical database. *International journal of lexicography*, 3(4):235–244.

Montoyo, A., Palomar, M., Rigau, G., and Gargalló, P. (2001). Wordnet enrichment with classification systems. In *Proceedings of WordNet and Other Lexical Resources: Applications, Extensions and Customisations Workshop.(NAACL-01) The Second Meeting of the North American Chapter of the Association for Computational Linguistics*, pages 101–106.

Narayan, D., Chakrabarti, D., Pande, P., and Bhattacharyya, P. (2002). An experience in building the indo wordnet-a wordnet for hindi. In *First International Conference on Global WordNet, Mysore, India*, volume 24.

Nickel, M., Tresp, V., and Kriegel, H.-P. (2011). A three-way model for collective learning on multi-relational data. In *ICML*, pages 809–816.

Paulheim, H. and Bizer, C. (2014). Improving the quality of linked data using statistical distributions. *International Journal on Semantic Web and Information Systems (IJSWIS)*, 10(2):63–86.

Rossi, A., Barbosa, D., Firmani, D., Matinata, A., and Merialdo, P. (2021). Knowledge graph embedding for link prediction: A comparative analysis. *ACM Transactions on Knowledge Discovery from Data (TKDD)*, 15(2):1–49.

Ruiz-Casado, M., Alfonseca, E., and Castells, P. (2007). Automatising the learning of lexical patterns: An application to the enrichment of wordnet by extracting semantic relationships from wikipedia. *Data & Knowledge Engineering*, 61(3):484–499.

Trouillon, T., Welbl, J., Riedel, S., Gaussier, É., and Bouchard, G. (2016). Complex embeddings for simple link prediction. In *International conference on machine learning*, pages 2071–2080. PMLR.

Wang, Z., Zhang, J., Feng, J., and Chen, Z. (2014). Knowledge graph embedding by translating on hyperplanes. In *Proceedings of the AAAI Conference on Artificial Intelligence*, volume 28.

Wang, M., Qiu, L., and Wang, X. (2021). A survey on knowledge graph embeddings for link prediction. *Symmetry*, 13(3):485.

Yang, B., Yih, W.-t., He, X., Gao, J., and Deng, L. (2014). Embedding entities and relations for learning and inference in knowledge bases. *arXiv preprint arXiv:1412.6575*.

Proceedings of the EURALI Workshop @LREC2020, pages 86–87
Marseille, 20 June 2022

A Digital Swedish–Yiddish/Yiddish–Swedish Dictionary: A Web-Based Dictionary that is also Available Offline

Magnus Ahltorp, Jean Hessel, Gunnar Eriksson, Maria Skeppstedt, Rickard Domeij
Institute for Language and Folklore
Stockholm, Sweden
firstname.lastname@isof.se

Abstract

Yiddish is one of the national minority languages of Sweden, and one of the languages for which the Swedish Institute for Language and Folklore is responsible for developing useful language resources. We here describe the web-based version of a Swedish–Yiddish/Yiddish–Swedish dictionary. The single search field of the web-based dictionary is used for incrementally searching all three components of the dictionary entries (the word in Swedish, the word in Yiddish with Hebrew characters and the transliteration in Latin script). When the user accesses the dictionary in an online mode, the dictionary is saved in the web browser, which makes it possible to also use the dictionary offline.

Keywords: Digital dictionaries, Yiddish, Swedish

1. Introduction

The Swedish Institute for Language and Folklore, ISOF, produces a number of different types of dictionaries. Examples include dictionaries for common immigrant languages that are intended for learners of Swedish,[1] dictionaries for professional translators,[2] as well as dictionaries for the national minority languages of Sweden. The main goals of this work is 1) to publish dictionaries, 2) to develop data sets that can be released as open data and used in third-party applications such as machine- and computer-assisted translation, computer-assisted language learning, and dictionary applications.

In addition to these two main goals, we also often make the content of the dictionaries digitally available via web page search interfaces. Previously, these search interfaces have required internet access to be possible to use. However, there are many situations in which there is a need for a dictionary and in which offline access might be needed, for example in hospitals, in court rooms, and when travelling. The standard solution to this problem is to develop mobile apps, which can be used offline. However, since the development of dictionary applications is not the main focus for ISOF, we currently do not have enough resources to develop and maintain dictionary apps for different mobile platforms, in addition to developing dictionary web pages. Instead, we have focused on developing web pages that can be accessed when using a mobile phone or a computer in an offline mode.

As the first practical application using this approach we have implemented a web-based dictionary for Swedish–Yiddish/Yiddish–Swedish. This web-based dictionary will be described here.

[1] `https://sprakresurser.isof.se/lexin/`
[2] `https://sprakresurser.isof.se/tolkordlistor/`

2. The printed dictionary and the dictionary as open data

Yiddish is one of the national minority languages of Sweden (Lag (2009:724) om nationella minoriteter och minoritetsspråk, 2009)[3], and one of the languages for which ISOF is responsible for developing useful language resources. As a part of this work, a new edition of a Swedish–Yiddish/Yiddish–Swedish dictionary was published in paper book format by ISOF[4] in 2020 (Kerbel et al., 2020).

The dictionary contains three main components for each entry in the dictionary: 1) the word in Swedish, 2) the word in Yiddish, written in its standard form with Hebrew characters, and 3) a transliterated form, in which the Yiddish word is written with Latin characters. The system used for transliteration is a system introduced by the first publisher of the dictionary. This system is a Swedish adaption of the YIVO transliteration system for Yiddish. The entries also contain additional information, such as part of speech and usage notes.

The content of the dictionary is also available as open data[5] with a CC0 license, and is provided as a part of the National Language Bank of Sweden. The open data format of the dictionary follows the same three-component structure as described in the previous paragraph. This data forms the basis for our web-based dictionary.

[3] `https://www.riksdagen.se/sv/dokument-lagar/dokument/svensk-forfattningssamling/lag-2009724-om-nationella-minoriteter-och_sfs-2009-724`
[4] `https://www.isof.se/lar-dig-mer/publikationer/publikationer/2020-12-18-jiddisch-svensk-jiddisch-ordbok`
[5] `https://sprakresurser.isof.se/jiddisch`

3. The web-based dictionary

The web-based dictionary is available at:
`https://sprak.isof.se/jiddisch/`.
Figure 1 shows the top results after "or" has been written in the search field. To reserve the maximum amount of space on the screen for displaying the search results, the user interface contains nothing apart from a single search field and the search results. This clean layout also makes it easier to integrate the dictionary into another existing web page layout.
The single search field is used for searching all three components of the dictionary entries. That is, if the user searches for a word using Hebrew characters, it is only used to match the component of the entry that is written with Hebrew characters, and if the user conducts a search using Latin characters, it is used to match both against the Swedish component and against the transliterated Yiddish. The search is performed incrementally, to minimise the number of key strokes needed for retrieving a dictionary entry. That is, as soon as the user starts typing matches are shown, and when the user continues to type, the search result is updated according to the updated search string. Figures 1 and 2 show how the search results have changed after the user first has typed "or" and thereafter "ord".

Figure 1: The top results after "or" has been written in the search field. The transliterated Yiddish word is shown in a standard font, the word in Hebrew characters with a grey background, the word in Swedish in a boldface font, and additional information in italics. ("Jiddischordboken" is "The Yiddish dictionary" in Swedish.)

When the user accesses the dictionary web page in an online mode, the contents of the dictionary are saved in the web browser. When opening the dictionary in an offline mode, with the same mobile device (or computer) and the same browser, the user is still able to use the dictionary.

Figure 2: The top results after "ord" (Swedish for "word") has been written in the search field.

The dictionary web page is implemented using HTML and JavaScript. The content is made available in an offline mode by using IndexedDB and Service Workers. The source code[6] for the web-based dictionary is freely available on GitHub.

4. Future work

Although the web-based Swedish–Yiddish/Yiddish–Swedish dictionary is fully functional, we will continue to improve it.
We intend to conduct a small user study, in order to gather ideas for possible improvements. We will, for example, gather ideas regarding the dictionary content, how the search results are presented, as well as ideas regarding the user interaction and layout in general.
In addition, we will implement similar web-based search interfaces for other dictionaries, e.g., dictionaries for translators and interpreters, for which the offline functionality might be particularly useful.

5. Acknowledgements

This work was partly funded by the National Language Bank of Sweden and SWE-CLARIN, which receive funding through the Swedish Research Council (Vetenskapsrådet) under the grant no 2017-00626.

6. Bibliographical References

Kerbel, L., Hessel, J., and David, P. (2020). *Jiddisch-svensk-jiddisch ordbok*. Institutet för språk och folkminnen, Stockholm.

Lag (2009:724) om nationella minoriteter och minoritetsspråk. (2009). Kulturdepartementet.

[6]`https://github.com/sprakradet/jiddischordbok`

Proceedings of the EURALI Workshop @LREC2020, pages 88–89
Marseille, 20 June 2022

An Online Dictionary for Dialects of North Frisian

Tanno Hüttenrauch
Independent Researcher
Amsterdam, Netherlands
nurdfriisk@gmail.com

Michael Wehar
Swarthmore College
Swarthmore, PA USA
mwehar1@swarthmore.edu

Abstract

Language is an essential part of communication and culture. Documenting, digitizing, and preserving language is a meaningful pursuit. The first author of this work is a speaker of Söl'ring which is a dialect of the North Frisian language spoken on the island of Sylt in the North Frisia region of Germany. Söl'ring is estimated to have only hundreds of native speakers and very limited online language resources making it a prime candidate for language preservation initiatives. To help preserve Söl'ring and provide resources for Söl'ring speakers and learners, we built an online dictionary. Our dictionary, called friisk.org, provides translations for over 28,000 common German words to Söl'ring. In addition, our dictionary supports translations for Söl'ring to German, spell checking for Söl'ring, conjugations for common Söl'ring verbs, and an experimental transcriber from Söl'ring to IPA for pronunciations. Following the release of our online dictionary, we collaborated with neighboring communities to add limited support for additional North Frisian dialects including Fering, Halligen Frisian, Karrharder, Nordergoesharder, Öömrang, and Wiedingharder.

Keywords: Endangered Languages, North Frisian, Online Dictionary

1 Introduction

1.1 A Dialect of North Frisian

The North Frisian language is estimated to currently have 8,000 native speakers across many dialects including Fering, Halligen Frisian, Karrharder, Nordergoesharder, Öömrang, Söl'ring, Wiedingharder, and more (Salminen, 2007; Minderheiten in Schleswig-Holstein, 2021). The first author of this work is a speaker of Söl'ring which is a dialect that is spoken on the island of Sylt in the North Frisia region of Germany.

1.2 Our Goal

Our goal is to support North Frisian speakers and learners by creating and maintaining an online dictionary. Although existing organizations provide support for limited in-person programming and events to assist North Frisian speakers and learners, there is a lack of online resources and digital content for North Frisian dialects such as Söl'ring. In general, providing online resources and digital content for endangered languages is necessary not only for archival purposes, but also to support language speakers and learners.

2 An Online Dictionary (friisk.org)

2.1 Overview

We built our online dictionary as a web application called (friisk.org) to provide online resources and digital content for Söl'ring speakers and learners. Our web application was built with HTML, CSS, and JavaScript on the frontend and PHP, SQL, and Python on the backend. Our web application primarily functions as a dictionary and resource repository. The second author served as the primary developer for our web application.

2.2 Language Data and Guides

Our language data sets are primarily composed of word lists, translations, conjugations, and rewrite rules for IPA transcription. The first author served as the primary lexicographer for compiling, transcribing, and formatting our language data sets. Our language data sets were created using the first author's first-hand language knowledge and acquired information from established resources such as (Jörgensen et al, 1981; Kellner, 2006; Lorenzen, 1977; Möller, 1973). We acknowledge that, as best as we could, we received written permission from publishers and/or original authors in cases that we directly or indirectly incorporated existing language data to build our language data sets.

To accompany our language data, for each supported dialect of North Frisian, we developed a language guide that provides basic background and information on the dialect along with information on pronunciations, grammar, and external references.

2.3 Spell Checking

We use the Open Source Spell Checker which is a web-based clientside spell checker that was developed and released by the second author (Wehar, 2019). This spell checker is ideal for our purposes because it is simple, multilingual, and runs on the client rather than the server which allows our server to focus on serving content rather than running complex algorithms. This spell checker simply looks at heuristic character differences that are easy to check, but is optimized to check these differences across word lists containing up to 100,000 words.

2.4 Translations

We currently provide translations from German to Fering, Halligen Frisian, Karrharder, Nordergoesharder, Öömrang, Söl'ring, and Wiedingharder. Additionally, we provide translations from English to Söl'ring and from Söl'ring to German. In total, our data sets include over 75,000 translations.

For each language pair, we translate from common words or phrases to definitions or explanations. In some cases, we also include parts of speech and example phrases to further clarify the concept. Additional labels are provided in some cases to denote subdialect differences and differences between sources.

Language Pair	Number of Translations
english-solring	1,656
german-fering	3,326

german-halligen frisian	5,512
german-karrharder	3,321
german-nordergoesharder	3,433
german-oomrang	3,308
german-solring	28,395
german-wiedingharder	3,394
solring-german	24,709

Table 1: Total number of translations

2.5 Conjugations

We currently provide conjugations for over 3,000 Söl'ring verbs along with a small collection of conjugations for the other six dialects of North Frisian that we support.

Dialect	Number of Verbs Conjugated
fering	189
halligen frisian	125
karrharder	114
nordergoesharder	174
oomrang	120
solring	3,505
wiedingharder	146

Table 2: Total number of verbs conjugated

2.6 Pronunciations

We currently provide a beta system for automatic transcriptions from Söl'ring to the International Phonetic Alphabet (IPA). According to the first author, because Söl'ring was originally a spoken language rather than a written language, whenever a writing system was developed, spellings could be used to systematically infer pronunciation. In particular, sounds directly correspond to symbols (or pairs of sequential symbols) along with their context within a word. As a result, we were able to devise a list of over one hundred regular expression replacement rules (with varying priorities) to directly translate words into phonetic transcription. To verify the accuracy of the resulting transcriptions, a test set of word and transcription pairs were compiled by hand. It is important to note that there are regional differences in pronunciations that we hope to further investigate and support in the future.

3 Conclusion

3.1 Community Usage

We created an online dictionary to support North Frisian speakers and learners. Our online dictionary currently serves over 5,000 unique users per year and has been featured by multiple community organizations from the island of Sylt. Although our online dictionary primarily provides resources for the Söl'ring dialect of North Frisian, through interactions with online language communities, we have been able to support six additional dialects of North Frisian spoken in neighboring regions.

3.2 Future Work

We hope to continue to maintain our online dictionary for years to come to be able to continue offering online resources and digital content for speakers and learners of the dialects of North Frisian. We also hope that our model of providing language guides, spell checking, translations, conjugations, and pronunciations will be adopted by other language communities for language preservation initiatives. In addition, we plan to make some of our developed technologies available in open source repositories for free usage within other language preservation projects.

Acknowledgements

We greatly appreciate all of the help and support that we have received while pursuing this project. We are especially thankful to the authors and publishers who permitted us to directly or indirectly use portions of their data while compiling our data sets. We also are thankful to the multiple organizations that shared our online dictionary with Söl'ring speakers and learners. In particular, we would like to thank Nordfriisk Instituut and Söl'ring Foriining. Finally, we thank Yvo Meeres for helpful suggestions and feedback related to this work.

Bibliographical References

Jörgensen, V. T., Petersen, J., & Altstädt, C. (1981). Kleines Friesisches Wörterbuch der Nordergoesharder Mundart von Ockholm und Langenhorn : Huuchtjüsch, Freesch/Fräisch. Bräist: Nordfriisk Instituut.

Kellner, B. (2006). Sölring Uurterbok: Wörterbuch der sylterfriesischen Sprache. Söl'ring Foriining.

Lorenzen, J. (1977). Deutsch-Halligfriesisch : e. Wörterbuch : 6000 Vokabeln Halligfries. mit Texten aus d. 17. bis 20. Jh. = Tutsk-freesk : en üürdeböök. Bräist/Bredstedt: Nordfriisk Inst.

Minderheiten in Schleswig-Holstein - Friesen (2021). Retrieved on May 24, 2022 from https://www.schleswig-holstein.de/DE/Fachinhalte/M/minderheiten/minderheiten_friesen.html

Möller, B. (1973). Söl'ring Uurterbok: Wörterbuch der Sylter Mundart. Sändig.

Salminen, T. (2007). Europe and North Asia from: Encyclopedia of the world's endangered languages. Routledge.

Language Resource References

Wehar, M. (2019). Open Source Spell Checker. https://github.com/MichaelWehar/Open-Source-Spell-Checker

Proceedings of the EURALI Workshop @LREC2020, pages 90–94
Marseille, 20 June 2022

Towards a Unified Tool for the Management of Data and Technologies in Field Linguistics and Computational Linguistics - LiFE

Siddharth Singh, Ritesh Kumar, Shyam Ratan, Sonal Sinha
Department of Linguistics, K.M. Institute of Hindi and Linguistics
Dr. Bhimrao Ambedkar University, Agra, India
sidd435@gmail.com, ritesh78_llh@jnu.ac.in, shyamratan2907@gmail.com, sonalsinha2612@gmail.com

Abstract

The paper presents a new software - Linguistic Field Data Management and Analysis System - LiFE for endangered and low-resourced languages - an open-source, web-based linguistic data analysis and management application allowing systematic storage, management, usage and sharing of linguistic data collected from the field. The application enables users to store lexical items, sentences, paragraphs, audio-visual content including photographs, video clips, speech recordings, etc, with rich glossing and annotation. For field linguists, it provides facilities to generate interactive and print dictionaries; for NLP practitioners, it provides the data storage and representation in standard formats such as RDF, JSON and CSV. The tool provides a one-click interface to train NLP models for various tasks using the data stored in the system and then use it for assistance in further storage of the data (especially for the field linguists). At the same time, the tool also provides the facility of using the models trained outside of the tool for data storage, transcription, annotation and other tasks. The web-based application, allows for seamless collaboration among multiple persons and sharing the data, models, etc with each other.

Keywords: LiFE, Web-based, Linguistic Data Management, Linked Data, NLP Interface

1. Introduction

Linguistic data analysis and management tools are always being required by field linguists. A large amount of data is collected, and needs to be properly stored, analysed and made accessible to the larger community by field linguists for a large number of languages including relatively lesser-known, minoritized and endangered languages of the world. On the other hand, hardly any dataset is publicly available for building any kind of language technology tools and applications for a huge number of languages across the globe.

An integrated system with an easily-accessible and user-friendly interface aimed at linguists needs to be made available, to tackle this multi-faceted problem of storing, processing, analysing and retrieving the primary linguistic data. "`LiFE`"[1] intends to provide a practical intervention in the field through an organised framework for management, analysis, sharing (as linked data) and processing of primary linguistic field data including digital and print lexicons, sketch grammars and fundamental language processing tool development, such as part-of-speech tagger and morphological analysers. The software aims to provide an easy-to-use, intuitive interface for performing all the tasks and emphasise on automating the tasks as far as possible. For example, the system incrementally trains automated methods for inter-linear glossing of the dataset (which improves as more data is stored in the system) and subsequent generation of sketch grammar as well as NLP tools for the language, by providing initial input. Likewise, the system automatically links and infers the entries in the lexicon and inter-linear glossed data using Lemon (more specifically OntoLex-Lemon) (McCrae et al., 2017) and Ligt (Chiarcos and Ionov, 2019). We have also integrated the recent transformer-based unsupervised and transfer learning-based ASR models (such as wav2vec 2.0 (Baevski et al., 2020) and wav2vec-U (Baevski et al., 2021)) which provides the whole automated pipeline from transcription to inter-linear glossing and free translation for the field linguists. At the same time the data itself could be used for improving the models for ASR, part-of-speech tagging, morphological analysers and machine translation. In addition to these, the system also enables storage and semi-automatic linking of the dataset to some of the largest linked data sources such as Wikipedia and DBpedia.

2. Motivation

The development of linguistic field data storage, sharing, management and linked data generation has been largely done independent of each other. There are some applications and tools aimed at field linguists (or community members interested in fieldwork for their own language) for management and collection of data as well as generating lexicon. One of the most popular tools in the field is FieldWorks Language Explorer (*FLEx*)[2] which is used for the collection, management, analysis and sharing of linguistic and cultural data (Butler and Volkinburg, 2007), (Manson, 2020). *Toolbox*, earlier called Shoebox[3] is a precursor to the FLEx and one of the the oldest softwares produced by

[1] `https://github.com/kmi-linguistics/life`

[2] `https://software.sil.org/fieldworks/`

[3] `https://software.sil.org/shoebox/`, `https://software.sil.org/toolbox/`

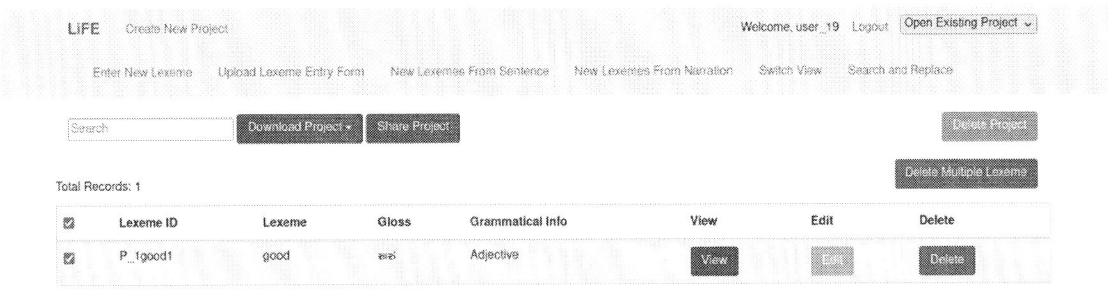

Figure 1: Dictionary View Interface of LiFE

SIL (The Summer Institute of Linguistics) that was essentially meant for anthropologists and field linguists to put their text data in the tool and build dictionaries (Robinson et al., 2007). *LexiquePro*[4] is a software for creating / formatting lexicon databases and easy sharing with others (Guérin and Lacrampe, 2007). *WeSay*[5] is created by SIL for providing support to the non-linguists/native speakers in building dictionaries for their own languages (Perlin, 2012), (Albright and Hatton, 2008).

There have been some efforts at development of tools focussed on data collection as well. (Vries et al., 2014) discusses the development of a tool named *Woefzela*[6], which is a smartphone-based (Android Operating System) data collection tool for speech data collection. It can function without Internet connectivity and allows multiple sessions for data collection. It works well for the quality control of collected data. This tool is demonstrated in the South African data collection project, where almost 800 hours of speech data were collected from remote and rural areas.

There are few other platforms for archiving and providing access to the data, the prominent ones being Endangered Languages Archive (*ELAR*)[7], which is a digital repository for preserving and circulating documentation of endangered languages (Nathan, 2010). The Language Archive (*TLA*)[8] is a hub for language resources that holds language corpus in audio, video format, along with preserving and documenting the dying languages (Drude et al., 2012). *SIL Language and Culture Archive*[9] contains works collected, compiled and created by SIL. The *Open Language Archives Community (OLAC)*[10], which is an association of more than 60 participating linguistic archives of different kinds (including the ones mentioned above and others for access and storage of linguistic data, specifically of endangered languages) has also newly joined the Linguistic Linked Data Open Cloud which covers the way for providing a large amount of such data as linked data (Simons and Bird, 2003).

However, none of the platforms and tools directly provide an interface for storing or (largely) automatically generating the primary linguistic data as linked data or provide a flawless two-way integration between the linguistic data management softwares and NLP libraries and tools. Most of these tools aimed at field linguists do not provide interfaces for generating linked data or even utilising the modern NLP models for automating the tasks

On the other hand, for supporting generation of linked data, the linked data community has developed tools for generating linked data lexicons. One of the renowned tools for this is *VocBench* (VB)[11]. It is a full-fledged open-source web-based thesaurus management platform, which provides feature of collaborative development of multilingual datasets compatible with semantic web standards (Stellato et al., 2020). In addition to these there have been quite a few attempts at transporting the non-linked datasets to the linked data repositories. These efforts are largely carried out manually and end up in producing high-quality linked data. For example, (Samarin, 1967) talked about the lexical data migration from textual e-dictionaries to lexical databases. Earlier Serbian Morphological Dictionaries (SMD) were developed in *LeXimir*, an application for the development and management of lexical resources. Now, a new lexical database model for the SMD is based on the lemon model with a thesaurus. This database improves the existing resources.

While work like these are tremendous efforts, these may not be scalable for a large number of cases. Moreover, given the fact that these efforts are extremely resource-intensive, it may not be at all feasible for endangered and low-resource languages. Hence it is a better option to create the new resources itself as linked data instead of later converting those to linked data. On the other hand, a tool like VocBench which focuses on

[4]https://software.sil.org/lexiquepro/

[5]https://software.sil.org/wesay/

[6]https://sites.google.com/site/woefzela/

[7]https://www.elararchive.org/

[8]https://archive.mpi.nl/tla/

[9]https://www.sil.org/resources/language-culture-archives

[10]http://www.language-archives.org/archives

[11]http://vocbench.uniroma2.it/

creating news resources as linked data, is not very user-friendly for field linguists nor do they provide options for automating the tasks or linking to the NLP ecosystem.

Given this general unavailability of common interfaces and tools that could act as a bridge between the three group of researchers working with linguistic data - field and documentary linguists, linguistic linked data community and NLP practitioners - and the linguistic community itself, a communication among these groups is almost non-existent. Our aims are, thus, to provide the following -

- Provide an interface for Field and Documentary Linguists such that it not only gives a user-friendly interface for putting their data in a structured format but also provide access to the state-of-the-art NLP for use without the need to navigate through complex instructions and workflow of most NLP tools.
- Access to the data from endangered and low-resource languages (if the community and researchers choose to make it available) in a structured format for NLP practitioners. Also an interface for training and testing the model on this data via the interface.
- A (semi-)automated method of linking the data to some of the largest linked data databases.

3. Features of System

As mentioned above, the central motive of building this platform is to provide a tool that acts as a bridge between field linguists (who are chiefly engaged in data collection from poor-resource and endangered languages, writing grammatical descriptions, building lexicons and also producing educational and other kinds of stuff for the communities that they work with), linked data community (who are chiefly engaged in resources using the semantic web techniques and meaningfully connecting data from different languages.) and the NLP community (who chiefly makes use of the linguistic data from many languages; could certainly contribute in automating the tasks carried out by field linguists; and also provide tools and technologies for the marginalised and under-privileged linguistic communities). As such in its present state the app provides the following operations -

- It provides a user-friendly interface for storing, making and sharing publicly available the linguistic field data including lexicon, interlinear glossed text and associated multimedia content.
- It provides a pipeline for automatic extraction of text and its POS tags using the unsupervised (using wav2vec-U) and transfer learning methods (using wav2vec2.0). It provides interfaces for training as well as using pre-trained NLP models needed for automating these tasks of ASR and POS tagging. The tool presently supports training various algorithms of the HuggingFace Transformers library and scikit-learn as well as using the models trained using these libraries.
- It provides an interface for exporting the data in structured formats such as RDF, JSON, HTML, XML, LATEX and CSV that could be directly used for NLP experiments and modelling (Singh et al., 2022).
- It generates linked data for dictionaries and interlinear glossed text using vocabs like LiGT and OntoLex-LEMON and then internally linked to the other linked lexicons and databases such as DBpedia and WordNet - this will help in the other tasks as well.

4. System Mechanism

This section contains information related to the architecture of the tool. The tool uses the Python-based Flask[12] framework and MongoDB (as database) in the backend and HTML, CSS and Javascript at the frontend.

There are six collections in the database of the tool:

- projects : containing a list of all the projects in the system,
- userprojects: containing projects created by and shared with each user and current active project of the user,
- projectsform : contains lexeme details form created for the project,
- lexemes : collection storing the details about each lexeme, This is stored as linked data entries using the relevant vocabularies.
- fs.files stores the file's metadata and fs.chunks stores the binary chunks of files (image, video, audio, etc).

There is a login interface where a registered user can login to the application and new user can register. Then there is a navigation bar leading to the interface to create new project; alternatively the user may select an existing project to work from a dropdown list as displayed in Figure 1.

The option to create new project will lead to the form for creating one's the fields required for the current project as shown in Figure 2. This makes the interface of the tool completely customisable which could be designed as per the need of the given project.

[12] `https://flask.palletsprojects.com/en/2.0.x/`

Once the fields are created then the user could use the relevant buttons to enter 'New lexeme' or 'New Sentence'. One could fill up the form with the required details to complete an entry as shown in Figure 3. The entry made for a specific lexeme through this customised form will be visible in the dictionary view as shown in Figure 1. Dictionary view contains a view button to view details of a particular lexeme and an edit button to edit the details. It has also two delete buttons to delete single or multiple lexemes.

The share button on the user's dashboard as well as in the lexicon view interface provides a multi-level option to share the project with other users - the users will have full control over which parts of the project could be shared and what kinds of access rights the sharee have. These access rights include such fine-grained classification as viewing rights for specific entries or all entries, editing rights for the entries, deleting rights for the entries, right to add new entries, share it with other users (with equivalent or lower rights), etc.

Finally, one can download the complete project in JSON format along with the files uploaded for the project and can share that with others. The lexicon could be downloaded in various formats such as RDF, CSV, HTML, PDF, DOCX, XLSX, etc.

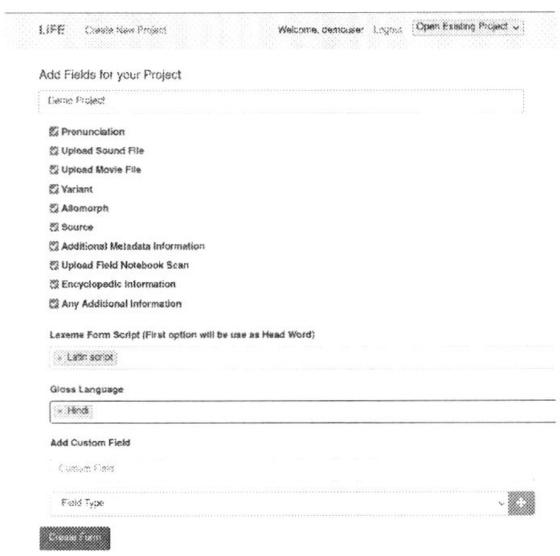

Figure 2: Create New Project Form

Figure 4 shows the model diagram of "LiFE", showing all the functions available to a user .

5. The Way Ahead

The platform is currently under active development and some of the features in the pipeline include the following

- Allow searching across multiple languages and generating concordances / parallel entries from multiple languages - options to search by language families, regions, and other available information.
- Allow for automatically generating glosses, example sentences, etc from different languages (especially those belonging to same language family / closely related), when working on a new dictionary - this will make the dictionary-making quicker. Also linked data could be used for doing this.
- Interface for training and automating morph analysers, parsers and machine translation system. This will make the whole pipeline after uploading of the speech data automated.
- Automatic sketch grammar generation.
- Template for Android app, which could generate mobile apps for dictionaries automatically (given the database).

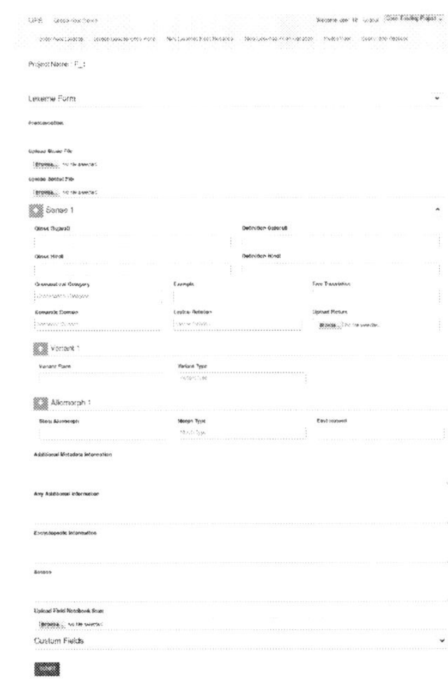

Figure 3: Lexeme Entry Form

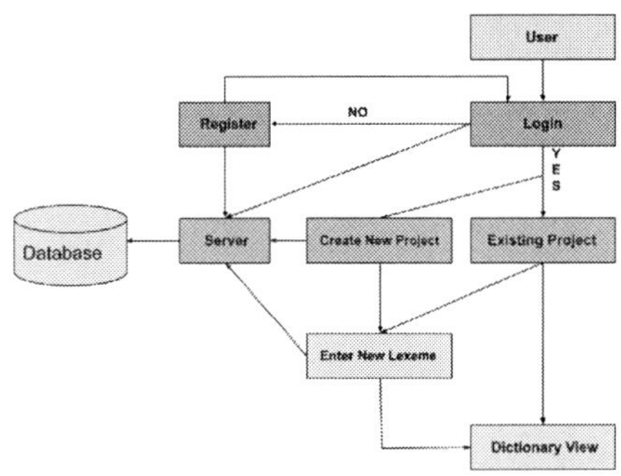

Figure 4: Model Diagram of LiFE

6. Bibliographical References

Albright, E. and Hatton, J. (2008). Wesay, a tool for collaborating on dictionaries with non-linguists.

Documenting and revitalizing Austronesian languages, 6:189 – 201, 12.

Baevski, A., Zhou, H., Mohamed, A., and Auli, M. (2020). wav2vec 2.0: A framework for self-supervised learning of speech representations. *CoRR*, abs/2006.11477.

Baevski, A., Hsu, W., Conneau, A., and Auli, M. (2021). Unsupervised speech recognition. *CoRR*, abs/2105.11084.

Butler, L. and Volkinburg, H. (2007). Review of fieldworks language explorer (flex). *Language Documentation and Conservation*, 1, 06.

Chiarcos, C. and Ionov, M. (2019). Ligt: An llod-native vocabulary for representing interlinear glossed text as RDF. In Maria Eskevich, et al., editors, *2nd Conference on Language, Data and Knowledge, LDK 2019, May 20-23, 2019, Leipzig, Germany*, volume 70 of *OASICS*, pages 3:1–3:15. Schloss Dagstuhl - Leibniz-Zentrum für Informatik.

Drude, S., Broeder, D., Trilsbeek, P., and Wittenburg, P. (2012). The language archive — a new hub for language resources. In *Proceedings of the Eighth International Conference on Language Resources and Evaluation (LREC'12)*, pages 3264–3267, Istanbul, Turkey, May. European Language Resources Association (ELRA).

Guérin, V. and Lacrampe, S. (2007). Lexique pro. *Language Documentation and Conservation*, 1(2):293 – 300, 12.

Manson, K. (2020). Fieldworks linguistic explorer (flex) training 2020 (ver 1.1 august 2020). 08.

McCrae, J. P., Bosque-Gil, J., Gracia, J., Buitelaar, P., and Cimiano, P. (2017). The ontolex-lemon model: Development and applications. Brno. Lexical Computing CZ s.r.o.

Nathan, D. (2010). Archives 2.0 for endangered languages: From disk space to myspace. *International Journal of Humanities and Arts Computing*, 4:111–124, 10.

Perlin, R. (2012). Wesay, a tool for collaborating on dictionaries with non-linguists. *Language Documentation & Conservation*, 6:181 – 186, 12.

Robinson, S., Aumann, G., and Bird, S. (2007). Managing fieldwork data with toolbox and the natural language toolkit. *Language Documentation and Conservation*, 1, 06.

Samarin, W. (1967). *Field Linguistics. A guide to Linguistic Field Work.* Holt, Rinehart and Winston., New York, NY.

Simons, G. and Bird, S. (2003). The open language archives community: An infrastructure for distributed archiving of language resources. *Computing Research Repository - CORR*, 18:117–128, 06.

Singh, S., Kumar, R., Ratan, S., and Sinha, S. (2022). Demo of the linguistic field data management and analysis system – life.

Stellato, A., Fiorelli, M., Turbati, A., Lorenzetti, T., van Gemert, W., Dechandon, D., Laaboudi-Spoiden, C., Gerencsér, A., Waniart, A., Costetchi, E., and Keizer, J. (2020). Vocbench 3: A collaborative semantic web editor for ontologies, thesauri and lexicons. *Semantic Web*, 11:1–27, 05.

Vries, N., Davel, M., Badenhorst, J., Basson, W., Barnard, E., and de Waal, A. (2014). A smartphone-based asr data collection tool for under-resourced languages. *Speech Communication*, 56:119–131, 01.

Proceedings of the EURALI Workshop @LREC2020, pages 95–104
Marseille, 20 June 2022

Universal Dependencies Treebank for Tatar: Incorporating Intra-Word Code-Switching Information

Chihiro Taguchi, Sei Iwata, Taro Watanabe
Nara Institute of Science and Technology
Ikoma, Nara, Japan
{taguchi.chihiro.td0, iwata.sei.is6, taro}@is.naist.jp

Abstract

This paper introduces a new Universal Dependencies treebank for the Tatar language named NMCTT. A significant feature of the corpus is that it includes code-switching (CS) information at a morpheme level, given the fact that Tatar texts contain intra-word CS between Tatar and Russian. We first outline NMCTT with a focus on differences from other treebanks of Turkic languages. Then, to evaluate the merit of the CS annotation, this study concisely reports the results of a language identification task implemented with Conditional Random Fields that considers POS tag information, which is readily available in treebanks in the CoNLL-U format. Experimenting on NMCTT and the Turkish-German CS treebank (SAGT), we demonstrate that the proposed annotation scheme introduced in NMCTT can improve the performance of the subword-level language identification. This annotation scheme for CS is not only universally applicable to languages with CS, but also shows a possibility to employ morphosyntactic information for CS-related downstream tasks.

Keywords: Tatar, treebank, Universal Dependencies, code-switching, low-resource languages, language identification

1. Introduction

Globalization and the digital revolution affect the world's languages in a two-fold manner. On one side, except for a handful of languages with a prominent international status, no languages are immune to the multilingualism, diglossia, and language shift to a majority language. In such a linguistic community, it is common to find these languages mixed within a single discourse. This linguistic phenomenon is called code-switching (CS). On the other hand, the information society enables us to access data of low-resource languages more easily. This situation coincides with the recent trend of multilingual and low-resource natural language processing (NLP) and their applications. Universal Dependencies (UD) (Nivre et al., 2020) is one of such projects that aims to create multilingual annotated corpora with universal rules and labels.

Following this momentum, this paper provides two main contributions: (1) it introduces the NAIST Multilingual Corpus Tatar (NMCTT[1]), and (2) validates the benefits of NMCTT's CS segmentation annotation. NMCTT is the first annotated corpus for the Tatar language. The innovative characteristic of the corpus is that language code information is explicitly annotated for each word, and CS segments and corresponding language codes are added if CS occurs within a word, which we call intra-word CS in this paper. For the evaluation of the usefulness of incorporating intra-word CS in UD, we conduct simple experiments of character-level tagging for both span prediction and language identification on Tatar–Russian and Turkish–German data. Leveraging the part-of-speech (POS) tag information which is readily available in the CoNLL-U format, we show that combining UD's linguistic information and CS annotation has the potential to improve the performance of segment-level language classification. In doing so, we encourage the annotation of language tags in treebanks of languages with CS.

[1]TT is from `tt`, the ISO 639-1 language code for Tatar.

1.1. Tatar: Linguistic Background

The Tatar language, a language categorized in the Kipchak (Northwestern) language group of the Turkic language family, is chiefly spoken in the Republic of Tatarstan, Russia. Kazakh, Kyrgyz, and Bashkir are other notable languages that fall into the same language group. Tatar is reported to have more than 5 million speakers (Eberhard et al., 2021), most of which are bilingual with Russian. However, the bilingualism is asymmetric; that is, while the Tatars communicate in Tatar and Russian, the Russians typically speak only in Russian (Safina, 2020). This asymmetry leads to frequent CS with, and gradual language shift to, Russian, leaving Tatar less resourced.

The canonical word order of Tatar is Subject-Object-Verb, and adjectival modifiers precede the modified nouns, i.e., head-final. It is a typical agglutinative language, and nominal case and verbal inflection are marked by suffixes.

Most modern Tatar texts are written in the Cyrillic script with some extensions to express phonemes unique to Tatar. The language can also be written in the Latin script, and the Latin orthography is mainly used among diaspora communities in Turkey and Finland. The linguistic examples from Tatar in this paper employ the Latin alphabet for convenience.

<table>
<tr><th>ID</th><th>FORM</th><th>LEMMA</th><th>UPOS</th><th>FEATS</th><th>HEAD</th><th>DEPREL</th><th>MISC</th></tr>
<tr><td>1</td><td>Татарстанда</td><td>Татарстан</td><td>PROPN</td><td>Case=Loc|Number=Sing</td><td>5</td><td>obl</td><td>LangID=TT</td></tr>
<tr><td>2</td><td>коронавирустан</td><td>коронавирус</td><td>NOUN</td><td>Case=Abl|Number=Sing</td><td>4</td><td>nmod</td><td>CSPoint=коронавирус§тан|LangID=MIXED[RU§TT]</td></tr>
<tr><td>3</td><td>беренче</td><td>беренче</td><td>ADJ</td><td>_</td><td>4</td><td>amod</td><td>LangID=TT</td></tr>
<tr><td>4</td><td>прививканы</td><td>прививка</td><td>NOUN</td><td>Case=Acc|Number=Sing</td><td>5</td><td>obj</td><td>CSPoint=прививка§ны|LangID=MIXED[RU§TT]</td></tr>
<tr><td>5</td><td>ясатырга</td><td>яса</td><td>VERB</td><td>VerbForm=Inf|Voice=Cau</td><td>0</td><td>root</td><td>LangID=TT</td></tr>
<tr><td>6</td><td>мөмкин</td><td>мөмкин</td><td>AUX</td><td>_</td><td>5</td><td>aux</td><td>LangID=TT|SpaceAfter=No</td></tr>
<tr><td>7</td><td>.</td><td>.</td><td>PUNCT</td><td>_</td><td>5</td><td>punct</td><td>LangID=OTHER</td></tr>
</table>

Table 1: An example of annotation with CS information. Note that the optional columns XPOS and DEPS are omitted as they are left blank in NMCTT. The free translation of the original sentence is "The first dose for coronavirus will be available in Tatarstan."

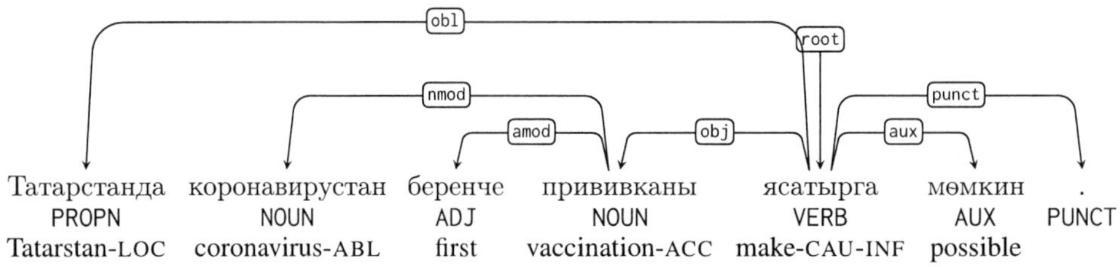

Figure 1: Dependency tree of Table 1 with morphological information.

1.2. Intra-Word Code-Switching

CS is broadly defined as "the alternative use by bilinguals of two or more languages in the same conversation" (Alvanoudi, 2017). When a minority language's morphology more or less has grammatical declension and inflection, CS can occur inside a word. Although intra-word CS is commonly found in minority language varieties, it is not easy to collect their text data, because intra-word CS is often a colloquial phenomenon and is not written down. The word in (1) is an example of intra-word CS in Tatar.[2] The noun *privivka* is a Russian word meaning "vaccination", and it takes an accusative case-marking suffix *-nı*.

(1) *privivka -nı*
RU -TT
vaccination-ACC

One may well see this sort of CS as mere loanwords, but in NMCTT we categorize them as a subset of CS for the following three reasons. First, these Russian words mixed in Tatar are typically pronounced with the Russian phonology (Burbiel, 2018), whereas loanwords are more or less incorporated in the phonology of the receiving language (Kang, 2011). Second, the use of Russian words depends on the speaker's preference and knowledge of and attitude toward the two languages as well as on other social factors (Burbiel, 2018). This tendency conforms with the characteristics of CS, which constitutes "a contact-induced speech behavior that occurs extensively in the talk of bilinguals" in contrast to borrowing that constitutes "a completed contact-induced change" (Alvanoudi, 2017). Third, handling these words as CS has benefits in other applications of text processing such as a transliteration task. Tatar and Russian are transliterated into Latin characters differently. For this reason, it is practically more convenient to annotate them as Russian that is code-switched from Tatar rather than as loanwords integrated in Tatar. Therefore, this study treats them as (intra-word) CS.

[2]Following the convention of linguistics, the text is transliterated into Latin Tatar.

2. Related Work

Code-switching and language resources. Recent spotlight on CS has brought several annotated corpora of various CS language pairs. SEAME (Lyu et al., 2010) and the Mandarin–English code-switching corpus (Li et al., 2012) are some of the first CS resources for computational linguistics.

UD Turkish-German SAGT (Çetinoğlu, 2016) is another treebank that handles CS texts and explicitly annotates a language tag and CS segmentation. UD Hindi-English HIENCS (Bhat et al., 2018) is a corpus of tweets involving Hindi-English CS, but CS occurs on the word level (i.e., not within a word). Tagalog is also a language known to have CS with English especially in its colloquial variety, but the two Tagalog treebanks available on UD, TRG (Samson et al., 2020) and Ugnayan (Aquino, 2020), do not contain any explicit annotation marking CS.

There are several language resources of Tatar, such as the Corpus of Written Tatar (Saykhunov et al., 2021) with ∼356 million tokens and the Tatar National Corpus (Suleimanov et al., 2013) with ∼180 million tokens. Although these corpora contain POS and morphological information linked with the text, it is automatically generated through a rule-based tagging. Therefore, at the time of writing, there is no manually annotated treebank of Tatar, let alone on UD.

Available Turkic UD treebanks. From the Turkic language family excluding Tatar and high-resource

Turkish, the present UD v2.9 contains Kazakh KTB (Makazhanov et al., 2015; Tyers and Washington, 2015) with 10,383 tokens, Old Turkish Tonqq (Derin and Harada, 2021) with 221 tokens, Uyghur UDT (Eli et al., 2016) with 40,236 tokens, and Yakut YKTDT (Merzhevich and Gerardi, 2021) with 271 tokens. Except for Turkish UD treebanks that contain 733K tokens in total, Turkic languages in UD are overall low-resourced.

Colloquial Kazakh also has CS similar to Tatar, but the Kazakh KTB treebank is based on formal written texts that do not contain CS, and therefore does not consider language tagging.

Language processing for CS. Though not much work has been done on computational approaches to CS relative to how common CS is in the world, one of the earliest studies on the topic is Joshi (1982) which investigated CS between Marathi and English. Early work on identifying segmental points where languages are switched is Solorio and Liu (2008), where the model was trained to learn to predict natural CS points. Anastasopoulos et al. (2018) conducted research on a POS tagging task for Griko, a language with token-level CS to Italian. Exploiting additional grammatical information for a tagging task is discussed in Silfverberg et al. (2014).

More recent work includes intra-word CS where language codes may switch at a morpheme level, particularly found in morphologically rich languages. Intra-word CS language identification by Mager et al. (2019) employs Segmentation Recurrent Neural Network (SegRNN) (Lu et al., 2016) to test on CS texts in the language pairs of German–Turkish and Spanish–Wixarika, a Uto-Aztecan language indigenous to Mexico. Sabty et al. (2021) also uses SegRNN for the language identification task of Arabic–English CS texts. Taguchi et al. (2021) is a work on transliteration from Cyrillic Tatar to Latin Tatar combining subword-level language identification; however, the subword tokenization is fully done by Byte-Pair Encoding (BPE).

3. Overview of the Tatar Universal Dependencies

This section outlines the feature of NMCTT with an emphasis on the comparison with other treebanks of Turkic languages. The policies of the annotation by and large follow the guideline proposed in Tyers et al. (2017). An exemplary annotation is shown in Figure 1 as well as its dependency tree in Figure 1.

3.1. Text

The raw text is obtained from the Tatar language version of Tatar-Inform,[3] an online news media actively posting articles in Tatar and Russian.

Note that, upon the use of the news text, it is necessary to attach a hyperlink to the original news article, as stipulated in the Russian federal law. In the treebank, the source link of each sentence is explicitly shown in the metadata row starting from `# link =`.

3.2. Tokenization and Word Segmentation

We obtained tokens by splitting at spaces and punctuation. UD Turkish-German SAGT employs a slightly more fine-grained approach to tokenizing sentences. For example, the Turkish locative adjectivizer suffix -*ki* is attached to the preceding element directly in the Turkish orthography, and SAGT further tokenizes them as different tokens. An example of the usage of *-ki* and the corresponding morpheme in Tatar *-ğı/ge* (*-qı/ke*) are illustrated in phrases (2) and (3).[4] The contrast is apparent in Tables 2 and 3. While NMCTT treats *Berlin-da-ğı* ("in Berlin") as one token, SAGT detaches *-ki* of *Berlin'-de-ki* and treats *ki* as an adposition.

(2) *Berlin'-de-ki* *ev* (Turkish)
Berlin-LOC-ADJVZ house
"A house in Berlin"

(3) *Berlin-da-ğı* *öy* (Tatar)
Berlin-LOC-ADJVZ house
"A house in Berlin"

ID	FORM	LEMMA	UPOS
1-2	Berlin'deki	_	_
1	Berlin'de	Berlin	PROPN
2	ki	ki	ADP

Table 2: Tokenization and tags in SAGT.

ID	FORM	LEMMA	UPOS
1	Берлиндагы	Берлин	PROPN

Table 3: Tokenization and tags in NMCTT (transliterated).

The first motivation to tokenize text simply by spaces and punctuation is that it will ensure more accurate automatic tokenization than splitting inside a word. The second motivation, at least in Tatar, is that the morpheme *-ğı/ge* (*-qı/ke*) corresponding to Turkish *-ki* is often treated as a derivational suffix to form a relational adjective (Burbiel, 2018) rather than an independent word or a clitic. Therefore, it is unnatural to tokenize it as a separate word that bears a POS tag.

3.3. Parts-of-speech

The statistics of the Universal POS (UPOS) tags are summarized in Table 4. Of all the UPOS tags, INTJ (interjection), PART (particle), SYM (symbol), and X (other)

[3] https://tatar-inform.tatar.

[4] See Appendix for glossing abbreviations. Note that *-ki* in Turkish and *-ğı/ge* (*-qı/ke*) in Tatar have several morphosyntactic properties, and ADJVZ "adjectivizer suffix" is a tentative glossing that by and large covers their properties.

Class	UPOS	Total	Russian	Mixed
Open	NOUN	413	21	62
	PROPN	79	34	8
	VERB	169	0	1
	ADJ	117	8	0
Closed	AUX	18	0	0
	DET	9	0	0
	ADV	40	0	0
	SCONJ	8	0	0
	ADP	35	0	0
	CCONJ	26	0	0
	PRON	26	0	0
	NUM	12	0	0
Other	PUNCT	167	0	0

Table 4: The distribution of UPOS tags in the treebank with respect to language code. The first column specifies whether the UPOS tag is an open class or a closed class.

do not appear in the present NMCTT. The use of PART is explicitly avoided as the UD guideline notes that "the PART tag should be used restrictively and only when no other tag is possible".[5] Other unattested UPOS tags might appear in additional texts in the future. Table 4 also demonstrates the disproportional distribution of CS in each POS tag. While open class words, such as NOUN and PROPN, contain several cases of CS to Russian, closed class words only appear in Tatar. This sort of distributional tendency of CS has often been empirically reported such as in Joshi (1982). We will return to this point in Section 4.

3.4. Morphology

The morphological features (e.g., in the FEATS column in Figure 1) in NMCTT are designed to be correspondent with morphological inflection as uniquely as possible. An example that reflects this policy well is the treatment of converbs. A converb is a non-finite verb form whose main function is to mark adverbial subordination (Haspelmath, 1995). In UD, converb is loosely defined as "a non-finite verb form that shares properties of verbs and adverbs."[6] Turkic languages are commonly known to have several converbs (Johanson, 2021). In Tatar, for instance, boldfaced converbs in sentences (4)–(7) are contrasted in the aspect. The suffix -(*ï/e*)p exemplified in (4) is a generic kind of converb used to denote consecutive or simultaneous actions and states. The suffix *-a/ä* (*-ïy/i*) in (5) composes a converb of simultaneous action or state. (6) shows a case of converb suffix *-ğaç/gäç* that means the action precedes the action expressed by the main predicate. The fourth suffix *-ğançı/-gänçe*, in contrast, expresses an action or state that happens after the event of the main predicate. To distinguish these functionally different converbs, NMCTT is designed to have different morphological annotations in the FEATS column for each of these converb suffixes.

(4) *ul* ***aşa-p*** *utır-a.*
he eat-CVB sit-PRS.3
"S/he is sitting and eating." (manner)
VerbForm=Conv

(5) ***aşı-y*** ***aşı-y*** *öy-gä* *qayt-tı.*
eat-CVB.PROG = house-DAT return-PST.3
"(S/he) went home while eating." (simultaneity)
Aspect=Prog|VerbForm=Conv

(6) ***aşa-ğaç*** *öy-gä* *qayt-tı.*
eat-CVB.PF house-DAT return-PST.3
"(S/he) went home after eating." (prior event)
Aspect=Perf|VerbForm=Conv

(7) ***tuy-ğançı*** *aşa-dı.*
become.full-CVB.IMPF eat-PST.3
"He ate till he became full." (posterior event)
Aspect=Imp|VerbForm=Conv

The annotation of converbs differs to a great extent among the treebanks of the Turkic languages, in particular of Turkish, as shown in Table 5. The treebank that shares the similar spirit to ours is Uyghur UDT (Eli et al., 2016).

3.5. Syntactic Dependency

Syntactic trees often differ in shape and branching among modern linguistic theories. However, following the gist of UD that pursues the unified format and rules for describing dependency, we tried to avoid innovative usage of dependency tags in NMCTT, and conformed to the guidelines for Turkic languages proposed by Tyers et al. (2017) as well as conventions in other existing UD treebanks.[7]

3.5.1. Nominal Arguments: nsubj, obj, obl

In UD, there are three grammatical relations of nominal arguments to a predicate: nsubj for a nominal subject, obj for a direct object, and obl for other non-core arguments. These notions are compatible with Lexical Functional Grammar (LFG) (Dalrymple, 2001).

For example, non-core arguments in sentence (8) are parsed with obl dependency relation as in Figure 2.

(8) *bala uram-da at-qa alma bir-ä*
child street-LOC horse-DAT apple give-PRS.3
"A child gives an apple to the horse on the street."

[5] https://universaldependencies.org/u/pos/PART.html

[6] https://universaldependencies.org/u/feat/VerbForm.html

[7] The detailed list of tags used in NMCTT and their statistics are summarized on the UD website: https://universaldependencies.org/treebanks/tt_nmctt/index.html.

Language	Treebank	POS	VerbForm=Conv	Conv distinction
Tatar	NMCTT	VERB	correct	yes
Turkish	FrameNet	ADV	NA	no
	GB	VERB	correct	no
	Kenet	ADV	incorrect	no
	Penn	ADV	incorrect	no
	Tourism	ADV	incorrect	no
	Atis	ADV	incorrect	no
	BOUN	VERB	incorrect	yes
	PUD	ADV	incorrect	yes
	IMST	VERB	correct	no
Turkish German	SAGT	VERB	correct	no
Kazakh	KTB	VERB	correct	yes
Uyghur	UDT	VERB	correct	yes

Table 5: Comparison of the annotation for converbs in Turkic treebanks. The values in the column "VerbForm=Conv" summarizes whether the corpus annotates converbs as VerbForm=Conv correctly; if the feature is not used at all, the value is NA. The column "Conv distinction" shows whether functionally different converbs are distinguished in morphological features. Yakut and Old Turkish are not included because the converb is not attested or left unannotated in the corpora.

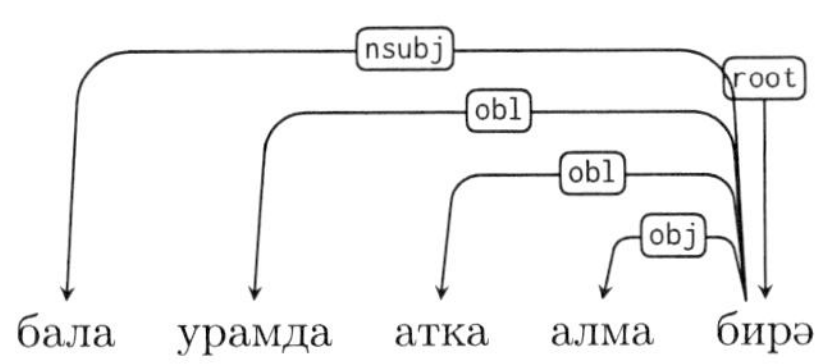

Figure 2: Dependency parsing of (8).

3.5.2. Copula: cop

Though nominal predication does not require a copula in the present tense in Tatar, it employs an overt copula in the past and future tenses. In UD, it is conventional to treat a predicate noun as a head of a copula unlike approaches of generative syntax that often puts a copula higher than the predicate noun. In this respect, too, UD shares the formalism in common with LFG.

(9) *min student ide-m*
I student COP.PST-1SG
"I was a student"

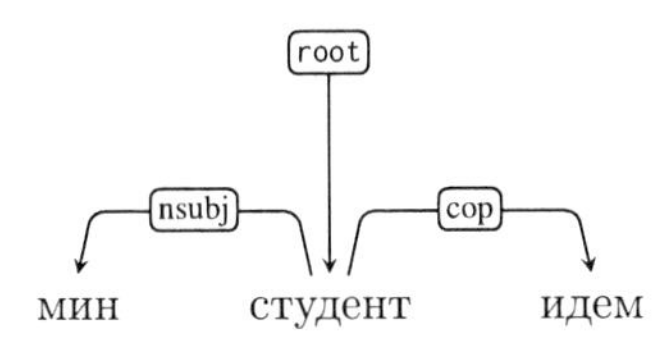

Figure 3: Dependency parsing of (9).

3.5.3. Light Verb Construction: compound:lvc

A light verb is a verb that has little meaning by itself but forms a complex predicate with a noun which serves as the semantic content. This complex predicate construction is labeled as compound:lvc in UD's dependency annotation. In light verb constructions, the verb is conventionally treated as the head of the noun in UD. In Tatar, there are a number of light verb constructions, typically with a light verb *it-*, as exemplified in sentence (10). The corresponding dependency is illustrated in Figure 4.

(10) *däres däwam it-te*
class continuation do-PST.3
"The class continued"

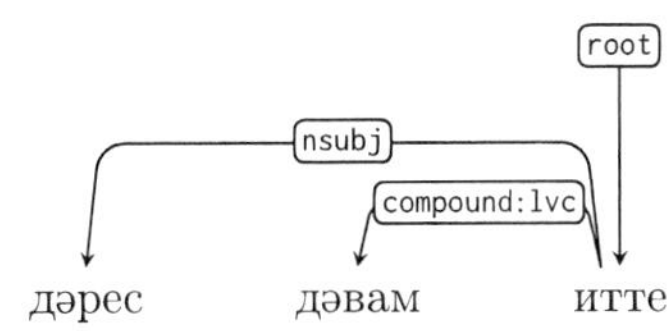

Figure 4: Dependency parsing of (10).

3.5.4. Grammaticalized Auxiliaries: aux

In Tatar, certain verbs following a converb are grammaticalized to lose their original lexical meaning and gain a new functional role. As shown in the example (11), the finite verb *çıq-* no longer retains its generic meaning of going out, but denotes aspectual semantics that implies the completion of the action expressed by the preceding converb. In such a case, the dependency relation between the converb and the finite verb is marked as aux (auxiliary), where the head is the converb. Therefore, the dependency tree of sentence (11) should be as in Figure 5.

(11) *ul kitap-nı uqı-p çıq-tı*
he book-ACC read-CVB go.out-PST.3
"he read the book (finished reading the whole)"

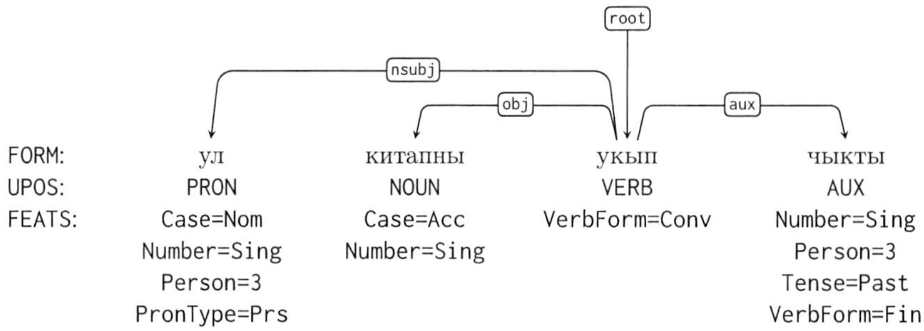

Figure 5: Dependency parsing of (11).

Note that the canonical usage of converbs described in Section 3.4 is represented by the dependency relation `advcl` (adverbial clause). In this case, the converb is the dependent of the main inflected verb, as illustrated in sentence (12) and its dependency tree in Figure 6.

(12) *ul kitap-nı uqı-p yoqla-dı*
he book-ACC read-CVB sleep-PST.3
"He read the book and slept."

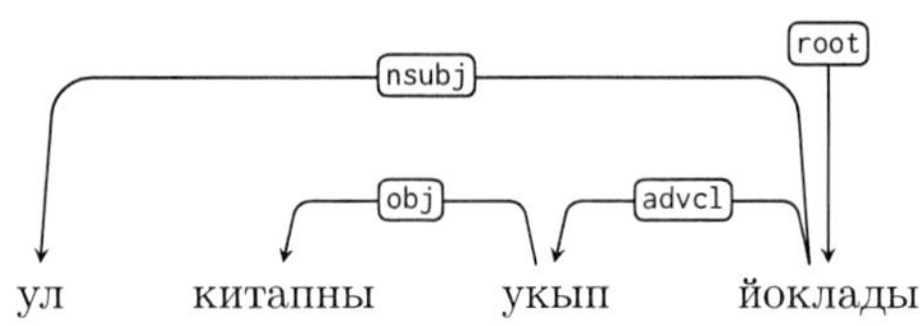

Figure 6: Dependency parsing of (12).

3.6. Language Tags (LangID=)

The most innovative characteristic of NMCTT is that it explicitly annotates language tags at a segment level for each token in the `MISC` column of the CoNLL-U format table. The idea of incorporating CS information into UD has already been carried out in UD Hindi-English HIENCS (Bhat et al., 2018) and UD Turkish-German SAGT (Çetinoğlu, 2016). However, HIENCS does not consider intra-word CS, and SAGT simply tags the intra-word CS with the `MIXED` tag, agnostic of what language codes are inside the token. UD Komi-Zyrian Lattice (Partanen et al., 2018), a UD treebank of another minority language of Russia, also explicitly annotates Russian words by specifying as `OrigLang=ru`, but their CS segments are unclear. NMCTT differs from these corpora by tagging each intra-word CS segment with a language code, allowing for more flexibility and expressiveness in the language tagging.
An example of segment-level language tagging in NMCTT is shown in (13). Following SAGT, the segmentation point is marked by the character § in the element starting with `CSPoint=`. The breakdown of the mixed languages is described in the brackets after `MIXED`. The same character § is used to show the segments where the languages are switched, which

Language	Count
Tatar (TT)	819
Russian (RU)	63
Mixed (MIXED)	71
Other (OTHER)	166

Table 6: Distribution of language tags in NMCTT for each token.

corresponds to the segment described in `CSPoint=`. Гыйбәтдинов (*translit.* *Ğibätdinov*) is a Tatar male surname that consists of a Tatar-origin morpheme *Ğibätdin* and a Russian-origin suffix *-ov* that derives a Russified surname from a non-Russian surname ending with a consonant. In the example, a dative case suffix *-qa*, a Tatar morpheme, is added.

(13) `CSPoint=Гыйбәтдин§ов§ка`
`LangID=MIXED[TT§RU§TT]`
"To Gibatdinov"

The criteria for determining if a segment is considered CS or is a loanword are outlined in Section 1.2. For example, the Tatar word *mömkin* etymologically comes from Arabic مُمْكِن (*mumkin*), but the word is fossilized in the Tatar vocabulary and also is pronounced in accordance with the Tatar phonological paradigm, and thus it is classified as a loanword and not a CS word.
The statistics of tokens for each language ID in NMCTT is summarized in Table 6. Note that NMCTT does not use the language label `LANG3` used in SAGT.

4. Experiment: Language Identification and Segmentation

To evaluate the usefulness of the proposed CS annotation, we implement a simple character-level tagger that jointly predicts language tags and span boundaries taking into account the corresponding POS tag. We test it not only on the UD Tatar treebank but also on UD Turkish-German SAGT (Çetinoğlu, 2016).
The Tatar training and test data contain 888 and 231 tokens, respectively. For the Turkish-German dataset, the training data contains 10,005 tokens; we concatenated the dev and test files to use them as the test data, comprising 26,929 tokens. Since the dataset of NMCTT is

too small to demonstrate the effects of POS tags statistically, we employ SAGT to verify the results.

Note that the objective of this experiment is to verify the effects of adding POS features in an explainable manner, and not to pursue the state-of-the-art performance of language identification and span prediction.

4.1. Task Description

The architecture of the span prediction and language classification task is as follows. Given an input word x that consists of characters $\langle c_1, \cdots, c_{|x|}\rangle$, our objective is to correctly predict a pair of a language tag y_l{L1, L2, other} and a span tag $y_s \in$ {B, I, E, S} for each character. (L1, L2) are the CS language pair, i.e., (Tatar, Russian) or (Turkish, German), and tokens in other languages or punctuation fall in to "other". B, I, E denote the beginning, intermediate, and ending position of a segment respectively, and S a single-character segment. Prediction $\hat{y}$ is taken to be correct only if it matches both the corresponding language tag y_l and span tag y_s. Therefore, there are 12 possible labels to be predicted in the task.

To keep the labels consistent in tests on both NMCTT and SAGT, label `LangID=LANG3` used in SAGT (a third language that is neither Turkish nor German) is converted to "other" during the data formatting.

4.2. Language–Span Tagging with Conditional Random Fields

The tagger is modeled with Conditional Random Fields (CRFs) (Lafferty et al., 2001). To predict correct labels $\boldsymbol{y}$ given a sequence of input x, the CRF model is defined as

$$p(\boldsymbol{y}|\boldsymbol{x}) = \frac{1}{Z(\boldsymbol{x})} \exp\left\{\sum_{k=1}^{K} \lambda_k f_k(y_t, y_{t-1}, \boldsymbol{x}_t)\right\},$$

where $Z(\boldsymbol{x}) = \sum_{\boldsymbol{y}} \exp\left\{\sum_{k=1}^{K} \lambda_k f_k(y_t, y_{t-1}, \boldsymbol{x}_t)\right\}$ is a normalization function to ensure the sum of p is 1, λ_k is a parameter vector, and $\{f_k\}_{k=1}^{K}$ is a set of feature functions. The feature function f takes into account bigram features (transition) and unigram features (observation/emission) by applying a function $\mathbf{1}_{\{q\}}$ that returns 1 when the desired condition q is met, namely:

$$\mathbf{1}_{\{q\}} = \begin{cases} 1 & \text{if } q \text{ is true} \\ 0 & \text{otherwise.} \end{cases}$$

K is the total number of features after combining transition features $f_{ij}(y, y', x) = \mathbf{1}_{\{y=i\}}\mathbf{1}_{\{y'=j\}}$ for each transition (i, j) and observation features $f_{io}(y, y', x) = \mathbf{1}_{\{y=i\}}\mathbf{1}_{\{x=o\}}$ for each state-observation pair (i, o); namely,

$$\begin{aligned}
&\sum_{k=1}^{K} \lambda_k f_k(y_t, y_{t-1}, \boldsymbol{x}_t) \\
&= \sum_{t} \left\{ \sum_{i,j} \lambda_{ij} f_{ij}(y_t, y_{t-1}, \boldsymbol{x}_t) \right. \\
&\qquad \left. + \sum_{i,o} \lambda_{io} f_{io}(y_t, y_{t-1}, \boldsymbol{x}_t) \right\}.
\end{aligned}$$

One of the architectural strengths of CRFs is that we can specify features that we want to include in the feature extraction function. The list of employed features used as the default in the experiment their example values are illustrated in Table 7. For example, assuming that we are looking at the first character "M" of the word "Mars", the extracted features will look like the right column of the table. We used trigram features to take neighboring characters into account as observation features. In doing so, it is possible to approximately model meaningful morphological units such as affixes. In addition, character features such as letter case, digit, and punctuation play a significant role in predicting correct language and span tags. Though the task is done at the character level, it is also possible to include word-level information such as the word form, word length, and its POS tag as a part of the observation features. In the ablation studies to confirm the efficacy of adding POS tag information, the POS and Word features (the last two rows in Table 7) are to be omitted.

An intuitive motivation to include POS tag in the features rather than morphology (`FEAT`) and dependency (`DEPREL`) comes from the following two points. First, since the number of POS tags is limited compared to other grammatical features such as dependency and morphology, we can assume that the effect of POS tags is straightforward and is easier to interpret. Second, intuitively, the distribution of tokens that undergo CS, at least in Tatar, seems to depend on POS tags as illustrated in Table 4.

For the training step, we chose limited-memory BFGS (Liu and Nocedal, 1989) as the parameter optimization algorithm, and set the L1 and L2 regularization parameters to 0.25 and 0.3, respectively, and the max iteration to 100. The evaluation is based on precision, recall, and F1 scores, considering the fact that the class distribution is imbalanced as seen in Table 6.

The architecture for the experiment is implemented on `sklearn-crfsuite`,[8] a wrapper library of CRFsuite (Okazaki, 2007) made to be compatible with `scikit-learn`.

4.3. Results and Discussion

Tables 8 and 9 show the results with ablation studies of the experiment. Note that all values are weighted average scores, and the F1 scores are not derived directly

[8] `https://sklearn-crfsuite.readthedocs.io`

Feature	Example value
Character	"M"
Character +1	"a"
Character +2	"r"
Character -1	False
Character -2	False
Word-initial?	True
Word-final?	False
Word in titlecase?	True
Character in uppercase?	True
Punctuation?	False
Number?	False
Word length	4
POS	"PROPN"
Word	"Mars"

Table 7: An example of a feature table for the character "M" in "Mars".

Features	Precision	Recall	F1
Default	**90.9**	**90.0**	**88.9**
[-POS]	87.3	86.5	84.3
[-word]	86.4	86.5	84.9
[-POS, -word]	86.7	87.0	85.7

Table 8: Ablation study of features on NMCTT. Scores are calculated at a character level.

from the precision and recall scores in the tables. In both NMCTT and SAGT, the default architecture with both POS and word form information resulted in the highest values of precision, recall, and F1. Also, compared to the model without the POS feature, we can see that the model with the default feature set performs better. However, it is notable that, though we expect models with POS features to be more accurate than ones without POS, the [-word] model in NMCTT turned out to work better than the [-POS, -word] model. This may partially come from the scarcity of the available data in NMCTT, as the scores are more susceptible to one error. We aim to enhance the data size of the NMCTT treebank in future releases.

These results imply that leveraging additional grammatical information available in UD potentially improves the performance of the segmentation and language classification task for both high- and low-resource languages. Although the experiment did not involve other features that can be extracted from UD's CoNLL-U format data, UD's flexibility also allows them to be incorporated in the features. This perspective is worth investigating further in future work. In addition, the results also conform with the observation in Table 4 in the previous section that the distribution of CS tokens is related to that of POS tags.

5. Concluding Remarks

This study reported NMCTT's contribution to UD and discussed the treebank from two aspects. First, we out-

Features	Precision	Recall	F1
Default	**95.9**	**96.1**	**95.9**
[-POS]	95.9	95.8	95.6
[-word]	94.6	94.7	94.6
[-POS, -word]	93.7	93.9	93.8

Table 9: Ablation study of features on SAGT. Scores are calculated at a character level.

lined the new treebank focusing on the cross-linguistic validity with the comparison to other Turkic UD treebanks. One of its important contributions is that it proposed a way to annotate language labels at the CS segment level. Given the prevalence of CS, especially between low-resource languages and more prominent languages spoken in the same region, the proposed annotation scheme can be further applied to other CS languages. Second, to evaluate quantitatively the benefits of adding CS information at a morpheme level to the UD annotation, we experimented the joint task of CS segmentation and language identification on NMCTT and SAGT using a simple CRF architecture. The results showed that POS tag information is likely to be meaningful to intra-word language classification. This also implies that combining other linguistic information available on UD-format treebanks may contribute to the improvement in performance of downstream tasks related to CS.

NMCTT is still small in the UD v2.9 release; therefore, it is necessary to enlarge the data for more reliable and flexible applications. In addition, the evaluation was experimented solely on two corpora due to the limited quantities of available linguistic data. More active corpus building for low-resource CS languages will enable more investigation into the (non-)universality of this paper's finding.

6. Acknowledgments

The Tatar NMCTT Treebank is an outcome of the CICP NAIST Multilingual Corpus Project supported by the Nara Institute of Science and Technology. We thank Dr. Özlem Çetinoğlu for providing insightful advice for the annotation of code-switching texts. We are also grateful to Arturo and Justin from the NAIST NLP laboratory for proofreading and to the anonymous reviewers of LREC2022 for helpful suggestions and comments.

Appendix: Glossing Abbreviations

1, 2, 3 — first, second, third person; **ABL** — ablative; **ACC** — accusative; **ADJVZ** — adjectivizer; **CAU** — causative; **COP** — copula; **CVB** — converb; **DAT** — dative; **IMPF** — imperfective; **INF** — infinitive; **LOC** — locative; **PF** — perfective; **PST** — past tense; **PROG** — progressive; **PRS** — present tense; **SG** — singular.

7. Bibliographical References

Alvanoudi, A. (2017). Language contact, borrowing and code switching: a case study of Australian Greek. pages 1–42.

Anastasopoulos, A., Lekakou, M., Quer, J., Zimianiti, E., DeBenedetto, J., and Chiang, D. (2018). Part-of-speech tagging on an endangered language: a parallel Griko-Italian resource. In *Proceedings of the 27th International Conference on Computational Linguistics*, pages 2529–2539, Santa Fe, New Mexico, USA, August. Association for Computational Linguistics.

Aquino, A. (2020). UD Tagalog Ugnayan. `https://github.com/UniversalDependencies/UD_Tagalog-Ugnayan`.

Bhat, I., Bhat, R. A., Shrivastava, M., and Sharma, D. (2018). Universal Dependency parsing for Hindi-English code-switching. In *Proceedings of the 2018 Conference of the North American Chapter of the Association for Computational Linguistics: Human Language Technologies, Volume 1 (Long Papers)*, pages 987–998, New Orleans, Louisiana, June. Association for Computational Linguistics.

Burbiel, G. (2018). *Tatar Grammar: A Grammar of the Contemporary Tatar Literary Language*. Institute for Bible Translation.

Çetinoğlu, Ö. (2016). A Turkish-German code-switching corpus. In *Proceedings of the Tenth International Conference on Language Resources and Evaluation (LREC'16)*, pages 4215–4220, Portorož, Slovenia, May. European Language Resources Association (ELRA).

Dalrymple, M. (2001). *Lexical Functional Grammar*, volume 34 of *Syntax and Semantics*. Brill, Leiden, the Netherlands.

Derin, M. O. and Harada, T. (2021). Universal Dependencies for Old Turkish. In *Proceedings of the Fifth Workshop on Universal Dependencies (UDW, SyntaxFest 2021)*, pages 129–141, Sofia, Bulgaria, December. Association for Computational Linguistics.

Eberhard, D. M., Simons, G. F., and Fennig, C. D. (2021). Ethnologue: Languages of the world.

Eli, M., Mushajiang, W., Yibulayin, T., Abiderexiti, K., and Liu, Y. (2016). Universal dependencies for Uyghur. In *Proceedings of the Third International Workshop on Worldwide Language Service Infrastructure and Second Workshop on Open Infrastructures and Analysis Frameworks for Human Language Technologies (WLSI/OIAF4HLT2016)*, pages 44–50, Osaka, Japan, December. The COLING 2016 Organizing Committee.

Haspelmath, M. (1995). The converb as a cross-linguistically valid category. *Converbs in Cross-linguistic Perspective: Structure and Meaning of Adverbial Verb Forms — Adverbial Pariticples, Gerunds —*, pages 1–55.

Johanson, L. (2021). *Turkic*. Cambridge Language Surveys. Cambridge University Press.

Joshi, A. K. (1982). Processing of sentences with intra-sentential code-switching. In *Coling 1982: Proceedings of the Ninth International Conference on Computational Linguistics*.

Kang, Y. (2011). Loanword phonology. In *The Blackwell Companion to Phonology*, chapter 95, pages 1–25. John Wiley Sons, Ltd.

Lafferty, J. D., McCallum, A., and Pereira, F. C. N. (2001). Conditional random fields: Probabilistic models for segmenting and labeling sequence data. In *Proceedings of the Eighteenth International Conference on Machine Learning*, ICML '01, page 282–289, San Francisco, CA, USA. Morgan Kaufmann Publishers Inc.

Li, Y., Yu, Y., and Fung, P. (2012). A Mandarin-English code-switching corpus. In *Proceedings of the Eighth International Conference on Language Resources and Evaluation (LREC'12)*, pages 2515–2519, Istanbul, Turkey, May. European Language Resources Association (ELRA).

Liu, D. C. and Nocedal, J. (1989). On the limited memory BFGS method for large scale optimization. 45:503–528.

Lu, L., Kong, L., Dyer, C., Smith, N. A., and Renals, S. (2016). Segmental recurrent neural networks for end-to-end speech recognition. *CoRR*, abs/1603.00223.

Lyu, D.-C., Tan, T. P., Siong, C. E., and Li, H. (2010). SEAME: a Mandarin-English code-switching speech corpus in South-East Asia. In *INTERSPEECH*.

Mager, M., Çetinoğlu, Ö., and Kann, K. (2019). Subword-level language identification for intra-word code-switching. In *Proceedings of the 2019 Conference of the North American Chapter of the Association for Computational Linguistics: Human Language Technologies, Volume 1 (Long and Short Papers)*, pages 2005–2011, Minneapolis, Minnesota, June. Association for Computational Linguistics.

Makazhanov, A., Sultangazina, A., Makhambetov, O., and Yessenbayev, Z. (2015). Syntactic annotation of kazakh: Following the universal dependencies guidelines. a report. In *3rd International Conference on Turkic Languages Processing, (TurkLang 2015)*, pages 338–350.

Merzhevich, T. and Gerardi, F. F. (2021). UD Yakut YKTDT. `https://github.com/UniversalDependencies/UD_Yakut-YKTDT`.

Nivre, J., de Marneffe, M.-C., Ginter, F., Hajič, J., Manning, C. D., Pyysalo, S., Schuster, S., Tyers, F., and Zeman, D. (2020). Universal Dependencies v2: An evergrowing multilingual treebank collection. In *Proceedings of the 12th Language Resources and Evaluation Conference*, pages 4034–4043, Marseille, France, May. European Language Resources Association.

Okazaki, N. (2007). CRFsuite: a fast implementation of Conditional Random Fields (CRFs).

Partanen, N., Blokland, R., Lim, K., Poibeau, T., and Rießler, M. (2018). The first Komi-Zyrian Universal Dependencies treebanks. In *Proceedings of the Second Workshop on Universal Dependencies (UDW 2018)*, pages 126–132, Brussels, Belgium, November. Association for Computational Linguistics.

Sabty, C., Mesabah, I., Çetinoğlu, Ö., and Abdennadher, S. (2021). Language identification of intra-word code-switching for Arabic–English. *Array*, 12:100104.

Safina, K. (2020). Bilingualism in the Republic of Tatarstan: language policy and attitudes towards Tatar language education.

Samson, S., Zeman, D., and Tan, M. A. C. (2020). UD Tagalog TRG. `https://github.com/UniversalDependencies/UD_Tagalog-TRG`.

Saykhunov, M. R., Khusainov, R. R., Ibragimov, T. I., Luutonen, J., Salimzyanov, I. F., Shaydullina, G. Y., and Khusainova, A. M. (2021). Corpus of written tatar.

Silfverberg, M., Ruokolainen, T., Lindén, K., and Kurimo, M. (2014). Part-of-speech tagging using Conditional Random Fields: Exploiting sub-label dependencies for improved accuracy. In *Proceedings of the 52nd Annual Meeting of the Association for Computational Linguistics (Volume 2: Short Papers)*, pages 259–264, Baltimore, Maryland, June. Association for Computational Linguistics.

Solorio, T. and Liu, Y. (2008). Learning to predict code-switching points. In *Proceedings of the 2008 Conference on Empirical Methods in Natural Language Processing*, pages 973–981, Honolulu, Hawaii, October. Association for Computational Linguistics.

Suleimanov, D., Nevzorova, O., Gatiatullin, A., Gilmullin, R., and Khakimov, B. (2013). National Corpus of the Tatar Language "Tugan Tel": grammatical annotation and implementation. 95:68–74.

Taguchi, C., Sakai, Y., and Watanabe, T. (2021). Transliteration for low-resource code-switching texts: Building an automatic Cyrillic-to-Latin converter for Tatar. In *Proceedings of the Fifth Workshop on Computational Approaches to Linguistic Code-Switching*, pages 133–140, Online, June. Association for Computational Linguistics.

Tyers, F. M. and Washington, J. N. (2015). Towards a free/open-source Universal-Dependency treebank for Kazakh. In *3rd International Conference on Turkic Languages Processing, (TurkLang 2015)*, pages 276–289.

Tyers, F., Washington, J., Çöltekin, , and Makazhanov, A. (2017). An assessment of Universal Dependency annotation guidelines for Turkic languages. 10.

Proceedings of the EURALI Workshop @LREC2020, pages 105–110
Marseille, 20 June 2022

Preparing an Endangered Language for the Digital Age: The Case of Judeo-Spanish

Alp Öktem[1], Rodolfo Zevallos[1,2], Yasmin Moslem[3], Güneş Öztürk[1], Karen Şarhon[4]
[1]Col·lectivaT, Barcelona, Spain [2]Universitat Pompeu Fabra, Barcelona, Spain
[3]Dublin City University, Dublin, Ireland [4]Sephardic Center of Istanbul, Istanbul, Turkey
alp@collectivat.cat, rodolfojoel.zevallos@upf.edu, yasmin.moslem@adaptcentre.ie
ozgurgunes@collectivat.cat, karensarhon@gmail.com

Abstract

We develop machine translation and speech synthesis systems to complement the efforts of revitalizing Judeo-Spanish, the exiled language of Sephardic Jews, which survived for centuries, but now faces the threat of extinction in the digital age. Building on resources created by the Sephardic community of Turkey and elsewhere, we create corpora and tools that would help preserve this language for future generations. For machine translation, we first develop a Spanish to Judeo-Spanish rule-based machine translation system, in order to generate large volumes of synthetic parallel data in the relevant language pairs: Turkish, English and Spanish. Then, we train baseline neural machine translation engines using this synthetic data and authentic parallel data created from translations by the Sephardic community. For text-to-speech synthesis, we present a 3.5 hour single speaker speech corpus for building a neural speech synthesis engine. Resources, model weights and online inference engines are shared publicly.

Keywords: Extremely low-resource language, Machine Translation, Data-augmentation, Text-to-Speech, Judeo-Spanish

1. Introduction

In this paper, we present our ongoing language technology-related efforts for preparing Judeo-Spanish to the digital age. We embark upon creating open language corpora and tools that would serve for language documentation, assisting language learners and development of advanced applications. We focus on two main tools, machine translation (MT) and text-to-speech synthesis (TTS). In our extremely low-resource setup, we get use of Judeo-Spanish's proximity to Spanish by using transfer learning methodologies. For MT, we build a rule-based machine translation engine that allows us to convert Spanish text to Judeo-Spanish. Using this system, we create large synthetic pre-training data from publicly available English, Turkish and Spanish parallel corpora and train neural machine translation systems. For TTS, we do transfer learning from pre-trained Spanish and English engines using a small single-speaker speech corpus. During the development of these tools, we have packaged various types of raw resources into training-ready language data and models and shared them in our project's data portal *Ladino Data Hub*[1]. The complete list of output of this work can be presented as follows:

1. A monolingual news corpus,
2. Authentic and synthetic parallel corpora in English, Spanish and Turkish paired with Judeo-Spanish,
3. A Spanish to Judeo-Spanish rule-based machine translation system,
4. Neural machine translation models between Judeo-Spanish and English, Spanish and Turkish,
5. A 3.5 hour single speaker speech corpus,
6. Neural network-based speech synthesis model,
7. Web application for MT and TTS[2].

2. Background

Judeo-Spanish, also referred to as Ladino or Judezmo (ISO 639-3 *lad*), is a descendant of old Castilian Spanish from the 15th century (Sefardiweb del CSIC, 2022). It is the historical and predominant language of the Sephardic Jews, who were expelled from their homes by the Spanish Inquisition (1492) and welcomed into the Ottoman Empire, where they retained the language, as well as France, Italy, the Netherlands, Morocco and England, where they shifted to the dominant language. It has traces of numerous Iberian languages of the 15th century like Old Aragonese, Astur-Leonese, Old Catalan, Galician-Portuguese and Mozarabic with Castilian Spanish forming its basis vocabulary (Minervini, 2006). After 530 years, Judeo-Spanish still survives as a language of Ottoman Sephardic Jews in more than 30 countries, with most speakers residing in Israel. Although it has survived and evolved over the centuries, it is currently classified as a severely endangered language by UNESCO (Moseley, 2010).

The digital age has a direct effect on endangered languages like Judeo-Spanish. There is currently a growing digital divide between languages with sufficient resources and languages with fewer resources, further

[1]`http://data.sefarad.com.tr`

[2]`http://translate.sefarad.com.tr`

exacerbating the danger of digital extinction for them (Kornai, 2013). For the dominant languages the process of generating artificial intelligence tools is much easier due to their large web-presence. However, many marginalized languages do not have sufficient material and human resources to power the creation of such tools. Lack of state support, public visibility, as well as societal and institutional oppression are direct causes of these languages being deprioritized in the digital spaces of today (∀ et al., 2020).

The Sephardic community of Turkey has been active in promoting their language heritage in many ways. These include: publishing the only newspaper in the world entirely in Judeo-Spanish *El Amaneser*, giving language lessons, writing and performing plays in Judeo-Spanish, creating language learning content, collecting speech corpora and publishing dictionaries, music albums and books.

The aim of this work is to build data-centric technology for Judeo-Spanish for it to gain digital ground. Besides building new and compiling already existing corpora for this purpose, we create first machine translation and text-to-speech synthesis systems for the language. Machine translation makes it possible for the language to be interpretable by non-speakers and is also proposed as a way of language documentation (Bird and Chiang, 2012). It is now also considered as an attractive tool for many language learners in addition to dictionaries and thesauri (Clifford et al., 2013). Even though it is difficult to obtain high performance in low resource settings, it has been used to strike interest in language and collect translations and corrections from the community. The second language tool we focus on, text-to-speech synthesis (TTS), makes it possible building of tools like virtual assistants and screen readers. In the context of language learning, one can learn how a certain word or sentence is pronounced in a language without the help of an instructor or a speaker.

3. Judeo-Spanish Resources

We explain our various data compilation efforts in this section. All data presented are published with *CC BY-SA 4.0 license*[3] on Ladino Data Hub. We also provide the scripts we have used in developing these resources with GPL-licenses for facilitating expansion and reproducibility[4].

3.1. Monolingual text corpus

Text corpora have been used both in language technology and in linguistic research. They are an essential part of creating statistical language models that are used in applications such as optical character recognition, handwriting recognition, machine translation and spelling correction.

For this task, we automatically scraped the articles published in the weekly online newspaper *Şalom*[5]. As of now, we have collected 397 articles totaling to $176,843$ words.

3.2. Parallel corpus

The type of data that is needed to build a MT system is parallel data, which consists of a collection of sentences in a language together with their translations. We have only detected two publicly available corpora of Judeo-Spanish in the commonly used OPUS portal[6]: Wikimedia corpus consisting of 18 sentences and Tatoeba corpus of 872 sentences.

In order to expand on this set, we gathered translations made by the Sephardic Center of Istanbul. These covered topics like news articles, online shop strings, recipes and cultural event announcements. We automatically segmented the text into sentences getting use of punctuation and then manually verified alignments. We also digitized the language learning material *Fraza del dia*[7], where daily a Judeo-Spanish phrase is presented with their translations in another language. The sizes of parallel corpora created for each language pair is listed in Table 1.

Language pair (Judeo-Spanish and)	**#Sentences**	**Total #tokens**
English	3333	41,508
Spanish	977	12,712
Turkish	845	15,781

Table 1: Parallel data compiled from Tatoeba and translations by Sephardic community.

3.3. Spanish Judeo-Spanish Dictionary

We developed a digital Spanish–Judeo-Spanish dictionary from the sources listed in Table 2. To process the dictionaries shown in Table 2 which were in PDF format, we used the Python programming language, where we aligned the Spanish word with Judeo-Spanish word and eliminated irrelevant information like example sentences. Once the dictionaries were processed, the data were stored in a plain text file under the following structure: $\langle word\text{-}spanish, word\text{-}judeospanish \rangle$.

3.4. Single-speaker speech corpus

We built a single-speaker speech corpus of 3 hours and 24 minutes to be used in the creation of Judeo-Spanish TTS system. We had our native Judeo-Spanish speaking author read 30 articles from the weekly newspaper *El Amaneser*. The articles are about different topics, ranging from historical issues, current affairs, cultural events and politics. The recordings had an

[3] http://creativecommons.org/licenses/by-sa/4.0/

[4] http://github.com/CollectivaT-dev/judeo-espanyol-resources

[5] http://www.salom.com.tr

[6] http://opus.nlpl.eu/

[7] http://sefarad.com.tr/judeo-espanyolladino/frazadeldia/

Dictionary	# Entries
Diksionaryo de Ladino a Espanyol (Güler and Tinoco, 2003)	2523
Diksionario de Djudeo-Espanyol a Castellano (Orgun and Tinoco, 2009)	4215

Table 2: Dictionaries used for the construction of the digital dictionary.

average length of 6 minutes. To obtain TTS training data material, we had to divide the audios into smaller segments. For this task, we developed an automatic aligner[8] based on Coqui Speech-to-text (Coqui, 2022). The pre-trained Spanish model performed well enough to optimize the process. Nevertheless, to ensure completely matching audio and transcription pairs, we manually verified each pair and performed corrections where needed. The resulting corpus consists of 1987 16-bit, single-channel WAV audio files sampled at 16kHz with their transcriptions.

4. Machine Translation

In this section, we present our experiments for Judeo-Spanish machine translation. To account for the lack of data, we first build a rule-based Spanish to Judeo-Spanish translator and then use that to obtain the data needed to train neural baseline models.

4.1. Rule-Based machine translation

In the following, we describe the procedure of our rule-based machine translation system from Spanish to Judeo-Spanish based on the dictionaries available in Table 2. The Python-based scripts and documentation are provided with GNU General Public License in our Github repository[9].

The first step in the translation process is to tokenize the input Spanish phrase, for which we use the Python library Stanza[10] (Qi et al., 2020). This library, in addition to tokenizing the phrase, obtains the part-of-speech (POS) and lemmas of each token. As a second step, each token is looked up in the Spanish–Judeo-Spanish dictionary. If the token is found in the dictionary, its corresponding Judeo-Spanish token is obtained, otherwise, the dictionary is searched for its lemmatized form of the token. If the lemmatized token is found in the dictionary, the corresponding Judeo-Spanish token is obtained and is conjugated according to its POS. Our method transforms a Spanish token to a conjugated Judeo-Spanish form using an algorithm based on conjugation rules specified in (Perahya, 2012). We also convert the verb form Present Perfect (e.g. spa."he cocinado") to past indefinite (e.g. spa."cociné" lad. "gizi") as the former form is not common in Judeo-Spanish. In case the lemmatized token is not found in the dictionary, it is processed by a Judeo-Spanish correction method, which follows established orthographic rules of the language[11]. Finally, in step three, phrase forms that do not exist in Judeo-Spanish are corrected into their right form using a phrase correction dictionary. For example, *"tengo ke"* (from *spa."tengo que" eng."I have to"*) is corrected to *"debo de"*, or *"ay ke"* (from *spa."hay que" eng."one must"*) is corrected to *"Kale"*. Some example translations are listed in Table 3. Automatic evaluation results are presented in Table 5.

4.2. Data augmentation

We introduce a data augmentation method based on creating synthetic parallel data using the rule-based MT system presented in Section 4.1. We first collect publicly available parallel data in pairs English-Spanish and Turkish-Spanish from the OPUS collection. Then, we translate the Spanish portions into Judeo-Spanish using the rule-based MT. This yields Turkish–Judeo-Spanish and English–Judeo-Spanish synthetic parallel data. Finally, the Spanish portions of two sets are then merged to create Spanish–Judeo-Spanish synthetic parallel data. The statistics and sources for synthetic data augmentation are listed in Table 4.

4.3. Neural machine translation

We used the OpenNMT-py toolkit (Klein et al., 2018) to train the models. The model consists of an eight-head Transformer "big" (Vaswani et al., 2017a) with six-layer hidden units of 512 unit size. It uses Relative Position Representations (Shaw et al., 2018) with a clipping distance k=16. A token-batch size of 1,024 was selected. Adam optimizer (Kingma and Ba, 2015) was selected with 4,000 warm-up steps. Trainings were performed until no further improvement was recorded in development set perplexity in the last five validations.

We used the synthetic parallel data we created as training data. As for development and test sets, we used the authentic data mixes presented in Section 3.2. As English portion was about three times larger than Spanish and Turkish, we used a commercial machine translation engine to translate the extra data available for

[8]https://github.com/CollectivaT-dev/Judeo-Spanish_STT

[9]https://github.com/CollectivaT-dev/Espanyol-Ladino-Translation

[10]Stanza is a collection of tools for the linguistic analysis (Tokenization, Part-of-Speech, Lemmatization, etc.) of many human languages, including Spanish. https://stanfordnlp.github.io/stanza/

[11]Orthographic structure of Judeo-Spanish compared to Spanish available in https://github.com/CollectivaT-dev/judeo-espanyol-resources/blob/main/resources/Gramatica_Ladino.doc

Spanish input	Judeo-Spanish translation
Me gusta leer.	Me plaze meldar.
¿No has leido el libro?	No meldates el livro?
Bebo café turco después del almuerzo.	Bevo kafe turko despues del komida de midi.
Tengo dos niños; una hija y un hijo.	Tengo dos kriaturas; una ija i un ijo.
Tengo que cocinar para mañana.	Devo de gizar para amanyana.

Table 3: Example translations obtained with the rule-based machine translation system.

ENG-SPA	#sentences
Books	93,470
Europarl	615,626
News-commentary	49,089
OpenSubtitles	4,652,910
SciELO	164,500
TED2013	157,895
WMT-News	14,522
TOTAL ENG-SPA	**5,748,012**
SPA-TUR	
EUBookshop	19,914
GlobalVoices	7,461
OpenSubtitles	4,000,000
TED2020	370,465
Tatoeba	28,829
WikiMatrix	147,352
TOTAL SPA-TUR	**4,574,021**
TOTAL SPA	**10,322,033**

Table 4: Publicly available parallel data used for synthetic data creation.

English to Spanish and Turkish and added them to the mixes. Finally, we reserved 500 sentences from Spanish and Turkish and 750 sentences from English mix as test data and used the rest as validation data during training. Development, test sets, training configuration files, subword models and training logs are provided for reproducibility[12]. Model weights are made available in Ladino Data Hub.

	ENG	SPA	TUR
LAD → *lang*	34.96	47.13	20.14
***lang* → LAD**	26.03	44.85	21.03
Rule-based SPA → LAD	-	45.80	-

Table 5: Automatic evaluation results in 6 language directions and also on rule-based system. BLEU scores were calculated on lowercased output and reference with SACREBLEU toolkit with Moses tokenizer (Post, 2018).

We report our test set BLEU-scores (Papineni et al., 2002) for each translation direction in Table 5. As future work, we will also perform human evaluations on additional data to have a fairer judgment of the translation qualities.

[12] https://github.com/CollectivaT-dev/judeo-espanyol-resources/tree/main/MT_devtest_configs

5. Text-to-Speech

In this section, we present our experiments for the development of a Judeo-Spanish speech synthesizer. We use Glow-TTS model (Kim et al., 2020) for our experiments and the Griffin-Lim algorithm (Griffin and Lim, 1984) to avoid using vocoder, which we intend to develop for future research. We trained three Glow-TTS models with our 3.5 hour dataset. The first model was trained from scratch; the second and third, by fine-tuning English and Spanish TTS models. For all experiments, we do not enable the use of phonemes or the phonemizer as in Paniv (2021). We follow the settings for the mel-spectrogram of Prenger et al. (2019).

Training Judeo-Spanish from scratch First, we evaluate the performance of the model trained only using our single-speaker dataset. During training, like Kim et al. (2020) we set the standard deviation to 1. Our model was trained for 5,000 iterations with a batch size of 32, using the Adam optimizer (Kingma and Ba, 2014) with the Noam learning rate program (Vaswani et al., 2017b). This required only 4 days with an 8GB NVIDIA GPU.

Fine-Tuning from English and Spanish To train the Glow-TTS model from the pre-trained English (ljspeech/glow-tts) and Spanish (mai/tacotron2-DDC) models (Coqui, 2022), we used the same setup as the Glow-TTS model trained only with Judeo-Spanish data, but added the use of the phonemes and phonemizer corresponding to each language from the pre-trained models. Each model required only 4 days with an 8GB NVIDIA GPU.

5.1. Evaluation

Our best model was the one where fine-tuning was applied to the pre-trained English model, achieving a much better intelligibility and naturalness than the other models, reducing even more the "metallic" sound that appears in some consonants. On the other hand, the Spanish fine-tuned model did achieve a better naturalness for Judeo-Spanish phonemes but did not achieve a good intelligibility, perhaps due to the amount of training data. Likewise, the from-scratch model did achieve an excellent naturalness in the phonemes but a very poor intelligibility.

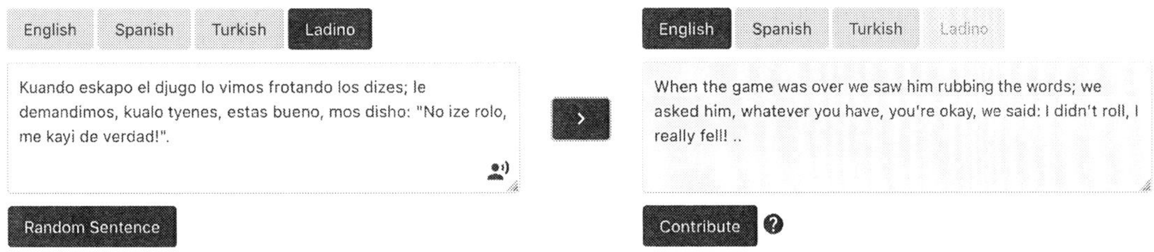

Figure 1: Web application for MT and TTS available in `http://translate.sefarad.com.tr`

We selected the best performing model (fine-tuned from English) for human evaluation. We used Mean opinion score (MOS) of intelligibility and naturalness with a 5-point scale: 5 for excellent, 4 for good, 3 for fair, 2 for poor and 1 for bad. An evaluation survey consisting of ten out-of-corpus samples were published in a closed Ladino speaker community of Istanbul and 12 native speakers participated. The average scores among ten samples are listed in Table 6. The configurations of all pre-trained models as well as audio samples are made available online for reproducibility [13]. Model weights are shared in Ladino Data Hub.

Model	Intelligibility	Naturalness
Glow-TTS (f.t. on English)	4.04	3.61

Table 6: Judeo-Spanish text-to-speech system evaluation results for intelligibility and naturalness (MOS)

6. Web Application

Our web application for serving the machine translation and speech synthesis systems can be seen in Figure 5. It allows translation between English, Spanish, Turkish and Ladino and makes it possible to listen to sythesized Ladino text. For Spanish, we integrated the rule-based system translating to Ladino and our model translating to Spanish. For the rest of the translation directions, we chained open source OPUS-MT translation models (Tiedemann and Thottingal, 2020) to these two systems to get translation to and from English and Turkish.

We also added a participation feature to make Judeo-Spanish speakers be part of future developments. By clicking the "Contribute" button, users can correct the translations and then submit to our database to be stored as parallel data for future trainings.

7. Conclusion

In this work, we introduced baseline systems of machine translation and speech synthesis for Judeo-Spanish. First, we developed a rule-based machine translator from Spanish to Judeo-Spanish. This base translator was used to apply a data augmentation technique. Second, we developed three bidirectional machine translation models between Judeo-Spanish and Spanish, Turkish and English, being the first neural-based systems for this language. Although some of our models do not perform optimally, we believe that this work is the basis for future research regarding this language, as well as motivating research for extremely low-resourced languages using data augmentation strategies. Third, we developed speech synthesis models for Judeo-Spanish, achieving an acceptable result by fine-tuning on an English model. Data, model checkpoints, development and test sets and configuration files are shared openly on project's data portal Ladino Data Hub and our Github repository. Finally, we created a web-application for machine translation with voice to help language learners, researchers and linguists who want to study Judeo-Spanish.

[13] `https://github.com/CollectivaT-dev/Ladino_TTS`

8. Acknowledgements

This paper was written as part of the project "Judeo-Spanish: Connecting the two ends of the Mediterranean" carried out by Col·lectivaT and Sephardic Center of Istanbul within the framework of the "Grant Scheme for Common Cultural Heritage: Preservation and Dialogue between Turkey and the EU (CCH-II)" implemented by the Ministry of Culture and Tourism of the Republic of Türkiye with the financial support of the European Union. The content of this paper is the sole responsibility of the authors and does not necessarily reflect the views of the European Union.

Yasmin Moslem contributed to this work while she was pursuing her PhD degree, supported by the Science Foundation Ireland Centre for Research Training in Digitally-Enhanced Reality (d-real) under Grant No. 18/CRT/6224, and the ADAPT Centre for Digital Content Technology which is funded under the Science Foundation Ireland (SFI) Research Centres Programme (Grant No. 13/RC/2106) and is co-funded under the European Regional Development Fund.

We would like to thank the excellent volunteer work by Brian Russell, who helped us digitize *Fraza del dia* content.

9. Bibliographical References

Bird, S. and Chiang, D. (2012). Machine translation for language preservation. In *Proceedings of COLING 2012: Posters*, pages 125–134, Mumbai, India, December. The COLING 2012 Organizing Committee.

Clifford, J., Merschel, L., and Munné, J. (2013). Surveying the landscape: What is the role of machine translation in language learning? *@tic. revista d'innovació educativa*, (10).

Coqui. (2022). Coqui TTS. `https://github.com/coqui-ai/TTS`.

∀, Nekoto, W., Marivate, V., Matsila, T., Fasubaa, T., Kolawole, T., Fagbohungbe, T., Akinola, S. O., Muhammad, S. H., Kabongo, S., Osei, S., et al. (2020). Participatory research for low-resourced machine translation: A case study in African languages. *Findings of EMNLP*.

Griffin, D. and Lim, J. (1984). Signal estimation from modified short-time fourier transform. *IEEE Transactions on acoustics, speech, and signal processing*, 32(2):236–243.

Güler, P. and Tinoco. (2003). Diksionaryo de ladino a espanyol. In *Diksionaryo de Ladinokomunita*.

Kim, J., Kim, S., Kong, J., and Yoon, S. (2020). Glow-tts: A generative flow for text-to-speech via monotonic alignment search. *Advances in Neural Information Processing Systems*, 33:8067–8077.

Kingma, D. P. and Ba, J. (2014). Adam: A method for stochastic optimization. *arXiv preprint arXiv:1412.6980*.

Kingma, D. P. and Ba, J. (2015). Adam: A method for stochastic optimization. In Yoshua Bengio et al., editors, *3rd International Conference on Learning Representations, ICLR 2015, San Diego, CA, USA, May 7-9, 2015, Conference Track Proceedings*.

Klein, G., Kim, Y., Deng, Y., Nguyen, V., Senellart, J., and Rush, A. (2018). OpenNMT: Neural machine translation toolkit. In *Proceedings of the 13th Conference of the Association for Machine Translation in the Americas (Volume 1: Research Track)*, pages 177–184, Boston, MA, March. Association for Machine Translation in the Americas.

Kornai, A. (2013). Digital language death. *PLOS ONE*, 8(10):1–11, 10.

Minervini, L. (2006). El desarrollo histórico del judeoespañol. *Revista Internacional de Lingüística Iberoamericana*, 4(2 (8)):13–34.

Moseley, C. (2010). *Atlas of the World's Languages in Danger*. UNESCO Publishing, 3 edition.

Orgun, P. and Tinoco. (2009). Diksionario de djudeo-espanyol a castellano. In *Diksionaryo de Ladinokomunita*.

Paniv, Y. (2021). Ukrainian TTS (text-to-speech) using coqui TTS. `https://github.com/robinhad/ukrainian-tts`.

Papineni, K., Roukos, S., Ward, T., and Zhu, W.-J. (2002). BLEU: a method for automatic evaluation of machine translation. In *Proceedings of the 40th Annual Meeting of the Association for Computational Linguistics*, pages 311–318, Philadelphia, Pennsylvania, USA, July. Association for Computational Linguistics.

Perahya, K. (2012). *DIKSYONARYO JUDEO ESPANYOL - TURKO LADINO - TÜRKÇE SÖZLÜK*. Sentro de Investigaciones sovre la Kultura Sefardi Otomana - Turka, 2 edition.

Post, M. (2018). A call for clarity in reporting BLEU scores. In *Proceedings of the Third Conference on Machine Translation: Research Papers*, pages 186–191, Brussels, Belgium, October. Association for Computational Linguistics.

Prenger, R., Valle, R., and Catanzaro, B. (2019). Waveglow: A flow-based generative network for speech synthesis. In *ICASSP 2019-2019 IEEE International Conference on Acoustics, Speech and Signal Processing (ICASSP)*, pages 3617–3621. IEEE.

Qi, P., Zhang, Y., Zhang, Y., Bolton, J., and Manning, C. D. (2020). Stanza: A Python natural language processing toolkit for many human languages. In *Proceedings of the 58th Annual Meeting of the Association for Computational Linguistics: System Demonstrations*.

Sefardiweb del CSIC. (2022). El Judeoespañol o Ladino. `http://www.proyectos.cchs.csic.es/sefardiweb/node/10`. Accessed: 2022-05-24.

Shaw, P., Uszkoreit, J., and Vaswani, A. (2018). Self-attention with relative position representations. In *Proceedings of the 2018 Conference of the North American Chapter of the Association for Computational Linguistics: Human Language Technologies, Volume 2 (Short Papers)*, pages 464–468, New Orleans, Louisiana, June. Association for Computational Linguistics.

Tiedemann, J. and Thottingal, S. (2020). OPUS-MT — Building open translation services for the World. In *Proceedings of the 22nd Annual Conferenec of the European Association for Machine Translation (EAMT)*, Lisbon, Portugal.

Vaswani, A., Shazeer, N., Parmar, N., Uszkoreit, J., Jones, L., Gomez, A. N., Kaiser, L., and Polosukhin, I. (2017a). Attention is all you need. In Isabelle Guyon, et al., editors, *Advances in Neural Information Processing Systems 30: Annual Conference on Neural Information Processing Systems 2017, 4-9 December 2017, Long Beach, CA, USA*, pages 5998–6008.

Vaswani, A., Shazeer, N., Parmar, N., Uszkoreit, J., Jones, L., Gomez, A. N., Kaiser, Ł., and Polosukhin, I. (2017b). Attention is all you need. *Advances in neural information processing systems*, 30.

Author Index

Association for Computational Linguistics
209 N. Eighth Street
Stroudsburg, Pennsylvania 18360

ISBN 978-1-7138-6119-5

9 781713 861195

CURRAN ASSOCIATES INC.
proceedings.com